D0849556

# GUARDIANS OF THE ARAB STATE

FLORENCE GAUB

# Guardians of the Arab State

*When Militaries Intervene in Politics,
from Iraq to Mauritania*

# OXFORD
### UNIVERSITY PRESS

Oxford University Press is a department of the
University of Oxford. It furthers the University's objective
of excellence in research, scholarship, and education
by publishing worldwide.

Oxford    New York

Auckland    Cape Town    Dar es Salaam    Hong Kong    Karachi
Kuala Lumpur    Madrid    Melbourne    Mexico City    Nairobi
New Delhi    Shanghai    Taipei    Toronto

With offices in

Argentina    Austria    Brazil    Chile    Czech Republic    France    Greece
Guatemala    Hungary    Italy    Japan    Poland    Portugal    Singapore
South Korea    Switzerland    Thailand    Turkey    Ukraine    Vietnam

Oxford is a registered trade mark of Oxford University Press
in the UK and certain other countries.

Published in the United States of America by
Oxford University Press
198 Madison Avenue, New York, NY 10016

Library of Congress Cataloging-in-Publication Data is available
Florence Gaub.
Guardians of the Arab State: When Militaries Intervene in Politics,
from Iraq to Mauritania.
ISBN: 9780190697617

Printed in India on acid-free paper

*To my grandfathers: the insurgent and the officer*

# CONTENTS

# INTRODUCTION

## OF KINGMAKERS AND GAME-CHANGERS

2011 was a military year for the Arab state: it saw the forces of Tunisia and Egypt desert their governments, the militaries of Yemen and Libya disintegrate in the face of civil unrest, the army of Syria launch a war against its people, and the forces of Qatar, Saudi Arabia and the United Arab Emirates (UAE) collectively intervene in Bahrain and to some extent Libya.[1] Whatever the outcome of the revolts, it was the military's action which proved to be decisive—not only during the fateful early days, but also thereafter: the Tunisian military made a decision to abstain from politics (although how much of it was deliberate remains disputed); the Egyptian military first governed, then stepped aside only to return a year later; the Syrian forces are now in the fifth year of civil war in spite of large-scale desertion; the skeleton of the Libyan military combats not only the militias which toppled Gaddafi but also has an eye on power; the Iraqi military fell apart in the face of IS; and the Yemeni forces disintegrated, a second time, in a transitional process leading to a full-scale war involving the military forces of, inter alia, Saudi Arabia, the UAE, Qatar and Egypt. For better or for worse, Arab armies played a role in the political process which unfolded after 2011: even in those countries where no large-scale unrest occurred, such as Algeria, they were the ultimate kingmakers and game-changers.

But why did these militaries become political actors in the first place? Armed forces are not political agents by design; their business is war and conflict, their client is the state and their outlook is determined by security. And yet, in Arab politics they played, and still play, an important role—going way beyond the most visible form, the ousting of a government in a coup.[2] If political activity is understood in the broader sense—that is, acts that aim to shape policy by influencing mass opinion or mobilising societal interests—then Arab forces have been even more active than previously thought. The release of public statements, endorsements and partisan activity, resignations (especially over highly visible issues), advocacy and agenda-setting with members of the civilian government, coalescing with special interest groups, or indeed mutinies and collective disobedience are all measures to influence politics. Lastly, disintegration is also a political act—albeit the most nihilistic one, since it denies legitimacy not only of the regime but also of the institution as such. In that sense, it can be considered a political declaration of bankruptcy.

In all of these ways, several Arab forces have deviated from the ideal model of a military institution subordinate to the executive. Every decade since the 1930s has seen at least one Arab coup: in the nine decades between 1936 and 2015, at least seventy-three coup attempts can be counted, thirty-nine of which were successful and thirty-four of which were aborted. Over half of them took place in the two decades between 1951 and 1969; 76 per cent of Arab states have experienced at least one coup attempt.[3] But coups are not the only way that officers can undermine the government: public declarations heavily criticising the executive, most recently in Iraq, Egypt or Libya, are just as much political. And so is disobedience: the cases of Egypt and Tunisia are of course the most recent ones, but by no means the only ones. The Lebanese military, for instance, has a long history of refusing orders to act against the civilian population since the 1950s. And disintegration is not foreign to the Arab world either: be it in Libya, Yemen, Lebanon or Iraq, military forces have revealed their weakness by melting away.

The decline in coups frequency after 1980 led to the assumption that Arab armed forces had been removed from politics and tightly integrated in their respective government structures. Governments with military origins civilianised themselves, adding to this illusion.

Removing the uniform and holding elections became the norm in the region to add a veneer of legitimacy: Egypt's Free Officers laid down their military commissions in 1956, making both Gamal Abdel Nasser and his successor Anwar Sadat regular civilians when they assumed power. Hosni Mubarak followed this example in 1981, when he ceased in his capacity as Air Marshal, as did Abdel Fattah Sisi in 2014. Similarly, Syria's President Hafez al-Assad eventually formally left the air force, as Tunisia's Zine El Abidine Ben Ali and Libya's Muammar Gaddafi left the army. (It should be noted that although Iraq's Saddam Hussein liked to appear in military uniform, he never served in the Iraqi armed forces— although he came to power with its help.) Arab military–political leaders went even further to express the formal removal of the armed forces, by banning their staff from voting and reducing the number of military officers in the executive.[4] Even today, military personnel are not allowed to vote in Tunisia, and similar bans are about to be lifted in Syria and Egypt.[5] Elsewhere, such as Lebanon or Jordan, they are not allowed to run for office while serving. Seen from the outside, the formal civilianisation of regimes of military origin led to the perception that the armed forces as an institution were integral parts of the regimes, and therefore unequivocal supporters of it. Nevertheless, they never ceased being political actors—but for what reason?

Considering that Arab military involvement in politics is such a ubiquitous phenomenon, there is surprisingly little to answer this question. Most research looks only at the most extreme form of military political involvement, coups—but this is problematic because not only are failed coup attempts under-reported and under-researched, but political involvement can take many other forms. More recent work usually seeks out only one variable for causal explanation, such as defence budgets or form of government—which is equally problematic because military involvement is the result not only of several elements but also a question of sequencing of these elements. The Arab Spring itself triggered a considerable amount of research looking at the military decision-making process in the moment of crisis, but while useful in itself it remains detached from historical antecedents and therefore does not establish patterns of Arab military interventionism.[6] Lastly, there is virtually no study looking at the phenomenon exclusively within the Arab context. Most studies today compare all international cases of military coups to establish patterns, ignoring the fact that the Arab world is a closed regional space with high levels of cultural and historical homogeneity. Consequently, research has provided us with several and often mutually exclusive explanations—none of which can singlehandedly explain what happened in 2011 and thereafter.

In the 1950s and 1960s, for instance, armed forces in politics were seen as only natural: a modern panacea against Arab "backwardness", since the military in power would inject "middle-class ideas of efficiency, honesty, and national loyalty" into society.[7] In the 1980s, social contexts were seen as the main culprit for military involvement: multi-ethnic societies seeming more prone to social conflict, the armed forces would be dragged into the conflict and consequently stage a coup—unless its leadership hailed from the same ethnic group as the civilian regime.[8] In the 1990s, economic factors seemed to explain it all: where states were poor and/or rural, the political discontent would provide the military with enough reason to oust a civilian government. Other approaches found as reasons the dependency on foreign trade which would make regimes vulnerable to shocks and therefore the military; or dependency on a single resource for government revenue, which would encourage power concentration in smaller circles.[9] In the early 2000s, regime types were used to explain why the armed forces turn political: in democracies, parliamentary systems are apparently more vulnerable to coups than presidential ones, because presidents are more difficult to remove than prime ministers in times of discontent; in general, coups are, however, more prevalent in non-democratic systems than in democratic ones—but then they are also rare in fully authoritarian ones. Consequently, the middle phase in between those two models is the most dangerous one in coup-terms, because it combines the weaknesses of democracy with those of authoritarian systems. Then again, other studies show that coups are likely to happen in places where they have happened before, even though they are governed by authoritarian military dictatorships—the reason for this being that not only did the first coup legitimise this way of acquiring power, but also military regimes usually do not seek any type of civilian support, such as political parties, and consequently lack legitimacy to some extent.[10]

Prevalent in the 1960s but now revived are studies which argue that the political and social context is irrelevant, and that drivers and motivations for political involvement are entirely military-inherent. Under this logic, civilians play no role whatsoever in the onset or the outcome of the coup, since it is ultimately an internal institutional power-struggle.[11] Coup-proofing theories—which assume that the absence of coups implies that the regime has meddled with the military institution's potentially dangerous characteristics—argue along the same, military-immanent lines.[12]

Alas, for every one of these hypotheses there is a disproving case in the Arab world. Coups continued to be present in the region in spite of modernity's arrival; multi-ethnic Lebanon never saw a successful coup, but Iraq and Syria did; the poorest states, like Yemen, have seen coups as much as some of the richest, Libya and Iraq; rentier states such as Algeria and Iraq did experience coups—but none of the Gulf States did; coups swept away the (albeit imperfect) presidential, monarchic or parliamentary democracies of Syria (1949), Egypt (1952, 2013) and Iraq (1958); where coups occurred once they did occur again—but even where they never succeeded, such as Saudi Arabia or Tunisia, this did not imply military subordination as proved by failed attempts. Even allegedly coup-proofed forces, such as Egypt's, were able to oust the government.

Moreover, these theories scratch only the surface of what military involvement in politics actually means in the region; they do not study in depth the relation that Arab forces have not only with their regime but also with society, and they do not correlate it with the fact that conflict, violence and war are a constant feature in this part of the world and that states are, for the most part, not fully consolidated. Without subscribing to orientalist myths of Arab exceptionalism, understanding the phenomenon of Arab military involvement in politics requires looking at it within the Arab context—of course, drawing on the vast literature that there is on coups and other forms of overstepping the prescribed role as an agent of the executive, but proposing a new framework for analysis.

Indeed, Arab forces become political actors in the broadest sense of the term when four elements come together in a certain sequence—the backdrop being, however, always situations of political distress. The first two are indeed internal to the armed forces, whereas the last two are external and pertain to the society and government to which the military is linked. Firstly, the force needs to be capable to act—without basic components of capacity, the military will not be able to act cohesively. Secondly, the leadership of the armed forces needs to have a reason to intervene—either material or immaterial, but a degree of institutional self-interest is necessary to move into action. Thirdly, the civilian body in charge of overseeing the military is incapable of foreseeing and aborting any such military activity. Fourthly and lastly, society at large either calls directly on the forces to intervene or at least holds a positive image of the institution which would allow it to overstep its mark. Only when these four elements are present do military forces become political actors—either by staging coups or displaying other, less invasive forms of disobedience.

Where armed forces are not cohesive, they will disintegrate in times of political crisis, as in Yemen or Libya; where they have no institutional interest, they will remain passive, as in Tunisia or Lebanon; where civilian leadership is alert enough to entertain an exchange with the armed forces, they will ensure that the institution is either too weak to act or has no reason to do so, as in Jordan or Morocco; and where society at large approves of the forces in politics, they will move into it, provided the other three elements are in place, as in Egypt or Algeria. Consequently, there are four different types of Arab military forces when it comes to politics: the failed forces who cannot act, the professional forces who have no interest although they could, the checked forces who might have both will and capacity but are checked by the civilians, and lastly the political force which has the capacity, the will, no opponent and the popular support to act.

2

# THE VIEW FROM WITHIN

## MILITARY REASONS

Although the first wave of analyses on armed forces in politics decided to ignore the internal dimension of such a move, military-intrinsic reasons do matter—for the simple reason that the armed forces are an institution of collective action. As such, they are (ideally) capable of moving in a united fashion, and possibly share a motivation as a whole rather than just as individuals. Consequently, the two aspects come first in the build-up to military intervention in politics. Where armed forces are not capable of acting or thinking collectively, they will lack the first necessary ingredient to be a political actor (and will be inefficient security actors). This is in itself not the main reason to act, but it is the most important precondition. Only in a second step does the institution become interested in intervening—where the armed forces have no institutionally-intrinsic interest to act, they simply will not.

*Institutional capacity: because they can*

Intervening in politics is a collective matter for the armed forces—a disgruntled individual (and often retired) officer criticising the regime in the media, as happened frequently in the context of Algeria's military reforms in 2015, does not constitute a military intervention. Calling the president's brother "mentally ill" and Algeria's government "a mafia" might be an act of disobedience or disloyalty, but it cannot be defined as military intervention in politics.[1] The difference between such personal opinions and interference by the armed forces in civilian matters is that the latter is a collective act. By collective here is not meant that the institution, from top general to lowest ranking foot soldier, is in total agreement with what its leadership orders, says or does. Rather, a military collective act implies that the institution responds positively to its leadership's orders—whether the individuals in the institution agree with this is irrelevant as long as they obey the given instructions. This is possible because the armed forces rely on three crucial elements to function: the officer corps, the command structure distributing them across the institution, and cohesion amongst its troops to hold it together—not to mention their firepower.[2]

## Built for war—and politics

After all, this is how modern military institutions work: they organise large numbers of people in a way that they can be moved by orders from a comparatively small leadership—without encountering resistance or entailing discussions about the reasons or wisdom to do so. It is precisely this which makes the modern military prone not only to war but also to potentially political action. Consequently, coups and other forms of political intervention in the Arab world or elsewhere are essentially a modern phenomenon—simply because only a modern armed force has the necessary features to execute such an act. Where ancient and medieval military forces fought wars "on the side", the armed forces of the nineteenth and twentieth centuries began to professionalise and to develop the features they still have today. As the military profession emerged as a separate and standing body, it was not only equipped for but also capable of collective action; in contrast to their historical forefathers, modern military forces stay in formation in peacetime, too. Preparation for war is now a continuous occupation and requires the military's readiness at all times. It is this aspect which plays into potential military action in politics: the armed forces are not only always as one, they develop and maintain those capacities which come in handy in a collective political action, too.

# THE VIEW FROM WITHIN: MILITARY REASONS

Arab armed forces underwent the same historical process as Western forces from the nineteenth century onwards; Egypt's Mehmed Ali was the first to create a modern military institution based on conscription in 1820, and perhaps not coincidentally it was the first Arab army to attempt a coup in 1879.[3] Tunisia, which enjoyed considerable autonomy in spite of its belonging to the Ottoman Empire, embarked on a large-scale military professionalisation project in 1837. Considered the founder of the modern Tunisian military, Ahmed Bey sent officers for education to France, established a military educational system, modernised its equipment as well as infrastructure and increased its total number to 27,000 troops. These levels of ambition were not maintained due to harsh economic conditions under his successor, but the institutional memory remained.[4] Colonial occupation introduced modern military standards elsewhere in the Arab world, leaving French and British legacies in doctrines and structures. When Arab states became independent from the 1930s onwards, the armed forces not only flanked state-formation but were from the start shaped as modern, standing armies mirroring very much the European structural standards of modern military organisation, albeit in a financially constricted environment.

As such, armed forces are of course an institution of the modern state, with a precise task, (theoretically) subordinate to civilian control, staffed with citizens drawn from the population and financed by taxes. Then again, the modern military in the modern state is still not quite like the other parts of the executive. Its task is an existential one, as it concerns the survival of the state as such; their staff must be willing to die for the cause and are sometimes enlisted against their free will. When the armed forces fail, the whole state is at stake. Its mission, and success thereof, is intimately linked to the state as such, in a way that no other state institution is—reflected in the tomb of the Unknown Soldier, which in many places symbolises the citizen's readiness to give his life for the state.[5] It is this very feature which singles out the armed forces amongst other state institutions and is at the origin of the term "cradle of the state". States might rarely emerge without an armed force, but once they vanish it is most certainly a military failure.

It is for precisely this reason that armed forces are generally the institution with the largest amount of destructive capacity in almost any given state. This capacity serves an external purpose when used against aggression; but when turned inwards, its coercive threat potential is enough. Although internal security is also armed, it generally has very limited air power (if at all), as well as only small to medium weapons and few armoured vehicles. Fighter jets, tanks, artillery, mines, and heavy explosives are generally reserved for the military—the Egyptian armed forces, for instance, 3,299 tanks and 569 combat capable aircraft, numbers that are entirely unmatched by civilians; Egyptair, the national carrier, possesses a fleet of 63 aircraft (designed for passenger transport, not war), and the military holds a near-monopoly on tanks. The Algerian army operates with 2,418 tanks and the air force with 121 combat aircraft; Air Algérie's fleet consists of 56 aircraft.[6] While the situation might be different in smaller states such as Qatar or Lebanon—here, civil aviation surpasses military airpower in numerical terms—the sheer destructive force is simply unsurpassed, and the potential threat emanating from this weaponry is considerable.

The existential aspect of the military's mission also determines every aspect of the organisation's management, ranging from its institutional design and equipment to recruitment choices. As an organisation, the armed forces need to be geared towards large-scale collective coercive action whose scale and location are mostly unclear. The uncertainty that comes with warfare implies that the armed forces constantly need to maintain a state of preparedness and alert to face a logistically challenging task. A military institution needs to be mentally at war at all times, even in a situation of peace. During conflict, decisions need to be taken in a general atmosphere of urgency, command structures need to be streamlined and centralised communication needs to be stringent, hierarchy and leadership need to be solid and unquestioned. Orders from the highest echelon need to be communicated and executed fast through secure channels. Even though only a small portion is actually engaged in combat, military units resemble each other in organisational format in this.[7]

Discipline, leadership, obedience, meritocracy, cohesion are the backbone of this system, which could not operate quickly and efficiently with flat hierarchies and consensus-based decision-making. In the name of battlefield effectiveness, the armed forces need to mould several thousand individuals into one entity capable of rapid deployment and action. As a result, it is often somewhat isolated from its surrounding society, located in closed-off areas and barracks, clouded in secrecy and marked by its own set of rules, values and even clothes. Leaving the armed forces without its permission is usually punishable, or in any case dishonourable; the institution sees itself, and is seen, as distinct from the society and state it serves.

Ironically, those features which contribute to the military's capacity to act in a unified way are also those that turn the armed forces into a potential political actor: the combination of coercive power (essentially firepower as well as sheer manpower) and capacity for rapid collective action. Crucial for the latter are leadership (i.e. the officers), cohesion, as well as command and control structures which tie the two together in a meaningful way.

## The backbone of the military: the officers

The first ingredient necessary for both war and collective political action is those individuals who command the authority to move large bodies of people: the officers. In the pyramidal structure of the military, the officers are the leadership elements distributed all over the organisation, which is made up mainly of rank and file, i.e. soldiers. Because of their leadership function, the officers generally determine the course of action in the armed forces, even though they are in the minority. Although their numbers are limited—depending on technological context, service branch and country, officers make up between 3 and 15 per cent of the armed forces[8]—the officer corps is crucial not only for the execution of orders, but also for the creation of cohesion, discipline and obedience amongst the ranks. If the officer corps or even just parts of it are cohesive—i.e. share a certain outlook and vision—and hold authority over the units they are commanding, they will be able to manoeuvre a very large organisation to their own interests. There are few cases of bottom-up coups or mutinies instigated by non-commissioned officers and soldiers; the vast majority—and in the Arab case the totality—of military interventions are led by officers, and not just any officers: in the case of a coup or collective disobedience, the officers who command units.[9] Whether or not these units participate or not in any manoeuvre depends entirely on the authority the officer has over the unit.

11

Of course, a successful coup does not need the active participation of all officers or units; instead, it needs to be able to single out the crucial units and co-opt them, actively neutralise those units which might oppose this move, and move too fast for other units to prevent the coup from happening. Depending on the specific situation of a given country, as little as 2 per cent of the armed forces can execute a successful coup. Critical units can be as small as a battalion (1,000 troops) or a brigade (3,000–5,000 troops); and the number of officers involved can be limited to 10 company commanders, 5 battalion leaders or 15–45 leaders in the technical structure.[10] In Iraq, the 1958 coup was staged with two brigades only, of which only one battalion sufficed to arrest the royal family and seize the broadcasting station—the whole commandeered by 10–12 lieutenant colonels. The Syrian coup of 1949 was led by the commander of the first army brigade; the Egyptian coup of 1952 involved a number of armoured brigades and less than 100 officers.[11]

However, the higher the ranks of the officers involved, the more likely the whole of the organisation will follow suit—provided that these officers are firmly embedded in the armed forces. The actions of the Egyptian military in both 2011 and 2013, for instance, were decided very much at the highest officer level, and therefore required neither the secrecy nor the strategic speed of coups organised and executed at a lower level. The same is true for the Tunisian military.

In the case of collective disobedience—which, in the Arab world, has happened only in Lebanon, Egypt and Tunisia—the authority of the commanding officers needs to be even greater, as all involved units need to be prevented from acting against the population. When Tunisia's Chief of Staff General Rachid Ammar allegedly "said no" to Ben Ali's orders to use live ammunition against civilians, the armed forces responded by collectively withdrawing its units from the streets of Tunis until the President fled the country the next day.[12] As an entity, the institution therefore collectively adhered to the General's orders without exception. The same occurred in Egypt, where the army leadership issued a declaration a week into the protests declaring that "the armed forces will not resort to use of force against our great people. The armed forces are aware of the legitimacy of your demands and are keen to assume their responsibility in protecting the nation and the citizens, affirms that freedom of expression through peaceful means is guaranteed to everybody."[13] Here, too, military units involved in the operation followed these orders because the command structure (that is, the hierarchical line of order communication between the officers) was as intact as the officers' authority in their respective unit.

In statistical terms, colonels as well as generals are the ranks which stage Arab coups the most successfully, although the former are twice as likely as the latter to attempt a coup. There are military-intrinsic reasons for this: in order to stage a coup, officers are needed who have the necessary authority over units with the required size. Colonels are at the forefront of coups because they usually have close relationships with their troops and command brigades—which are the right unit size to stage a coup.[14] Smaller units, such as battalions or companies, are normally commanded by lower ranks, which will command less authority over a smaller group of people. Generals, however, are less in direct contact with the soldiers they are commanding and therefore have less leverage to request actions which test loyalty. It is precisely for this reason that colonels matter the most to a force's functioning: where their numbers are low, the organisation will struggle to connect strategy and tactics. The Lebanese military, for instance, is currently suffering a severe shortage of colonels because the civil-war generation, recruited in low levels during the conflict, is now reaching these levels.

Units commanded by general officers range from divisions (more than 10,000 troops) for a major general to corps (more than 20,000). To establish leadership over a unit, officers need to be in contact, as will be explained further below. In other words, it might be possible to stage a coup or collective disobedience without general officers, but not without colonels. Egypt's Free Officers, the core of which was comprised of officers of junior to middle rank, elected Major General Mohammed Naguib as the figurehead of the Revolutionary Command Council, mainly for prestige purposes and to add military legitimacy to their actions; but he was not the leader or planner of the original group. When his ambitions clashed with Gamal Abdel Nasser's, he was deposed by the Council only two years after the coup.

In addition, colonel is the rank with the highest frustration potential, since it is one promotion away from general which might never occur, whereas generals have already achieved the highest command level and therefore have more to lose from risky political business. Famous Arab colonels who have staged coups are Gamal Abdel Nasser of Egypt; Ziad al-Hariri (who was recruited by the plotters because they themselves were too junior to go it alone, including wing commander Hafez al-Assad) as well as Sami al-Hinnawi of Syria (who was overthrown by fellow colonel Adib Shishakli); Ahmad Thalaya of Yemen, who led the coup against Imam Ahmad bin Yahya in 1955; Gaafar Nemery in Sudan's 1969 coup; Abdul Salam Arif who participated in the Iraqi coups of 1958 and 1963; Houari Boumediene, who left the Algerian *Armée de la liberation nationale* with the rank of colonel, and seized power four years later; and the failed Lebanese coup of 1961, while plotted by captains, relied on a colonel, Fouad Lahoud, to establish the necessary network within the military.[15]

Muammar Gaddafi, however, was not a colonel when he staged his 1969 coup in Libya, but a captain—he promoted himself to colonel only later in reverence to Nasser, as did Yemen's Ali Abdullah Saleh when he arrived in power in 1978. In some cases, as in Egypt in 1952, the dividing line between generals and colonels is also a generational one and contributes to rank-defined frustrations.

In addition, commanding officers—usually lieutenant colonels or colonels—are responsible for the vertical as well as horizontal cohesion of a unit with those below and above it in the pyramidal command structure. In other words, they are in constant exchange with other officers of higher, lower and identical ranks and have a tightly knit network across the whole organisation. The Egyptian Free Officers' Movement, for instance, counted around ninety to one hundred officers in total, although the core numbered eight who, like a miniature armed force, represented an equilibrium of corps (infantry, air force, artillery, armour and signal). This meant that the movement possessed a wide span across different services; in addition, all eight had also been battlefield commanders during the war for Palestine and had fostered ties with younger officers whom they recruited into their movement from different services in the organisation.[16]

## Cohesion: the glue that makes collective action

But officers do not solely have a role of command and leadership; they also play a crucial role in creating the bond which turns the unit from a random group of individuals into a team willing and able to act as one. Officers foster pride in the mission and organise occasions for the unit members to bond. They also mete out rewards for behaviour that is to the unit's advantage (and punishments for the contrary). Leaders need to make sure that the unit members' needs are met, that the set goals are achievable, and that the rules of engagement are clear. The military saying "Mission First, Troops Always" reflects this: without a properly functioning unit, the armed forces cannot fulfil their mission. Consequently their morale, "the enthusiasm and persistence with which a member of a group engages in the prescribed activities of the group",[17] is the direct outcome of cohesion and *esprit de corps*; the more cohesive the military at the vertical or horizontal level, the higher its morale will be.

Cohesion implies the formation of a united whole—it can be defined in the military as "the bonding together of members of an organisation/unit in such a way as to sustain their will and commitment to each other, their unit, and the mission".[18] Cohesion, sometimes also known as military camaraderie, is what led modernisation theorists to believe that the military might act as a "natural integrator" of individuals with different background and mould them into a national whole—but while the military does have a cohesion-building effect on its members out of necessity, it can be transposed only in a limited fashion to the nation as a whole via conscription. Cohesion is necessary for any collective action: war, coups or collective disobedience. Cohesiveness will be required not only within the units, but also amongst the crucial elements of the officer corps. Where collective action fails, lack of cohesion amongst the officers, or between them and the troops, is usually the reason. In Egypt, a 1971 coup attempt failed precisely because the chief of the military, a supporter of it, did not manage to gain support from the military hierarchy.[19] Similarly, General Haftar's announcement of a coup in Libya in February 2014 had little impact—he had left the Libyan military 27 years earlier and had only little authority over the ranks below him. His second attempt three months later was more successful, but simply because crucial elements of the Libyan military joined his endeavour out of self-interest.

There are three explanations for why the armed forces would not be able to operate as one without cohesion. One, the members of a unit recognise themselves that cohesion is in their interest as it increases unit effectiveness and therefore chances of survival. Consequently, the more dangerous the mission is, the stronger cohesiveness will be. Two, cohesion has a social function within the unit; where unit members take on risk to the benefit of the whole unit, they will be rewarded with increased status and recognition. Hence, social capital is built within the unit over time. "Psychologically, the development of these norms transfers control over actions from individual members to the group as a whole (…). The service member does not want to let his/her buddies down, and further, can feel the strong social support of the group so as to elevate the service member to actions above and beyond the call of duty."[20] Three, cohesion has a control function in a context which includes the handling of highly lethal weapons. The supervision of handling these weapons responsibly is partly enforced by a social context built on laws, norms and regulations. Research clearly shows a correlation between officer leadership and rule clarity on the one hand and peer cohesion on the other. Lastly, cohesion serves, more generally, the provision of help and support for its group members, regardless of whether in the armed forces or elsewhere. Simply put, cohesion is to the advantage of individuals and the collective alike in a situation of combat, and will therefore be deliberately fostered by the organisation.

Cohesion can be related to a task, for example, by representing the shared commitment to a common goal, but it can also have a social dimension in which case it stands for mutual appreciation. In the armed forces, task cohesion is more important than social cohesion, but the two are often intertwined.[21] Cohesion can be horizontal—i.e. at the unit level—or vertical, in which case it refers to leaders and followers and could be equally called leadership; when a larger organisation is cohesive, the term *esprit de corps* is often used, but it points to the same phenomenon: the sticking together of a group of individuals, more often than not for the completion of a task. In the military, cohesion has to be both horizontal and vertical—where it is not, mutiny or disintegration is the consequence.

There are a number of ways in which the armed forces encourage cohesion; generally speaking, the military emphasises the unity of its entities by using "shoulder patches, unit colours, campaign streamers, review ceremonies, and even informal symbols such as scarves serve this important function and should be supported as long as they are used in an appropriate manner",[22] as noted in a US army leadership and command booklet. At the unit level, the cohesive strength depends on a variety of factors, such as training, group size (according to some, "only teams, squads, platoons, and companies possess cohesion"[23] putting the numbers for cohesive units at approximately ten to fifty individuals), turnover and the leadership of the commanding officer. It is worth noting that the causal link between training and cohesion is not clear: "The bonds of friendship may grow out of military proficiency and the performance of collective drills; comradeship may be the function of collective drills not their prerequisite."[24]

Cohesion in Arab forces has generally been criticised for being poor in combat situations but a closer look shows that the picture is more nuanced:[25]

> The cohesiveness of Arab units has varied to a considerable degree not only from war to war and army to army but even within armies during the same war. (…) Although the evidence is not entirely consistent, the unit cohesion of Arab armies generally has more often been good than bad, and on many occasions it has been outstanding. (…) one cannot blame poor unit cohesion for the consistent underachievement of Arab armed forces. In fact, quite the contrary is true: unit cohesion was probably more a strength of these armies than a weakness.[26]

Examples abound: during Egypt's war with Israel in 1956, an infantry battalion virtually collapsed under a first attack, while the rest of its brigade continued to fight even though it was assaulted repeatedly; the Iraqi army's 6th armoured brigade kept attacking an Israeli position during the war of 1948 and its Republican Guard kept fighting the American VII Corps during the Gulf War; several Jordanian units ferociously defended their positions during the war of 1967. Where cohesion was generally weak was when the units were ordered to retreat while being pursued aggressively, as happened to the Egyptian forces in the Sinai in 1956 and 1967, the Jordanians in 1967 in the West Bank, the Syrian forces on the Golan the same year, the Libyan forces in 1987 and the Iraqis in 1981–2. And although discrimination based on ethnicity has been thought to diminish cohesion, the Iraqi case shows that this picture is more nuanced. During the war with Iran, Shiite recruits fought well in spite of discriminatory policies towards them, although morale decreased with more widespread political repression of Shiites in 1991.[27]

In any case, war is an entirely different business from acting politically as one; coup operations require cohesiveness to strike in a quick and unified manner, but they are rarely as dangerous to the individual as war. It is therefore safe to assume that the degree of cohesion necessary to execute a coup is lower than that necessary to fight a battle—but where units have seen combat together, they will probably have higher degrees of cohesion than before. The reverse argument might therefore be true: most Arab forces have seen their share of violent conflict, and they happen to be also those which are mostly engaged in politics; those that have seen little to no combat action (such as the Gulf forces until recently) have equally not been involved in politics. This is not to say that the experience of war creates the conditions for collective political action, but up to a certain point it does contribute to cohesion which in turn is necessary to execute a coup; once a conflict lasts longer than 200 days, cohesion is likely to diminish, however.[28]

## The structure which ties it together: command and control

The last military element necessary for political intervention is command and control structures (C2) which are related to both cohesion and leadership. Without these structures, the hierarchical flow of commands would not occur in a structured manner. C2 can be defined as:

> the exercise of authority and direction by a properly designated commander over assigned and attached forces in the accomplishment of the mission. Command and control functions are performed through an arrangement of personnel, equipment, communications, facilities, and procedures employed by a commander in planning, directing, coordinating, and controlling forces and operations in the accomplishment of the mission.[29]

In other words, C2 structures ensure that a common goal is achieved by a large body of units sometimes scattered over a large territory and without direct communication methods, streamlining their efforts.[30]

In Arab military forces, command structures have, more often than not, been politicised—to the detriment of military effectiveness. When Gamal Abdel Nasser and his on-and-off minister of defence Abdel Hakim Amer wrangled over appointments, they effectively created duplicated and therefore distorted command and control structures.[31] Only after the war, when the competition between the two men ended, were Nasser and later his successor Sadat able to create a cohesive officer corps based on an unambiguous command and control structure—changes that contributed to increased military performance during Egypt's war with Israel in 1973. It is precisely because of the insight that politicisation harms the armed forces as a whole that the Egyptian military underwent an important professionalisation phase under Sadat—a move widely replicated in the region, but flanked by another fear: "professionalisation enhances the autonomy of the military and, if politically unchecked, can increase its tendency to intervene in the affairs of the state. (...) The military's professionalisation can become a double-edged sword and may significantly undermine the powers of the actors seeking to implement it."[32] A performing military organisation always comes at the price of a potential threat, if not checked properly—nobody knows this better than regimes that have to come to power with its help.

## Coup-proofing: a double-edged sword

One way of containing the political threat potential of Arab military forces is to target precisely those military dimensions which render it politically capable in the first place. Coup-proofing, "the set of actions a regime takes to prevent a military coup",[33] essentially undermines the possibility for small groups to use the military system for its own goals. It targets therefore the aforementioned elements which give the armed forces not only its military striking power, but also its potentially political clout: leadership (i.e. the officers), cohesion and the command structures.

There are several ways in which these three elements can be (and have been) successfully and deliberately weakened in Arab armed forces, but the most important ones focus on the officer corps.

One manner is to undermine meritocratic principles and recruit and man posts according to principles of loyalty. Examples include the Iraqi regime under Saddam Hussein or the Syrian regime under al-Assad: both favoured the appointment of officers from Tikrit (where Hussein was from) or from al-Assad's Alawite sect. Similarly, Hussein's predecessors, the Arif brothers, overly relied on officers and non-commissioned officers from the al-Jumaylah tribe, and Muammar Gaddafi relied heavily on his own tribe, the Qadadfa, as well as the

Warfalla and Maqarha in the armed forces.[34] He did this in particular to reduce the strength of Libyan nationalism in the armed forces, (on which his own coup had thrived in 1969), but also to keep the military under his control.

Such staffing happens not so much for sectarian purposes, but rather to strengthen the hold on a notoriously unrestful organisation by appointing tribal relatives or friends. In most cases, no single ethnic or religious group is large enough to control an entire population, so co-option is key. In order to control a population fully, a given group needs not only to make up more than 20 per cent of the population, but all its members need to be fully committed to this task. More important than percentages, absolute numbers matter with regard to coercive control. Per 1,000 inhabitants, 120 men aged twenty to thirty-nine are required—which, for instance in the case of the Alawites would constitute only 14 per cent of the whole community. In other words, it is simply not feasible to establish a mono-ethnic force in Syria for peace enforcement. "As trivial a calculation as this is, it has profound implications for the plausibility of producing large units based on single communities and the need to include virtually all communities when the situation demands the formation of large field armies."[35] It is therefore more practical for a regime to include even groups that are less allegiant to the state into the military, but to post them into units that are less useful than others when it comes to staging a coup.[36]

As the regime seeks to create a reliable force (instead of an effective one) it will therefore engage in "ethnic security mapping":

> The ethnic security map optimal for state maintenance is one in which those groups deemed most reliable, most dependably acquiescent to state authority, have the easiest access to the state structure. On the other hand, those ethnic groups considered least reliable, least likely to subject themselves to the established authority, are given little or no access to state structures.[37]

This is a strategy not limited to post-coup states—both French and British colonial powers used ethnic mapping to man the indigenous forces under their control by favouring minorities; in the French *Troupes Spéciales*, Alewites and Druze were consistently over-represented.[38] This practice has often spilled over into the newly shaped states: in Lebanon, Christians were over-represented in the officer corps in the years leading up to the civil war, reflecting the fact that the

Sunni Muslim community had its misgivings about the very existence of Lebanon (and that Shiites had trouble meeting the educational requirements). [39] In addition, regimes employing coup-proofing techniques use frequent officer rotation in order to prevent the fostering of cohesive ties between troops and officers, and centralise any benefits the troops usually receive from the officers (days off, clothing, housing and food allocations).

Where troops—and officers in particular—are selected not on meritocratic principles but on personal backgrounds, cohesion will suffer. In Libya, every single promotion was controlled by Gaddafi; in Syria, brigade commanders are said to report directly to the president rather than to their responsible general. As inflexible hierarchies (such as the armed forces) are built on meritocracy, politicisation of recruitment, promotions and postings will result not only in officers with lesser leadership skills but also in undermined authority.

These regimes also engage more often in war to keep the troops busy—Iraq's invasion of Kuwait is at least in part the result of a bloated armed force following its war with Iran and Hussein's subsequent predicament over whether to disband them or to keep them engaged. In Libya, the armed forces were involved in skirmishes for several years on the border with Egypt, in Uganda and Chad, but paid a high military price for coup-proofing. Not allowed to conduct military exercises above the company level (let alone use live ammunition), they proved unable to coordinate efforts of the artillery, armour and infantry. Cohesion suffered tremendously:

> Throughout the nine years of direct Libyan involvement in Chad, Gaddafi's legions suffered high rates of desertion among units deployed there. (...) When morale was high, unit cohesion was stronger and more soldiers were willing to risk their lives for their comrades and their missions. But when they were dispirited, units broke under less pressure, and fewer troops were willing to sacrifice for their mission or one another. [40]

Yemen's Ali Abdullah Saleh, who had come to power with the help of the armed forces, equally began to man posts with members of his tribe. [41] In the Iraqi case, the armed forces underwent tremendous coup-proofing measures under Saddam Hussein, but his successor Premier Nouri al-Maliki has equally attempted to check the military's political potential with similar results.

Under Hussein, the large-scale Baathification of the officer corps undermined morale; challenged traditional lines of authority; circumvented hierarchy and promotional systems; and introduced cronyism, sectarianism, and tribal elements into an institution that prided itself on Iraqi and Arab nationalism. None of the regional defence commanders whom Hussein appointed in 2003 had substantial military experience;[42] he elevated himself to the rank of general and then field marshal without his ever having served a day in the armed forces, changed the army's traditions, and created an overall sentiment of animosity within the officer corps. Most importantly, he undermined professional basics of the armed forces over decades while institutionalising iron discipline that crumbled once he fell from power. He did this because he knew that the Iraqi military was more prone than any other Arab force to develop political ambitions—in 1936, the Iraqi armed forces were the first in the region to oust a government, triggering a long phase of political meddling. When Hussein came to power with the military's help in 1968, the Iraqi forces had attempted eleven coups in thirty years, half of them successful. Arriving in power was not possible without the armed forces, but staying there required weakening their political potential.

His successor, Prime Minister al-Maliki, came to similar conclusions, of which his 2011 coup accusations against Vice President Tarek al-Hashemi are a testimony. Although al-Maliki did not come to power with the assistance of the armed forces, he used similar—albeit less violent—techniques to keep the military in check, all of which impaired it in terms of military capacity. He not only meddled with promotions and postings personally, but concentrated decision-making power regarding the security sector in the prime minister's office which could overrule other governmental institutions such as the Ministry of Defence.[43] In order to balance out an officer corps largely reliant on men from the old armed forces (70 per cent of the corps are from Saddam Hussein's military), al-Maliki inserted politically appointed officers (called *dimaj*) into the armed forces, circumventing any criteria of meritocracy or transparency. Struggles between these two groups significantly weakened cohesion.[44]

If al-Maliki's goal was to weaken the armed forces, he was helped by the factors of time and an ever-worsening security situation following the fall of Saddam Hussein. At some point the military grew by 14,000 new troops every five weeks, but struggled to fill officer posts—it grew out of joint, incapable of developing military cohesion or functioning command-and-control structures. Within only six years, the Iraqi military therefore quadrupled without the adequate leadership in place.

Both the rapidity of reconstruction and over-politicisation led to a significant weakening of the forces in operational terms. In 2008, this resulted in high desertion rates during the battle of Basra against the Shia militia Jaysh al-Mahdi: 500 soldiers from the same brigade that had just completed basic training abandoned their post, as did a handful of officers.[45] In 2014, it led to the rather spectacular desertion of three entire divisions in Mosul.

Training and equipment are not what make an armed force; in fact, training works best in existing structures led by experienced officers, neither of which were sufficiently present in the Iraqi case. As the Iraqi military suffered from severe leadership problems, absenteeism was and is chronic, with on average 25 per cent of staff absent at any given time—a rate which goes up to 50 per cent once the unit is deployed for combat operations outside its usual area of operation, as during the 2014 assault on Mosul and Tikrit by IS.[46] Iraq's officers had not only been recalled from an organisation in which terror and fear reigned; they also brought with them practices of corruption (leading to the infamous "ghost soldier" phenomenon, of staff on the pay roll who did not exist) and a feeling of distrust towards a leadership seen as sectarian. Al-Maliki, who did not trust these men, successfully coup-proofed the armed forces into ineffectiveness, both militarily as well as politically.

In addition to these techniques, armed forces that are perceived as a potential threat are frequently subjected to purges of its officer corps. Somewhat ironically, regimes are particularly harsh with the armed forces when they have emerged from them; immediately after a coup, the often brutal purging of the officer corps is meant to deter further coup attempts. To maintain that level of deterrence, military intelligence will monitor political activity within the forces, and occasional executions of officers guilty or suspected of plotting a coup are the norm rather than the exception. This rather gruesome practice established itself in particular after coup-regimes were repeatedly challenged by counter-coups—in the beginning, officers such as the Syrian

1962 plotters (including Hafez al-Assad) were simply sent into exile, only to attempt another coup a year later; 120 officers were then purged from the military's ranks, but only eight officers were executed. The purging of Nasserist officers from the Syrian military following the 1963 coup triggered another putsch attempt, led by Colonel Jassem Alwan who was promptly sentenced to death (though later pardoned following diplomatic pressure from Egypt). This was the first time that coups involved large-scale violence in Syria's military. The 1966 coup which pitted the old Baath guard against the younger officers equally led to the imprisonment of any officer suspected of being a supporter of Baath-founder Michel Aflaq and defence minister Muhammad Umran.[47]

Other Arab regimes resorted to similar methods to threaten the officer corps into submission. The Libyan military was first purged right after its 1969 coup of every Sanussi officer, regardless of rank, and of all colonels and ranks above. When two rivals of Gaddafi in the Revolutionary Command Council, Major Bashir Hawadi and Captain Umar al-Muhayshi, attempted a coup in 1975, between twenty and thirty officers were tried and executed in secret; in 1983, five more officers were executed for the same reason. In 1984, several thousand soldiers were arrested and around a hundred officers executed following riots in barracks, allegedly the precursor to a coup attempt. In 1985, sixty officers were arrested, and the military governor of Surt, Colonel Hassan Ishkal, was executed because he disagreed with the regime over the role of the revolutionary guards within the armed forces. In 1993, a coup attempt by the commander of the Libyan forces in Chad was foiled by the air force, and resulted in 250 casualties.[48] When Yemen's Ali Abdullah Saleh arrived in power in 1978, his first official act was to execute thirty officers he suspected of disloyalty.

In Iraq, officers were purged following every coup or coup attempt in 1958, 1959 and 1963. Saddam Hussein's regime was particularly harsh on the officer corps; not only were officers executed when suspicions (both founded and unfounded) of a plot arose (such as in 1989, 1992 and 1996 when several hundred officers were executed on each occasion), but also when their battlefield performance was not satisfactory.[49] During the war with Iran, the execution of high-ranking officers, such as generals and colonels, became the norm and weakened the armed forces significantly in terms of morale. As Lieutenant General Ra'ad Majid Rashid al-Hamdani, staff officer and battalion commander during the Iran–Iraq war, put it:

> the trial and executions did not help at the time, of course; the process repeated itself every time there was a failure, in spite of whatever success a commander might have achieved before. Nothing could save a commander from execution once he failed. This was a serious issue and it had a great impact on the army...[50]

Arguably, this is still part of the Iraqi military's institutional memory.

Similarly, the Egyptian military underwent several waves of political purges: first after the coup of 1952, when 450 officers were dismissed, including every general officer except for General Naguib.[51] Most of these were forced into retirement, although a few were put on trial for their failures during the 1948 war with Israel.[52] The military underwent several more purges: first, of officers suspected of being sympathetic to the Muslim Brothers; later, of supporters of Naguib who had fallen out with the Free Officers; after the defeat against Israel in 1967, Egypt's air force was purged, though more for military than political reasons; and once Sadat came to power, he dismissed officers with Nasserist inclinations.[53] It is worth noting that Egyptian purges were not as violent as Syrian, Iraqi or Libyan ones. Whether or not these officers were guilty as charged was largely irrelevant—the mere suspicion was generally enough to set an example.

The regular execution of officers has implications for the corps at large; it not only depletes the armed forces of experienced and knowledgeable officers, but creates an atmosphere of fear and impacts negatively on the leadership. In Iraq, for instance, assertive mid-level officers learned that they were threats to their supervisor or worse—individuals with leadership abilities were seen as a threat by Saddam Hussein himself. As a result, officers across all ranks were groomed into passivity, distrust and lack of initiative.[54] By and large, the armed forces as an organisation therefore suffered from a coup or from governmental concerns about an impending one.

Aside from undermining cohesion, regimes concerned about the threat potential of the armed forces can target the command and control structure as well. Rather than allow for the pyramidal structure that a regular command structure usually has, Arab regimes undertaking coup-proofing techniques resort to highly centralised structures which deprive lower ranks of any autonomy. The Egyptian C2 structure, for instance, has been described as a "tower with a pyramid on top",[55] where virtually every decision has to be taken by the highest command, leaving it unresponsive, slow and inflexible. A structure designed for the rapidity of war is therefore slowed down for purely political reasons. At the same time, direct exchange between service branches is discouraged or forbidden, diluting unity of command and purpose.[56] Not surprisingly, command problems contributed significantly to Egypt's defeat by Israel in 1967. Similar features plagued the Iraqi armed forces during its war with Iran, when Saddam Hussein insisted on making strategic decisions personally in spite of his lack of military expertise or experience on the frontline; or in Syria, where several units (such as air force, special forces and struggle companies) reported directly to Hafez al-Assad rather than through the chain of command. Yemeni command structures were consistently undermined by tribal communication structures, which bypassed hierarchy and ranks on tribal grounds. High ranks had to be bolstered by influential tribes, or else had no authority.[57]

Weakening of military capacity can occur also as an unintended consequence of political disagreement: the Lebanese military, for instance, is not deliberately meddled with, but suffers cohesion and leadership shortcomings as a result of a far-reaching quota system at the officer corps level, as well as a high command composed of representatives of all ethnic groups in the country. Although capable enough in military terms, its plural nature has often been considered a protective shield against coup-attempts.[58]

Crucially, all these coup-proofing methods come at a military price: where cohesion, leadership and command and control structures are deliberately weakened, the armed forces will simply not be able to act as one cohesive body. Ironically, this became particularly visible in 2011 and its aftermath, when the armed forces reacted in broadly two ways: they acted cohesively either in support of the regime or demonstrators, or they fell apart in the face of large-scale demonstrations and later violent conflict. Although national and historical criteria played a role in this too, those forces that did play a role did so because they had the institutional choice to pick a side; those which were challenged in terms of cohesion and leadership were not even in a position to consider their options.

The first group, largely cohesive and sheltered from politicisation weakening its military capacity, consists of Tunisia and Egypt (which took the side of the protesters in 2011); both forces managed to resist regime attempts to use them for repressive purposes due to their collective outlook and (in)action. In this case, the driving force of its behaviour was leadership, i.e. the fact that the military command had taken a decision on military inaction which was obeyed. The leadership itself was cohesive enough to take this decision, whereas its authority remained solid at all levels of the command structure. Granted, abstention from controversial action is less difficult to implement than its execution, but it still showed that both the Egyptian and the Tunisian armed forces had the military capacity for collective action.

The Syrian case is somewhat more intricate because the force, albeit having suffered at least 50 per cent desertions, is still maintaining fighting capacity with about 50,000 troops. These desertion rates are comparatively normal, especially in a civil war context.[59] Crucially, these are clustered in units always designed for regime protection rather than conventional war: the Republican Guard, the Special Forces (both effectively commander by Maher al-Assad, the president's brother) and the 3rd and 4th Armoured Divisions were traditionally geared for internal use, and as such kept aloof from overly damaging coup-proofing.[60] More importantly, the force has not suffered disintegration (i.e. the departure of whole units), which indicates that its overall structure is still operational. The same can be said of the Algerian military, which faced large-scale violence following the abortion of national elections in 1992, but managed to retain cohesion and fighting capacity.

In this, both the Syrian and Algerian military differ from the Libyan and the Yemeni cases, which are the counter-examples. Neither force was able to act cohesively in 2011; the armed forces split along unit lines amidst large-scale desertion. In Yemen, the 1st armoured division under Major General Ali Mohsen al-Ahmar followed him; others defected simply to go home; the third case, headed by President Saleh's family members, defended the regime. In Libya, only those units protected from coup-proofing techniques and under the command of Gaddafi's son Khamis (mostly in the 32nd brigade) continued to fight, whereas only the Special Forces joined the rebels in the country's east.

Most soldiers simply deserted to go home. The Libyan scale of desertion exceeded that of Syria by far: four months into the conflict, the Libyan military had shrunk to about half of its original size. A logical continuation of its internal disarray and broken loyalty towards a regime which mistreated it, the military had been weakened by Gaddafi to the extent that it could not and would not protect his rule.

While the Syrian case shows that a regime can survive by using the military structure for maintaining power, the Libyan and Yemeni forces proved to be showcases of forces that had been coup-proofed to the extent that military capacity had been reduced to incapacity. Whether or not a force turns its weaponry into political capital therefore depends always first and foremost on its capacity to do so; where a military organisation does not possess this capacity, it will simply not be able to translate any ambitions into action.[61]

*Military interests: because they want to*

Having the capacity for collective action—political or military—does not imply that a military force will oust a government or desert it. What pushes the armed forces into the political sector is if their own institutional interests are unmet or jeopardised by the existing government. Needless to say, armed forces usually cloak their own interests in national narratives rather than admit that purely military considerations played a role, too, in their decision to interfere one way or another. A glance at a typical Communiqué No. 1 (the military's first announcement after a coup) in the Arab world reveals that the military's declared intentions were to "save the nation from the tyrant" (Syria 1949), "remove corruption and tyranny" and to "restore the legitimate rights of the people" (Syria 1961), because it had "noticed the country's worsening situation" and decided to "save the country" (Sudan 1985) or was compelled by the people's "demands for change and regeneration" by overthrowing "the reactionary and corrupt regime" (Libya 1969).[62] Perhaps the most honest Communiqué was the Egyptian one of 1951, in which Sadat laid out mainly military–internal reasons for the move:

> Egypt has passed through a critical period in her recent history characterised by bribery, mischief, and the absence of governmental stability. All of

these were factors that had a large influence on the army. Those who accepted bribes and were thus influenced caused our defeat in the Palestine War [1948]. As for the period following the war, the mischief-making elements have been assisting one another, and traitors have been commanding the army. They appointed a commander who is either ignorant or corrupt. Egypt has reached the point, therefore, of having no army to defend it. Accordingly, we have undertaken to clean ourselves up and have appointed to command us men from within the army whom we trust in their ability, their character, and their patriotism. It is certain that all Egypt will meet this news with enthusiasm and will welcome it. As for those whose arrest we saw fit from among men formerly associated with the army, we will not deal harshly with them, but will release them at the appropriate time. I assure the Egyptian people that the entire army today has become capable of operating in the national interest and under the rule of the constitution apart from any interests of its own. I take this opportunity to request that the people never permit any traitors to take refuge in deeds of destruction or violence because these are not in the interest of Egypt. Should anyone behave in such ways, he will be dealt with forcefully in a manner such as has not been seen before and his deeds will meet immediately the reward for treason. The army will take charge with the assistance of the police. I assure our foreign brothers that their interests, their personal safety [lit. "their souls"], and their property are safe, and that the army considers itself responsible for them. May God grant us success.[63]

The main reason for the usual cosmetic rhetoric is that military collective interests are usually qualified as self-interested (which ignores others or proceeds at their expense) and therefore something negative rather than merely interested. This perception is reinforced by the fact that the majority of military forces which do become political actors are under-staffed, under-funded and under-equipped—a situation which changes for the better following the intervention, whereas the country's economy usually takes a 3.5 per cent hit in income.[64] Consequently, some argue that "the great majority of coups are partly, primarily or entirely motivated by the defence or enactment of the military's corporate interests".[65]

While this is accurate, it ignores the pull factors (discussed in Chapter 3) which act on the armed forces in addition to these internal push factors; it also implies that these corporate interests boil down to self-enrichment and totalitarian control. But military *interests* (which means simply a stake or involvement) are directly related to the armed forces' identity and *raison d'être*.[66] And just as the armed forces have several identities, they also have different interests. The military is on the one hand a bureaucratic organisation, and on the other an institution representing the state more than, say, a health ministry. It is also possible that its staff, especially the officer corps, develop their own set of interests as a collective. Some of these interests might therefore be more personal than institutional, but as a whole they are intertwined within the organisation—and consequently at least in part justified.

## A bureaucracy at war

In order to understand the institutional/organisational interests of the military, Arab or other, we need to look beyond their task of war and see what organisations and institutions are, regardless of their mission. In this context, the armed forces are first and foremost a bureaucracy. In fact, they are an ideal-type bureaucratic organisation in the Weberian sense, defined by a hierarchical structure, managed according to defined rules, a specialised area of work requiring recruitment based on specific qualifications, a mission to be achieved and a generally impersonal outlook.[67] Bureaucracies are—at least in theory—not only the most efficient form of human organisations, they also have interests consisting mainly of securing the resources necessary to achieve their mission and the freedom to operate. Hence, they have a tendency to grow over time, just as their work will continue to expand—an observation applicable to all organisations, not just the armed forces.[68] In addition, they hold a monopoly (of violence in the military case), and as a result they never have to face competition. While any organisation, in particular a bureaucratic one, will display these features, the right to exist becomes especially emotional if the organisation is an institution.

The difference between an organisation and an institution lies in the purpose or mission of each: whereas the former is a collective set up for a certain, hence any, purpose, the latter is "legitimated in terms of values and norms, i.e. a purpose transcending individual self-interest in favour of a presumed higher good. Members of an institution are often viewed as following a calling; they generally regard themselves as being different or apart from broader society and are so regarded by others".[69] Institutions are therefore also organisations, but their purpose is understood to be one that serves society at large. As a representative of the state, tasked to defend this state with potentially even the lives of its staff, the armed forces perceive their self-interest as intertwined with their mission—in other words, since the mission is the defence of a state and nation, surely anything serving this mission will be also in the interest of the state and nation. Institutional interests are therefore often cloaked in national considerations; this explains why military leaders deny that organisational interests played a part in the decision to act, as it would clash with the military's narrative of the defender of the nation—by default an almost altruistic and self-sacrificing endeavour.

The institutional aspect transfers to the individual level, too, as by logical extension, the military is a profession rather than an occupation; where the latter is merely an activity "legitimated in terms of the marketplace, i.e., prevailing monetary rewards for equivalent competencies", professions are "legitimated in terms of specialised expertise, i.e., a skill level formally accredited after long, intensive, academic training". In fact, service in the armed forces is not just a profession, but for some a calling "legitimated in terms of institutional values, i.e., a purpose transcending individual self-interest in favour of a presumed higher good. A calling usually enjoys high esteem from the larger community because it is associated with notions of self-sacrifice and complete dedication to one's role. (...) Members of a calling generally regard themselves as being different or apart from the broader society and are so regarded by others."[70] Soldiers and officers will therefore see themselves, and be seen by society, as individuals serving the nation at large; in return, they will expect the necessary resources, freedom and perhaps recognition for doing so.

## Show me the money: financial considerations

Armed forces are often accused of seeking political influence merely to increase their respective state's defence budget. This is not in itself a political move: for purely organisational reasons, armed forces usually seek financial resources they deem adequate to perform their mission; where they are under-funded, organisational frustration will feed into political motivation. This is mirrored in the statistics, which show that there is a link between military budgets and political intervention: the lower the defence budget, the likelier coups become. In return, coups are least likely in states with high military spending. The exact link is not clear: does low military spending result in incentive to stage a coup, or does high spending equate with a sort of protection money the civilian government pays?[71] In any case, defence budgets increase after a coup regardless of whether or not a coup was successful (although it does increase by 25 per cent more after a successful one).[72] In the case of unsuccessful coups, the increase could be a move by the government to prevent further attempts. This is particularly the case in autocracies, where military spending is generally higher than in democracies—although amongst autocratic types, military regimes indeed spend the most and personalist ones the least, whereas single-party systems and monarchies are somewhere in between.[73]

It is important to note, however, that not just military budgets increase after a coup, but state budgets overall. These budgets cater first and foremost to the armed forces as a collective; although regimes occasionally seek to build loyalty networks in the officer corps by handing out privileges and cash to individuals, military expenditure figures accommodate the organisational/institutional interests of the armed forces as they cover the costs of all armed forces (including strategic, land, naval, air, command, administration and support forces) for operations, procurement and research—this includes salaries and pensions, the cost of maintaining and training units, headquarters, servicing and repairing infrastructure and equipment, and, of course, develop and purchase weapons.[74] Privileges such as cars, refrigerators and other luxury items, access to funds and loans, housing, travel permits and civilian jobs following retirement (all techniques used by leaders such as Egypt's first military chief after the coup, Abdel Hakim Amer, to create loyal constituencies in the officer corps) do not fall in the same category, as they appeal to the individual's interests rather than the organisational ones.[75] Similar techniques were used in Syria and in Iraq under Saddam Hussein, though they play to individual, not collective military interests and therefore have less impact on collective institutional interests.[76]

Wherever financial collective interests of the armed forces are threatened one way or another, political intervention, or threat thereof, is likely to occur. Syria's first coup in 1949 was preceded by an unheard request for an increase in the military budget, and resulted in a special army tax, as coup leader Za'im sought to provide the military with US$28 million—but similar financial dire straits were present in Egypt, Iraq or Syria before the first coups struck.[77] Defence budgets were generally extremely low on the eve of political intervention— perhaps because civilian leaders believed that a small and under-funded force would not constitute a political threat.

Consequently, defence spending rose across the region—either as a protection racket against coups, or as a result of military intervention. While global military expenditure hovered around 5 per cent in the 1970s and 1980s, the Arab world spent 8.2 per cent; breaking this down into sub-regions, the Middle East spent 9.8 per cent and North Africa 6.64 per cent in those years.[78] Between 1960 and 1975, the region's spending multiplied by fifteen, while it remained constant for NATO and Warsaw Pact nations, and doubled in Asia. Within only five years (1972–7), Iraq's defence expenditure grew by 48.9 per cent, Egypt's by 25.9 per cent, Saudi Arabia's by 62.1 per cent, Algeria's by 40.3 per cent and Syria's by 49.2 per cent; this compares with 6.5 per cent in the United States and 5.8 per cent in the United Kingdom.[79] In the 1960s, military regimes (where the armed forces were directly involved in government) devoted almost twice as much as civilian regimes to defence budgets, but the general trend for increased spending was mirrored on the civilian side, too.[80] In the 1990s and early 2000s, the region mimicked global trends of first decreasing and later increasing, but spending remained consistently higher than elsewhere, and continues to do so. In 2015, the average Arab state spent 3.5 per cent, whereas NATO nations struggled to meet the agreed 2 per cent.

The size of the Libyan armed forces, for instance, virtually doubled overnight after the 1969 coup, and the regime went on a spending spree. In no time, the Libyan military had the highest ratio of military to equipment in the Third World, and continues to be allotted at least 10 per cent of the budget after Gaddafi was toppled.[81] Weapon procurements rose by 300 per cent between Bashar al-Assad's arrival in office in 2001 and 2012, indicating a possible attempt to win over an institution that he did not control as well as his father.[82] Sudan's armed forces presented their budgetary plans the very same day they took power in 1969.[83] During the war with Iran, the Iraqi armed forces were handed large material assets, such as advanced weapons systems, to silence criticism.[84] Egypt's defence budget has risen steadily since the 1952 coup, under the slogan "Everything for the battle", playing into sentiments of defeat following the 1948 war against Israel; although budgets fell after the Yom Kippur War in 1973, they have not only increased since—most recently by 10 per cent or $0.5 million following the ousting of President Mubarak, while overall expenses grew by 19 per cent[85]—but have been masked by the establishment of parallel sources of funding not included in the budget.

High defence spending is no guarantee against military intervention, however. In both 2011 and 2013 financial considerations played into the Egyptian military's decisions first to desert President Mubarak and later to topple President Morsi. In the first instance, Mubarak's grooming of his son Gamal to be his successor—likely planned for 2011— was at odds with military interests. Gamal's liberal economic tendencies constituted a direct threat to the many economic activities the Egyptian military was (and is) involved in—a concern that officers had raised rather openly only months before the military decided to abandon Mubarak.[86] Similarly, constant unrest under President Morsi had the officers worried about their investments in business, particularly the tourism industry.[87]

In contrast to most other forces of the region, since 1973 the Egyptian armed forces have turned into an economic enterprise whose activities go way beyond military production. The military-owned Ministry of Military Production, the Arab Organisation for Industrialization, and the National Service Production Organisation manage over thirty enterprises producing civilian products, including food staples and domestic technology, and are engaged in construction, agriculture and tourism. It is estimated that the armed forces' activities make up 5–15 per cent of Egypt's GDP—and these are not included in the defence budget, of course.[88] As is often the case after military intervention, Egypt's military has expanded its financial hold even further, being involved in the construction of the second Suez Canal and more.[89]

Other Arab forces have equally ventured out into economic activities, but none has gone as far as in Egypt. Syria's armed forces have equally been active in civilian business and own two of the country's biggest construction companies, employing over 45,000 before the war. Although originally tasked with only military construction, they have also built roads, schools, bridges and hospitals. As in Egypt, other companies owned by the armed forces produced food, furniture and medicines. In Iraq, the military was involved in the production of copper, pesticides, electronics, plastic, optics and engines for the civilian market.[90]

Although financial considerations do play a role in the decision to stage a coup, it is important to place them in the larger national context. Rivalry for budget shares is particularly pronounced in the Arab world, where resource constraints are the norm (with the exception of the Gulf States). Even when the armed forces manage to increase their share of the national budget, in absolute terms these numbers are dwarfed by Western expenditure. Where Algeria spent $9.96 billion (or 5.8 per cent of its GDP) and Iraq $16.9 billion (or 9.8 per cent), the United Kingdom spent $57 billion or 2.3 per cent of its GDP.[91] In addition, defence spending remains institutional even after political intervention—although most Arab forces' budgets are swallowed by salaries (in Lebanon, for instance, 75 per cent of the army's budget covers wages).[92]

Earnings of Egyptian army officers, depending on rank, are between $400 and $1,000 a month.[93] Engineers, doctors, architects and lawyers earn more than the average officer. The pay scale is similar across the region: in Iraq, middle-rank officers make between $1,000 and $1,200 a month; in Algeria, a major will live off €650 a month (although a 40 per cent rise in salaries took place in 2012).[94] Military salaries, particularly of the officer corps, place them firmly in the middle and lower middle-class section of their respective societies; of course non-monetary benefits, such as cars, drivers, access to housing and subsidised food staples, can be added to this, depending on rank; but by and large, officers are not the wealthiest members of Arab societies. Gulf officers' salaries, while higher than the rest of the Arab world, still seem to be at middle-class levels within their respective societies, rather than of elite value. Although Emirati military salaries have increased sixfold since 2008—from $6,000 a month to $36,000 for the rank of colonel[95]—this is in line with average Emirati national household incomes.[96] It is precisely for this reason that several Gulf States increased their military salaries in the years after 2011, presumably to pre-empt financial frustration: in Qatar, for instance, salaries grew by 120 per cent;[97] similarly, the Syrian regime increased military salaries in the middle of its civil war in order to stem endemic desertions.[98]

## Personnel policy, and politics

The armed forces not only have an interest when it comes to funds needed for weapons and infrastructure; personnel decisions are just as crucial. The main reason for this—individual ambitions aside—is that as a collective, the military is a profession, and as such has usually defined standards for education and training. Meritocratic principles, even when applied in a flawed manner, are the cornerstone of military personnel decisions since "who is chosen for what position affects everything from the discipline and skill applied to peacetime planning to the quality of command in the heat of battle. These processes are essential to a military's organisational competence and ultimately to its ability to generate power on the battlefield."[99] When officers are appointed on criteria other than competence, this is resented not simply out of petty jealousy, but because the conduct of war comes with a strict hierarchy, functional only when the best person is chosen for the position. As a logical consequence, the military organisation itself usually rejects ethnic or religious quotas (as applied in Lebanon or Iraq today) as they distort the principle of meritocracy. Balancing a military force according to ethnic affiliation has the potential to create intra-corps jealousy, distorted chains of commands following the ethnic rather than the official order, fragile cohesion, and possibly disobedience—but it is particularly resented when it contributes to defeat on the battlefield.

Even where the conditions for this ideal are imperfect, the military mindset nevertheless operates within this framework and resents civilian interference. One such example is the Iraqi armed forces which, regardless of their poor training standards and high levels of corruption, begrudged then Prime Minister Maliki's untransparent personnel policy. Consequently, the armed forces tend to protect their procedures of selection, posting and promotion from interference from outside the profession, or at least to limit any outside influence. The

Egyptian military, for instance, lobbied hard to move the appointment and dismissal of its staff further and further from the civilian realm in successive constitutions. As of 2014, the defence minister can no longer be appointed without the approval of the Supreme Council of the Armed Forces.

Hence, whenever a civilian government handles personnel questions unsatisfactorily, institutional interests can be threatened and political frustration increase accordingly. This ranges from dismissal of officers to understaffing and lack of promotions: whenever the corps develops a collective grudge, the frustration can feed into a pool of coup motivations.

Dismissals are particularly dangerous, regardless of whether large numbers or key individuals are being let go. The 2008 coup in Mauritania, for instance, followed a presidential announcement that he was firing several senior army officers including the head of the presidential guard.[100] The dismissals were certainly not the only reason for the ousting, but they provided the final element of frustration. Similarly, the Egyptian military was purged of over 1,000 officers following its defeat against Israel in 1967 (and several senior air force officers were tried for mismanagement), eventually feeding into a coup attempt in 1971.[101] And personnel considerations also played into the tragic disintegration of the Yemeni military in 2014. Following a security sector reform which largely consisted of firing officers considered close to former President Saleh (rather than reform technical aspects such as professional selection criteria and equipment), the military fell into two parts: those in favour of the former, those in favour of the new President Hadi.[102]

While dismissing a group of men trained in arms is by definition a politically risky endeavour, it gets even trickier when the group is particularly large. The 1990s concept of DDR (Disarmament, Demobilisation, Reintegration) seeks to address this by flanking military downsizing in an acceptable manner to individuals who could jeopardise any political process. Where they are not integrated appropriately, there is a high chance of them turning to collective violence—what soldiers are trained for. In order to prevent coups, the payroll has consequently often been extended for longer than necessary, as in Iraq after the war with Iran ended in 1988.

The Iraqi armed forces almost quadrupled during the war, emerging from it with 850,000 troops, plus units in the Popular Army and the reserves. While Iraq had to downsize because its force was simply too costly, its economy had suffered from the war to a point where soldiers would be dismissed into a job market which could not absorb them. At the same time, keeping the force on standby represented a risk at the political front; the combat experience had not only created a cohesion that the regime sought to torpedo throughout, but it also fostered discontent with a regime which had taken erroneous strategic decisions at the expense of the armed forces. Saddam Hussein faced a dilemma— and solved it with another war.[103] Alas, the occupation of Kuwait, the subsequent war against an international coalition and the downsizing efforts then implemented were all resented by army officers who staged a coup, and failed, in 1992.[104]

Egypt's President Sadat faced the same challenge as Saddam Hussein after its peace treaty with Israel: no longer in need of its heavy defence posture, changing from manpower-intensive Soviet to lighter American doctrine and under serious economic pressure to reduce the military budget by an annual rate of 20 per cent, Sadat had to cut personnel as well as budget. In order to achieve this without the political risk attached, he sought to appease military frustrations by not only replacing Soviet with American equipment but also allowing the Egyptian military to manage it directly without going through civilian channels.[105] In addition, the state began to dole out post-retirement appointments and financial rewards, and expanded military economic activity into purely civilian areas. Begun under Sadat, the system was firmly established under his successor Mubarak, and is still largely in place.[106] Lastly, Sadat reduced the armed forces mainly at the rank-and-file level rather than the officer corps, resulting in a top-heavy corps.[107]

Where large amounts of militarily trained men are dismissed in bulk, this can lead not only to coups, but can also cause other serious political disruptions, as happened with the disbandment of the Iraqi armed forces following the war of 2003. Although initial post-conflict plans recognised that one "cannot immediately demobilise 250K-300K personnel and put on the street",[108] the Coalition Provisional Authority issued an order disbanding the military, arguing that it had melted away and therefore no longer existed. In reality, the Iraqi armed forces had not only been encouraged to desert by a large-scale military information campaign, but negotiations were already under way between over 137,000 Iraqi troops and the US forces to bring them back. When the civilian leadership overturned this, over 400,000 personnel were out of job and pay; initial demonstrations carried banners reading "Please Keep Your Promises" (in reference to the encouragement for desertion), "Dissolving the Iraqi Army is a humiliation to the dignity of the nation", and they threatened organised resistance, but the decision remained in place.[109] In no time, the pool of disgruntled Iraqis was joined by several hundred thousand dismissed soldiers, leading first to a quadrupling in casualties and then the emergence of a proper insurgency.[110] A crucial portion of those officers who were not recalled eventually contributed to the spectacular rise of the Islamic State (IS): more than 25 of IS's top 40 leaders are former military officers; in total, 100 to 160 more are in mid- and senior-level positions and provide important tactical advice to an organisation previously active only in guerrilla warfare.[111] Although neither the insurgency nor IS are political actions by the Iraqi armed forces, they are still the extension of the collective identity of the military corps.

But armed forces resist not only dismissals and downsizing; understaffing provides coup motivation, too. Although it seems counterintuitive, statistics show that smaller militaries are not less, but more likely to stage a coup—like the Libyan military, which was tiny when it staged its 1969 coup against King Idris, with a total of 6,500 troops; or the Syrian insurgence of 1948 by just 5,000 troops. Although the civilian impulse would be to reduce military threat potential by keeping the institution small, personnel shortage actually leads to institutional frustration, then feeding into coup motivation; this impulse also miscalculates the low number of troops necessary to stage a coup.[112] While most armed forces consider themselves under-staffed—a side-effect of their bureaucratic nature's natural tendency to grow—the traditionally manpower-intensive warfare of the Middle East and North Africa means that a certain number of personnel is actually necessary to conduct or prevent a war. In Lebanon, for instance, the 15,000 troops of the armed forces were simply outmatched by the militias, which numbered 30,000 during the civil war.[113] Once the conflict was over, the forces quadrupled to 60,000. Consequently, most armed forces of the region have grown over time, but particularly after coups or conflicts: Syria's 1948 coup came with the request to increase numbers from 5,000 to 27,000 troops; and Libya's 6,500 troops multiplied to 85,000 within two decades of the coup.[114] Following Egypt's putsch in 1952, the military grew, too—in particular the officer corps. In Yemen, Saleh grew the armed forces quickly from 3,000 to 66,700 following his coup in 1978.

In addition to dismissals and understaffing, lack of promotion and access to strategic positions can lead to military frustration, too. During the brief union of Egypt and Syria between 1958 and 1963, Syrian officers felt passed over to the benefit of their Egyptian colleagues, to the extent that the whole United Arab Republic was abolished in a coup. In the process of integrating the two armed forces, the lack of respect for military hierarchy and procedures led to serious misgivings at the Syrian end. Over 1,100 officers and 3,000 non-commissioned officers were removed from the Syrian military (allegedly because they objected to sloppy Egyptian standards), and 500 officers transferred to Egypt, where they remained under-worked and, more importantly, without any influence. In Syria, they were replaced by 2,300 Egyptian officers.[115]

A few days after the putsch, the Syrian Chief of Staff, Abdel Karim Zahr al-Din, explained at length the military grievances when it came to the union with Egypt:

> From the first day we wanted to manifest the union by exchanging officers between Syria and Egypt (...). They sent us officers who had specialised in spying before learning about any other activity. (...) Rule and order demand strict observance of rank and military regulations at work, in appointments and in establishing contacts but these men disregarded them. Instead of contacting the Army High Command and their superior officers, the Egyptian rulers contacted their own officers directly, despite the fact that the latter's ranks and duties were inferior to their commander's.[116]

Corps frustration ultimately trumped political considerations.

Similar frustrations began to build up in the 1950s Jordanian military, which still had a sizeable share of British nationals in its corps, blocking advancement of Jordanian officers. The corps began to push for its Arabisation—mainly to free the way for its own career advancement—and came close to staging a coup.

Egypt's Free Officers equally experienced a promotion deadlock in the 1950s: the military had grown after Egypt suspended its defence treaty with Great Britain in 1936, which meant not only a large intake of young men, but also rapid and eventually stalled promotions.[117] "The average officer born at the turn of the century attained the rank of colonel twenty-six years after being commissioned. The average officer of Nasser's generation, born at the end of the First World War, became full colonel after less than twenty years of service, at forty years of age."[118] Accustomed to speedy promotions, the officers suddenly hit a glass ceiling once the officer corps was saturated, and senior officer posts simply became fewer thanks to the pyramidal structure of the armed forces. This aspect of promotion could also explain the high prevalence of colonel ranks amongst plotters; the last rank before general officer, it potentially combines the largest amount of occupational frustration with operational expertise.

On the flipside, Egypt's middle-rank officers condoned President Morsi's removal of senior military leaders, not because they accepted his civilian authority, but because it freed a number of positions for themselves.[119]

## How to conduct war: Strategic concerns

The armed forces resent not only when civilians do not provide them with what they need, but also when they meddle with their key business: war. After all, fighting and winning wars is the military's *raison d'être* as an institution, and where the leadership does not provide the necessary leeway to do so, it will be held responsible in the eyes of the armed forces. Arab coups have consistently been preceded by operational defeats, either caused by civilian shortcomings (as the military see it), or disagreement over how to react to a specific security challenge.

One example of this is the defeat of 1949 against Israel. Egypt's King Farouk ignored the warnings of his prime minister and the army's chief of staff against Egyptian participation in the conflict, instead following the pressure of public opinion, and engaged the armed forces in a war for which they were ill prepared. Military advice was consistently ignored during the operation as well. As Nasser himself noted, "officers felt by listening to the government's statements that it was a political war... How could such a thing be called a war with no troops mobilised, no preparation for weapons and ammunition, and no plans and information for the officers in the theatre of operation."[120] The Egyptian military, including the officers sent to the front, were under-trained, had few and inadequate weapons, ammunition and transportation, and virtually no intelligence on the Israeli forces. Not a single military exercise had taken place between 1931 and 1947 which would have prepared the Egyptian armed forces for such a major combat operation.[121] Not only were the forces on the front ill-prepared, they were also understaffed: because the regime needed the armed forces for internal security in Egypt proper, it initially sent only 10,000 troops. It was apparent to senior military leadership that neither Farouk, the commander-in-chief, nor his war minister Haydar knew about military strategy and tactics.

Within a few weeks, Egypt realised that what was thought to be a short expedition was going to last longer than expected. Additional troops were dispatched, eventually quadrupling the initial numbers, but shortcomings in intelligence and weaponry were more difficult to fix. Although the Egyptian military "were quite courageous, conducting repeated frontal assaults into heavy Israeli fire and hanging tough in precarious defensive positions", this did not make up for "dearth of information and initiative among junior officers" which was largely the result of lack of training.[122] Blamed by the Egyptian public, the armed forces felt abandoned by a civilian leadership which had thrown them into a war for which they were not prepared—mainly in terms of training, as strategy and weaponry were not the key contributors leading to the armed forces' defeat.

As Nasser wrote in his *Philosophy of the Revolution*:

> I recall a time when I was sitting in the trenches thinking of our problems. Faluja was surrounded, and the enemy was subjecting it to a terrific air and artillery bombardment. I used often to say to myself: Here we are in these foxholes, surrounded, and thrust treacherously into a battle for which we were not ready, our lives the playthings of greed, conspiracy and lust, which have left us here weaponless under fire.[123]

Not coincidentally, Nasser and most of his plotters had fought in the Palestinian campaign, and had mainly met there. Although the Free Officers' movement was founded before the war, the disastrous experience fed into the decision to topple the regime in 1952.

Similar frustrations played into the Syrian military's decision to topple the government in 1949; as in Egypt, distrust between the regime and the armed forces had pre-dated the war but was reinforced by it. "Army dissatisfaction grew with the incompetence of the administration—food for the Syrian units at the Israeli front arrived late, and certain officers were arrested for alleged corruption. Also, complaints about promotions reached an unprecedented peak."[124] Syria's first post-independence President Quwatli saw the military as an agent created by France, and immediately began to dismiss officers following the French departure. Although he halted these efforts as a result of parliamentary protest, the damage had been done:

> The army had 30,000 effective fighters under the French, but it was slashed to roughly 6,000. It became a dwarf. Only one rule governed the process of dismissal: a policy of opportunism, personal interest, and individual survival. That was the first and greatest reason for the discontent which began to spread and multiply in the ranks of the army.[125]

Quwatli kept the armed forces on a short leash in terms of equipment, ammunition and training out of fear of a coup—rightly so, as the disgruntled officers were indeed toying with the idea. In contrast to Farouk, however, he understood that the armed forces were not ready for a war, and sought to avoid their deployment while paying credit to a popular push for war. When Syrian troops—a small number, ranging somewhere between 1,000 and 4,500—finally deployed into theatre as part of the Arab Liberation Army, they were pushed back strongly by Israeli forces. Public opinion held the government responsible, and both the chief of staff and the defence minister were dismissed—but in the armed forces, resentment against the civilian leadership prevailed. Defeat was attributed to lack of training, corruption, poor communication, and "refusal to hand responsibilities to the army officers actually fighting the war".[126] Although other reasons fed into the coup of 1949 as well, the 1948 war played a major role in creating collective frustration within the armed forces.

Similarly, Iraq's military paid a high price both in strategic and actual terms for Saddam Hussein's desire to conduct the war with Iran himself, in spite of his non-existent military experience. As one general described it: "Our troops were just lined up on the border and told to drive into Iran. They had an objective, but no idea how to get there or what they were doing, or how their mission fit the plan, or who would be supporting them."[127] Criticism of Saddam Hussein's strategy—when he ordered the strengthening of a position rather than using the momentum, for instance[128]—did not go unpunished. Within the forces, the Baath party had installed political officers reporting on soldiers and officers disagreeing with the leadership as to how the war was conducted, and ensuring that orders given by the party on the conduct of the war were obeyed to the letter. Baath party officers could overrule military commanders' decisions, meddling with warfare as much as with military hierarchy, and making the conduct of war unnecessarily cumbersome and lethal.[129]

Iraq's failures on the battlefield were therefore largely the result of the political leadership's overly engaged involvement in the war itself—even Saddam Hussein recognised by 1982 that "his micromanagement of the armed forces had hampered their effectiveness, and with Iran's victorious armies beating down the doors of his realm, it was time to put military effectiveness ahead of political reliability".[130] While this included the promotion of officers who had performed well so far—rather than had proven loyal—this also meant the dismissal (and sometimes execution) of between 200 and 300 mostly senior officers. Although this improved the overall performance of the military, it also hurt morale and, more importantly, slowed down campaign efforts. As one general recalls:

> from this point on, commanders chose to avoid responsibility. For example, sending out reconnaissance patrols is a commander's responsibility. Only a commander could send a patrol at the battalion level. Because of this fear of responsibility, corps commanders would wait for approval before sending units on reconnaissance missions. This killed the creative spirit within the army's structure. I confronted this problem in my own unit (...) I argued that it was important to provide a commander a margin of error in case mistakes should happen.[131]

Successful commanding officers who gained too much popularity were dismissed or executed upon return from the front—in sum, leaving the Iraqi military with the feeling that when sent to the front, they were not given the necessary leeway to conduct the war properly; and when they did succeed, they were punished. All of these sentiments fed into the coup attempts which took place in 1989, 1992 and 1996.[132]

But it is not only war that can frustrate the armed forces strategically; politics can, too. When troops heard about troop reductions in the Sinai, a rebellion broke out in Egypt's 3rd Army in central Cairo in 1974, because it was seen as giving away hard-won gains of the war of 1973.[133] The subsequent assassination of Sadat by an army lieutenant and three non-commissioned officers in 1981 was an extension of this frustration: although not the armed forces as a whole, pockets in the institution resented the political outcome of the war. The choice of the event—a military parade commemorating the 1973 war—was highly symbolic, as much as the intention—revenge—was explicit.[134]

But war is not the only area where military frustration with the leadership can arise. Lebanon's government decided not to deploy armed forces when the civil war of 1975 broke out. It was concerned not only that it would be seen as taking sides in the conflict between the Maronite Phalangist militia and the Palestinian fighters, but also that the armed forces, themselves made up of Christians and Muslims, would disintegrate in such an operation. As the armed forces were therefore forced to watch the country spiral downwards into violence, this had an impact on military moral. Within a year of the conflict, a young Sunni Lieutenant, Ahmad Khatib, occupied several barracks and called for a coup without attracting large support among other officers. Two months later, General Aziz Ahdab also failed in attempting a coup d'état, claiming to act out of necessity to save the country and reunite the army. Although none of these attempts succeeded in attracting inner-military support, they indicate organisational frustration in the face of passivity.[135]

In a similar vein, the Egyptian armed forces were not satisfied with the leeway they were given in fighting terrorism in the Sinai under President Morsi. The insurgency, which began with the toppling of President Mubarak in early 2011, intensified right after Morsi's election in summer 2012. Although the armed forces were beginning to pay a heavy blood price, the president ordered military restraint and instead focused on dialogue and mediation with the militants. The armed forces did not appreciate this—especially as this tactic did not succeed. Without a doubt, the handling of the Sinai played a major role in the military's decision to remove Morsi from power. A week after he was toppled, Sisi, then head of the armed forces, declared on TV: "I don't want to count to you the number of times that the armed forces showed its reservations on many actions and measures that came as a surprise" about the Sinai campaign and how to conduct it. [136]

Although professionalism is often cited as a bulwark against military intervention into politics, this is not true *ad absolutum*. The forces of Iraq, Syria, Egypt and Lebanon felt that the government had prevented them from executing their professional mission, and as a result have tried, both successfully and unsuccessfully, to topple it in return. Where professional ambition is thwarted by the government, it might take revenge.

## A rival to the army: threats to monopoly

Bureaucratic jealousy can also feed into coup considerations: where several security institutions rival each other (a system often put in place to neutralise their political threat) this threatens not only the military institution's calling as the defender of the nation, but also their access to resources and influence on strategic decision-making. The existence of other security organisations is usually disapproved of by the military.

In the Arab case, there are several such examples. Libya's King Idris distrusted his Royal Libyan Army and kept it small at 6,500 troops, but flanked them with two paramilitary units which were not only manned by 14,000 Bedouins he considered loyal to him, but also heavily armed with armoured cars, artillery and helicopters. Their very existence, coupled with the under-staffing and under-equipment of the armed forces, contributed to the motivation for a coup in the first place (the units made very little effort to thwart the coup which was carried out by the Libyan Army on 1 September 1969). [137] Unsurprisingly, the Libyan military later resented Gaddafi's ideas of abolishing the armed forces altogether after the transition to the new political system called *Jamahiriya* began in 1975; in his ideology, mass mobilisation would replace a standing and professional armed force. Parallel security structures, such as the Revolutionary Guards and the People's Militia, were designed to undermine the armed forces' role. This contributed to the discontent in the armed forces, from which at least four coup attempts were staged after 1975.

In Iraq, the discontent that officers felt with the regime during the 1980s was not only the result of strategic dilettantism and frequent executions, but also of the creation of several rival institutions. The Republican Guard, founded in 1969, gained its real strength only after 1986, when the regime decided to overhaul its Iran war strategy. Reporting directly to the president and ultimately the size of a separate army with 70,000 troops, it undermined the Iraqi military's monopoly and created frustration in its ranks. When the armed forces staged two coup attempts following the invasion of Kuwait (spearheaded by the Republican Guard), Saddam Hussein created another parallel force, the Fedayin Saddam.

## A matter of class: sociological considerations

A last, though somewhat controversial, potential source of collective military interest is the class from which its officer corps are recruited. While in theory the armed forces could or would want to recruit from all sectors of society, the reality is often different: certain groups, ethnic or economic, might not be interested in serving in the military while others are; in multi-ethnic states, the leadership might prefer recruiting from one ethnic group over another; and educational requirements for certain military posts might make access difficult for members from less educated parts of society. Because of a combination of strategic and socio-economic considerations, not all social entities which make a state end up in equal parts in the armed forces. This can have ramifications in particular for the officer corps: if it is recruited overwhelmingly from one group, be it an ethnicity, a religious sect or simply a social class, this can add another cohesion-building layer to the already very tightly-woven-group-think of the officer corps. In this case, the shared social identity might become intertwined with the military identity—and the armed forces might then be used as a political vehicle for non-military interests. This does not mean that social identity trumps professional identity, but rather that they amplify each other: only where the cohesiveness of the corps is already strong can another collective identity come into play.

One such example is the 1950s introduction of the middle class to the Arab officer corps. Until independence, officers in the region were mostly drafted from the elites or were nationals from the colonial powers; employment opportunities at officer level were limited, as the perception of these forces as colonial agents was pronounced. In addition, the middle class was fairly underdeveloped, and clustered mostly in commercial jobs with little interest in the armed forces.[138] Both these tendencies changed when independence arrived: the armed forces became attractive as a symbol of nationalism, and in the wake of their technical and manpower expansion, they offered new jobs requiring skilled and educated personnel. At the same time, a new middle class emerged in the context of the newly created state institutions: the bureaucratic middle class joined up in growing numbers. This led some to the conclusion that the armed forces would consequently become an agent of the middle class—ideally, a progressive and modernising middle class or "intelligentsia in uniform".[139]

However, this overstates the cohesiveness of the middle class and its capacity to steer the military through the officer corps—and understates the officer corps as a closed and cohesive entity. The middle class is, firstly, not a united body with necessarily shared interest; in addition, its outlook is highly dependent on context. The middle class can be entrepreneurial or state-employed, progressive or conservative—in other words, the mere dominance of middle-class officers in the corps does not by default spell modernity or progress.[140] Nevertheless, the shared social background of the newly shaped officer corps did and does play a role in group formation and cohesion-building.

One such example is Egypt; here, officers were traditionally recruited from families with a tradition of serving in the armed forces, and their appointments and promotions were based more on social status than performance.[141] When military academies opened their doors to sons from middle and lower-middle classes in 1936, its officer corps grew by over 150 per cent within a year (from 398 to 982); in no time, senior ranks were outnumbered by younger officers from less privileged social backgrounds, such as Gamal Abdel Nasser and Anwar Sadat, who was the son of a postal worker. Similarly, Syria's military academies opened their doors to rural and lower classes in 1954.[142] While it is true that the Free Officers championed the cause of Egypt's lower-middle classes, several of the officers themselves were in fact from wealthy families—highlighting the fact that it was not the socio-economic background alone which bound the plotters together. Once in power, the Free Officers did not become "agents" of the middle class, but instead developed a military middle class separate from the civilian one. The main reason for this was that Egypt's middle class at the time was neither entrepreneurial nor creative, but largely employed in the newly created bureaucratic state institutions. Consequently, its interests were focused on state employment rather than modernisation.[143] The officers acknowledged this by boosting bureaucratic employment, but still took several measures at odds with typical middle-class demands: unionisation was forbidden, and the long-awaited land reform, which would have benefited the lowest classes, was not introduced as extensively as had been announced. In 1947, more than 65 per cent of the land in Egypt was owned by less than 6 per cent of the population, and less than 0.5 per cent of Egyptians owned more than one-third of all fertile land.[144]

Another example is Jordan, whose post-independence officers had been largely recruited from the East Bank tribes until the expansion as well as modernisation of the military made recruitment of urban dwellers necessary. These were, in contrast to the tribes, by and large less loyal to the Hashemite throne and behind the coup attempt or mutiny of 1956. When the remaining British officers were phased out of the Jordanian military that year, it was these officers which moved into key positions in mostly technical units, overtaking Bedouin officers who were slower at realising the empowering side-effects of the officer corps' Arabisation.[145] What this group shared was therefore a professional frustration, in addition to a political disenfranchisement—which then translated into militarised political action.

But group identity goes beyond socio-economic criteria—ethnic, religious, and geographic dimensions play a role as well in group identification. This is particularly salient in the Middle East, where plural societies are often 'ranked': membership of one religious or ethnic group often implies a certain position on the social ladder. In post-independence Iraq, for instance, the officer corps was largely Sunni in spite of the fact that Iraqi society was largely Shia Muslim. In part, this was because its first batch of officers hailed from the Ottoman military, in which only few Shia served; but it became an expression of Shia alienation from the Iraqi state, their restricted access to education as well as the Sunnis' continuous recruitment of more Sunnis. While this gave the officer corps an overwhelmingly Sunni outlook, this does not imply cohesiveness; instead, socio-economic criteria came into play and divided the Sunnis along social lines. The plotters of 1958, for instance, were all from lower-income families.[146]

While Lebanon's officer corps were dominated in the three decades between independence and the civil war by Christian Maronites, this did not translate into a collective political outlook of the Lebanese military—perhaps because Maronites never had the monopoly on the military, and because across Maronite ranks, social fragmentation was still important.[147]

Any attempts which could hurt the collective interests of an armed force—be it in institutional, organisational, sociological, strategic or other terms—will feed into a pool of frustration ultimately leading to coups or coup attempts. These interests are rarely the only reason, but they provide the necessary dynamic to turn the military into a powder keg involved in politics. In reverse, armed forces which feel adequately equipped, staffed, provided with strategic latitude and social recognition might have the capacity to act against a regime, but have less incentive to do so. Understanding this institutional/organisational nature of the armed forces (Arab or other) means recognising the price of coup-proofing measures, and the politically risky endeavour in tinkering with the armed forces in purely institutional terms.

# 3

# THE COMPANY THEY KEEP

## SOCIO-POLITICAL REASONS

Armed forces do not merely execute state institutions: they are funded and staffed from a certain society, and always embedded in a socio-political context. When they finally move into the political arena—whether collectively or individually, whether passively or actively—they do so also for reasons extrinsic to the organisation, and linked to the society from which the forces have emerged. Two levels of interaction can be distinguished here: on the one hand, the civilian leadership; and on the other, the civilian collective or citizenry. Whereas the former is a clearly identifiable body (or collection thereof), the latter is more difficult to grasp, but is nonetheless crucial. Both dimensions can push and/or pull the military into the political sphere—but they will not be able to if the two preconditions outlined in the previous chapters are not met. If a military organisation lacks the capacity and the will to act politically, civilians will not be able to use it for their own ends. In the sequencing of military intervention in politics, the civilian dimensions consequently follow on from the military–intrinsic ones.

*Civil–military relations undone: because there is nobody else*

Whether or not armed forces will move into the political sphere depends also on the degree of control their civilian counterparts exert over them. After all, civilians are supposed not only to give the military strategic direction, to fund it and staff it, but to keep their political ambitions in check, too. When the military decides to act against the government, this therefore implies also a failure on the civilian side—failure to deter or counter such a move, failure to detect military frustration and ambition within the armed forces, failure to establish the productive cooperation necessary for effective defence, or, simply put, failure to establish healthy civil–military relations in which the armed forces are given enough freedom to ensure the defence of the country, but are firmly kept in the place of an institutional service-provider.

The list of civilian Arab leaders who failed in this regard is long: King Farouk of Egypt, King Idris of Libya, Syrian President Shukri al-Quwatli, Kings Ghazi and Faisal II of Iraq, Baath party leaders in both countries, President Ben Bella of Algeria, Imam Yahya and President Abdul Rahman al-Iryani of Yemen, Presidents Abdallahi and Taya of Mauritania, Prime Minister al-Mahdi of Sudan and most recently Egypt's President Morsi all failed, as they were ousted by their armed forces. Others failed because their militaries disobeyed their orders or were incapable of executing them: Presidents Ben Ali of Tunisia, Mubarak of Egypt, Saleh of Yemen, Prime Minister Maliki of Iraq and Gaddafi of Libya saw their forces paralysed or melting away in time of crisis. But where did these civilian leaders fail, exactly?

Broadly speaking, there are four reasons for the failure of Arab leaders to engage in constructive civil–military relations: firstly, because they do not use non-punitive measures to keep the armed forces in check; secondly, because they fail to detect the coup potential as a result of too much separation; thirdly, because they deliberately politicise the armed forces to bolster their own position; and lastly, because they lack the necessary legitimacy to control the armed forces.

## Civilian control of the armed forces: an approximate ideal-type scenario

What defines civil–military relations, in Europe or the Arab world are two paradoxes: formally, civilians control the military, but informally, the military has the violent potential to overthrow the civilians at any given time; and while both sides would prefer to be separate from each other, the common objective of the relationship—defence of the country—demands cooperation rather than pure control.

The first paradox is a relational one. Superficially, the relation is asymmetric: civilians create the military for their own needs, make funds and staff available to it and give it strategic direction. In theory, they are therefore the principal in the relationship, whereas the military is the agent. In practice, however, the asymmetry of the relation is levelled by the fact that the armed forces possess weapons and the knowledge of collective violence. Somewhat ironically, the institution created to protect a political entity has the potential to threaten that entity, too—a rather serious potential.

The second paradox is that the object at the heart of the relation—the defence of the country—is a shared responsibility and therefore requires cooperation on strategic, organisational, operational and social matters. Absolute control as Saddam Hussein or Gaddafi sought to establish it is counterproductive—although it does achieve a certain degree of protection from the military, it always has a price in defence effectiveness. The fact is that neither side can achieve effective defence without the other; in truth, they depend on each other in order to do so. The civilian side needs military expertise, whereas the military side needs resources and a certain degree of operational freedom. Agreement on key points—especially social composition of the officer corps, the political decision-making process, and recruitment methods and military style—is essential to fruitful civil–military cooperation.[1] But at the same time, both sides reject intrusion into their fields: while the military seeks to limit civilian interference in its spheres, civilians are concerned over military influence on politics.

Civil–military relations are therefore to be understood not as a set of structures or procedures, but as a set of *relations*. Consequently, they can take many different shapes, idiosyncrasies included: the military mildly influences politics but is firmly controlled by civilians; the military actively participates in political decisions while retaining significant degrees of autonomy; civilians control but consider the military as partners; the military is almost unchecked but does not interfere with politics; and, of course, lastly, the military controls the civilians either openly or discreetly.[2] Many writers have looked at the different degrees of mutual influence and found terms such as 'constabulary control' (where the civilians over-controls the armed forces), the 'garrison state' (where the military and civilians coexist but military has more power than the civilians), the 'guardian state' (the military is strong enough to protect itself against civilian interference but does not interfere in politics for its own interests) or indeed the 'praetorian state' (where the boundaries between civilian and military leaders are weak and mutual influence is detrimental to both).[3] But these categories are not necessarily useful, because they start with the assumption that all of the aforementioned models are wrong—in contrast to a right version which is never spelled out, as there are many different ways to cooperate constructively on defence.

In fact, neither total separation nor total fusion is the goal of civil–military relations, as war is ultimately a political enterprise. Consequently, the armed forces are always involved in politics in some way—if only as a bureaucratic pressure group lobbying for resources; civilian control is therefore never absolute.

The main objective for civilians is therefore not just control over the armed forces' potential political power; it is also the proper defence of the country. Civilians can easily establish punitive control, but this will severely hurt their defence posture. The desirable goal goes therefore beyond pure control, and is more accurately defined as balanced and constructive civil–military relations.

In these relations, a delicate balance between military and civilian objectives has to be struck: civilians want the military to obey their orders and implement them with maximum efficiency, and they want the de facto and not only de jure civilian supremacy in key policy decisions pertaining to defence.[4] The military wants its expert advice to be taken seriously, adequate resources and staffing, and enough freedom to operate. Only when these two sets of goals are achieved (at least partially) can effective defence of the country take place—and in this case, not disciplinary but constructive control mechanisms will keep the military in its technical place.

The tasks of the civilian leaders therefore include regular exchange of views with the military leadership in order to tap into their expertise, to establish consensus on the political decision-making process and social composition of the officer corps and military style, to monitor the organisation (through control over budget and doctrine, for instance) and to provide adequate resources. Overly active control and interference with the military's procedures needs to be limited by default: too much of it will not only trigger resentment, but will also harm its effectiveness on the battlefield. Beyond these broad guidelines, civil–military relations can take many shapes as both civilians and military develop them together.

Arab civilians have often failed to live up to these tasks—because they lacked the essence of the civilian component of civil–military relations which can be summed up as legitimacy, resources, trust or the understanding of how to cooperate with the armed forces. In cases where they then faced a military institution which was superior in terms of defined roles, structure, coherence, autonomy and identity, they found (and find) controlling this organisation a difficult task.[5]

It is important to note that the armed forces are not by default institutionally stronger than their civilian counterpart; although their hold on violent means gives them an advantage, it is their staff who give or take its real strength. Where the military is not cohesive, it will be easier to control; but it will also not be as effective, militarily speaking. Ideally, a strong civilian organisation therefore meets a strong military organisation, in order to work jointly for the same goal, the defence of the country. But where civil–military relations are out of joint, two extreme scenarios are possible: the armed forces will either interfere in politics (as occurred in Egypt in 2013), or be unable to perform operationally (as occurred in Libya in 2011 and Iraq in 2014).

## Civilian failure number 1: discarding non-punitive measures of control

In a host of Arab countries, civil–military relations have been reduced to the first paradox of the relationship: preventing the armed forces from using their violent means against the civilian government. In order to achieve this objective, leaders resorted to mainly punitive measures known as coup-proofing: ranging from the establishment of a parallel security force to the use of threats and force to keep the officer corps under control, and meddling with regular military procedures to undermine cohesion. As Saddam Hussein famously noted, "with party methods, there is no chance for anyone who disagrees with us to jump on a couple of tanks and overthrow the government".[6] The main reason for this choice is that it is effective and its result immediate; but coup-proofing comes at an effectiveness price, and hurts the military operationally. Cases like the Libyan or Iraqi military, which fell apart in time of duress, are such examples.

But civilians who want to control the military while preserving its operational capacity have means available other than punitive ones. Both objective and subjective control of the armed forces will achieve this, albeit in different ways. Objective control is a set of mechanisms, whereas subjective control is essentially a basic agreement of military and society on values and identity—both resulting in the military's distance from politics.

Objective control includes constitutional constraints, who is the responsible authority to declare war, budgetary decisions, clear delineations of the military's responsibilities, civilian control over military budgets and doctrines, and civilian monitoring of military activities. What all these mechanisms have in common is that they are codified and make the interaction between armed forces not only transparent and predictable, but also regular. One way of monitoring the military is to restrict the scope of delegation, for instance through the establishment of rules of engagement, standing orders, mission orders and contingency plans. In the rules of engagement, the requirements for the use of force are laid down; whenever they need to be changed because of developments on the battlefield, the commanders need to involve the civilian leadership.

At the civilian end, control or supervision of the military is ideally spread out over several entities: such as the ministry of defence, the relevant committee in parliament, media access to defence matters and more. Where objective control is effective, it ensures that civilians have to engage with their military counterparts while having the last word on key decisions—but not on all military details.

By and large, Arab leaders are making very limited use of constructive civilian control over the armed forces. In part, this is because civilians are unable to play their assigned constructive role—most Arab parliaments have only token defence committees for instance, and defence ministries remain staffed with military personnel. Experience is missing, as much as distrust is overly present in civil–military relations; in countries with a history of military interference in particular, existing control mechanisms were often dismantled by the armed forces once they got involved in politics.

Egypt, for instance, has moved further and further away, constitutionally speaking, from civilian control over the military. In the 1923 constitution, the king was the commander in chief and had the power to declare war and appoint and dismiss officers; but the document was silent on other military issues. Although technically controlling the armed forces, neither King Farouk nor the Egyptian parliament used these powers effectively, ultimately leading to the coup of 1952. The subsequent Egyptian constitutions of 1971, 2012 and 2014 all successively expanded military power over their own affairs successively, but the 2014 constitution certainly goes the farthest. While the president is the supreme commander of the armed forces in the constitutions of 1971 and 2014, he had the power to declare war with the approval of parliament only in the 1971 version. Since 2014, the president needs to consult the National Defence Council (a 15-member body chaired by the president and comprising civilian and military leaders from the executive and legislative) and requires a two-thirds majority of parliament in order to do so. It is also worth noting that the council was originally created by a rather weak President Sadat as a tool to contain the military, but remained largely inactive until the military revived it only two weeks before Morsi became president, in fact as a tool to contain the civilian leadership.

This strengthens the armed forces and the legislative's role in the business of war, and in the absence of a sitting parliament (such as between 2012 and 2015) gives the military the final say. The 2014 constitution also establishes the defence minister as the commander in chief, thereby somewhat rivalling the position of the supreme commander—and without suggesting how the two posts are different. Since 2012, the defence minister post is earmarked as a military role, although this had been common practice since at least the 1930s: all nineteen defence ministers of Egypt since 1952 were appointed from amongst the military ranks, and under King Farouk over half of his seven war ministers hailed from the armed forces.

The constitution of 2014 also expands the powers of the 1971-created National Defence Council, as it now supervises (note: not controls) the military budget. This had been in theory supervised by the National Assembly, though in a non-itemised and therefore not very effective manner. Entirely beyond civilian reach are the military's economic activities, which are not part of the budget. The same constitution also institutionalised for the first time the organisation of the Supreme Council of the Armed Forces (SCAF), which is made up of the military's most senior officers. Although the SCAF's history dates back to 1954, it had not been mentioned constitutionally before. Civilian control over the body was to be ensured by the president's mandatory presence at its meetings; but when the council met without Mubarak present in 2011, this was the first sign that the military was deserting him, a measure it repeated in the run-up to President Morsi's ousting in 2013. Since 2014, the SCAF is headed by the minister of defence—who himself is now always to be an officer, according to the constitution. Lastly, the 2014 constitution declares that "The Armed Forces belong to the People", thereby creating a special status for the military when it comes to subordination to civilian power; and it maintained the right for civilians to be tried in military courts concerning matters of military security. Egypt is therefore a case where civilians have been formally almost entirely removed from overseeing the defence sector.

Iraq's case is different insofar as civilians did establish control over the military, albeit with mostly punitive measures—a tradition maintained after 2003. Starting out, like Egypt, with a constitutional set-up granting supervision to king and parliament, Iraq suffered a coup in 1958. The following provisional constitution opened with a statement highlighting the role of the Iraqi military in the regime change, and the military was declared to belong to the people; beyond that, the text said nothing about the institutional set-up to govern defence matters. With the Baath coup of 1963, Iraq moved away from constitutions, instead being ruled by the laws of the respective revolutionary command councils, which were a law unto themselves.

Iraq's 1970 constitution enshrined this clear civilian authority over the armed forces. The Revolutionary Command Council became, in theory, the state's supreme authority. It was empowered with all decisions pertaining to defence, including declarations of war, supervising the budget and electing the president—and if need be, transfer of all these powers to the latter. In addition, the constitution bestowed on the president the title of supreme commander, and made appointment of officers and supervisions of ministries his prerogative. Although a clearly authoritarian system—no provisions were spelled out as to how members of the council were admitted—it created a clearly defined, non-civilian place for the military. However, these provisions also hurt the armed forces in its operational capacity—effects which still can be felt today.

Although the 2005 constitution established a balanced framework for civil–military relations, Prime Minister Maliki managed to distort this system. On paper, Iraqi civil–military relations were to be dominated by parliament, which has to approve the president, the army chief of staff, senior officers, the budget, and the defence minister. Article 9 clearly spells out that the Iraqi military "shall be subject to the control of the civilian authority (and) shall not interfere in the political affairs and shall have no role in the transfer of authority"; it prohibits military personnel, ranging from privates to employees in the ministry, from standing for active political activities, such as running for office or campaigning; but it does preserve their right to vote (in contrast to Arab countries such as Egypt or Tunisia). The constitution clearly limits military jurisdiction to "crimes of military nature that occur by members of the armed forces".

In practice, Iraq's parliament has, however, struggled with keeping up its end of civilian control. Its first post-Saddam term of office in particular was marred by low levels of attendance: several sessions had to be adjourned because not even 24 per cent of its members attended. In part this was due to the high level of violence, making the trip to and from the assembly a dangerous one; but boycotting the parliament's session (not to mention the elections altogether, as many voters in several Sunni provinces did in the 2005 elections) became a tool to express discontent. Representatives of the Sadrist bloc, the Iraqiya list or the Kurdish parties regularly failed to attend sessions for this reason. During the year-long formation of government in 2010, the executive acted alone, leaving control of Iraq's military entirely in the hands of Prime Minister Maliki. Unchecked by parliament, he meddled directly with the Ministry of Defence, command structure, officer appointment and tactical decisions, and contributed to the failure of the Iraqi military in 2014 in the face of IS. Prime Minister Abadi's reforms since then have targeted re-establishing Iraq's balance of civil–military relations, including reform of the Ministry of Defence and the regular testifying to parliament's defence committee.

In Algeria, a look at its constitution shows that the armed forces have been relegated progressively by civilians, but not necessarily by establishing constructive civil–military relations. The first constitution of 1963 highlighted the military's contribution to independence by declaring it the direct descendant of the guerrilla organisation Armée de Libération Nationale. It also clearly stated that the armed forces "continue to participate, in the framework of the party, in political activities and the building of the country's new social and economic structures". Although the president was declared the supreme commander of the armed forces, with the right to appoint military personnel and to declare war (with approval of parliament), this constitution enshrined the role of Algeria's military beyond classical defence tasks.

Over the next three constitutions of 1976, 1989 and 1996 this evolved considerably. The political activities of the armed forces were removed as early as 1976, but their special status as midwife of independence (and therefore of its war veterans) was still highlighted. It continued also to give the armed forces a role of not only defence but also "protection of the economic zone", an echo of Algeria's then socialist stance. Both constitutions of 1989 and 1996 reduced the role of the military further; the preamble still stresses the importance of Algeria's war of independence, but emphasises now the role of the civilian wing, the Front de Libération Nationale. Defence of the country is "organised around the armed forces", giving it a *primus inter pares* status amongst those state institutions involved in defence, but this is the only time it is mentioned. The president retains the right to declare war after having consulted parliament and the High Security Council (a body containing the speaker of parliament, the prime minister, as well as the ministers of defence, foreign affairs and interior), and he is the supreme commander of the armed forces. The military's budget is reviewed, as as the rest of the state's budget, by parliament.

Although Algeria's military seems controlled by civilians on paper, de facto it has exerted a lot of influence on its own matters. In the twenty-four cabinets Algeria has had since independence in 1962, the post of defence minister has always been in the hands of a military officer who, more often than not, combined this post with the presidency. Military officers Houari Boumediene, Chadli Bendjedid and Lamine Zéroual used the post of defence minister to ascend to head of state (and kept the file); Abdelaziz Bouteflika, arguably the most civilian of Algeria's presidents, never passed through the defence minister stage, but formally kept the title. Both he and Bendjedid appointed military officers as vice ministers who de facto managed the dossier. In the 1980s, vice minister of defence colonel Abdallah Belhouchet was also a member of the ruling party's central committee. Civilian supervision of the armed forces has therefore been somewhat curtailed. The large-scale reshuffling of Algeria's military intelligence by the president in the last two years can be interpreted as a civilian reassertion over military matters; the military intelligence was seen as a powerful entity potentially threatening to the presidency. However, this does not put Algerian civil–military relations into a balanced state: its defence matters are still largely ruled tightly by the executive, with very little leeway for parliament or civil society.

A good counter-example to this is the Lebanese situation: the president is the commander in chief according to the constitution (although according to the non-written National Pact, this is a position earmarked for Christian Maronites) and is elected by parliament. He has the power to declare a state of emergency—but only along with the (usually Sunni) prime minister and only for one week, after which legislative approval is required. The president decides, theoretically, on military promotions, salaries, equipment, deployment and budgets, but he always requires the council of ministers to enact them. Most Lebanese defence ministers have been civilians and were members of parliament when they assumed the post; of its fifty-four defence ministers since independence, only seven did not fit this profile: army commander Fuad Chehab held the post twice for a few months in 1952 and 1956, both times of crisis, as did his successor Michel Aoun in 1988. Prime Minister Rachid Karame combined the post with his other executive powers during the early years of the civil war, and former president Camille Chamoun managed defence along with interior and foreign affairs in 1976.[7]

In contrast to Egypt, Lebanon's defence committee plays (or used to play) an important role in the supervision of the defence budget.

The budget is not only itemised; the parliamentarians have seized the opportunity to scrutinise it, too, on several occasions. In 1970, parliament passed a law requiring civilian orders before the military could deploy inside the country. In 1971, deputy Raymond Eddé requested more information on a line declaring 27 million lira for weapons; when he was told that they were earmarked for Mirage aircraft, he said that no such item was mentioned in the budget proposal, and that parliament was entitled to know not only how much was spent on weapons but also which ones exactly. In 1972, it investigated the so-called Croutal scandal, where a French company failed to deliver the purchased missiles but received, upon termination of the contract, 7 per cent of the sum by the Lebanese cabinet. While parliament uncovered corruption and dismissed officers (including the chief of staff), it also moved jurisdiction over crimes related to armaments and ammunition agreements from the military court to the civilian High Judicial Council. In addition, it moved the jurisdiction for press crimes to military courts in 1974.[8] The 15-year civil war has changed Lebanese civil–military relations since then, but not in the sense that the military would venture into politics. Instead, civilians have left the military largely alone in terms of strategic guidance. Until 2005, this was the outcome of Syrian occupation, but since then the Lebanese military had to give itself the strategic vision civilians are to provide in theory. This has worked so far as Lebanon's military is largely the subject of subjective control—i.e. the armed forces share the basic views of society on its role and abides by them. Nevertheless, the interaction between Lebanon's civilian and military leaders could be more productive.

Not part of external control of the military but still a non-punitive technique is the professionalisation of the military—although it is not always successful in terms of preventing the armed forces from staging coups. The idea behind the concept of the professional soldier is that the armed forces are so specialised and technical that they are indifferent to social values and political ideologies. In order to achieve professional standards, civilians need not only provide the necessary resources but they must also respect the autonomy of the military sphere, and not interfere with it. Then, the armed forces can become the highly complex, well-organised institution which has internalised the conservative and nationalistic values necessary to achieve its mission.[9]

But the extent to which professionalisation protects civilians from military interference is debatable; as the case of Egypt in 2013 shows, this can be undermined by other factors such as lack of civilian legitimacy, military frustration and indeed too much distance between the civilian and military leaders. Professionalisation is therefore not a stand-alone panacea to protect civilians from coups. In addition, when Arab forces overstep into politics, it is usually not because they are not professional, but precisely because they do have an institutional interest: statistically, small and under-financed forces are more likely to stage a coup—precisely because of institutional frustration.

## Civilian failure number 2: too much separation

Constructive and professional civil–military relations do not depend necessarily on the degree to which the armed forces are separate from the civilian realm; indeed, too much separation of the two worlds leads to a breakdown of relations altogether. Lack of civilian input leads to stagnant military doctrine, as it is no longer in line with the country's grand strategy; lack of military input into civilian decision-making leads to strategic mistakes. But in terms of political involvement, civilians also need to be in touch with what preoccupies the military if they want to prevent a potential coup. This concerns particularly three areas of civil–military relations: the political decision-making process, social composition of the officer corps and military style.

A typical example of too much separation is the case of President Morsi of Egypt. Although he did show an interest in the armed forces, he misread certain signs as military subordination. When he removed Defence Minister Field Marshal Tantawi and Chief of Staff Sami Annan, Navy Commander Mohab Memish and Air Force Commander Reda Hafez and encountered no resistance, Morsi understood this as an assertion of his civilian power over the armed forces. By the same token, Morsi overturned a constitutional declaration which the military had issued shortly before his election, granting itself far-reaching powers (including total autonomy over its own affairs, the removal of the president's role as commander in chief and the military's acquiescence to war declarations) and was met with no resistance.

In return, Egypt's 2012 constitution granted the military far-reaching powers and leeway, most of which the 2014 constitution preserved. It was under Morsi that the defence minister post was turned into a military one in the constitution, that the president had to consult the National Defence Council before declaring war and that the military judiciary was declared independent. Three months before the coup, Morsi promoted the heads of army, navy and air force to the same rank as that held by the defence minister—in an attempt to ease increasing tensions between the civilians and the armed forces. In return, the military restated that they were not planning a coup.

Consequently, Morsi concluded that his civilian authority was asserted: the armed forces had executed his decisions, and in return he gave them wide-ranging rights. But Morsi did not see eye to eye with the military on key strategic issues: where the armed forces wanted to act more forcefully against the Sinai insurgency and the smuggling networks into Gaza, Morsi preferred a more lenient approach. Failure to listen to and understand military preoccupations, especially concerning the operation in the Sinai, accelerated his downfall.

Although there were indeed signs that the Egyptian military had not given up entirely on politics (such as its refusal to implement a curfew, defiantly playing football with protesters, and offering a national dialogue between the president and opposition forces), Morsi did not read them properly. His lack of understanding of Egypt's military mind proved to be his undoing.

Other Arab civilians have similarly failed to seek an understanding of the armed forces and their interests. King Idris of Libya (often called the "reluctant king") not only distrusted his Royal Libyan Army but the state as a construct, for that matter. He had been the leader of the Sanussi, a religious order, before coming to power and despised the unpleasant side effects of politics: the corruption, the strife, the rivalries, and indeed even the notion of national identity. Early on in his reign he withdrew from active politics, preferring his religious studies—and taking zero interest in military matters. This, even though the armed forces had emerged from the Sanussi army fighting against Italy and therefore could have been considered loyal. Nonetheless the king viewed any national (as opposed to tribal or regional) institution with suspicion. As a consequence, he dragged his feet on the formation of a regular armed force, spending eight years in creating a small army of 6,500 volunteers. He manned the command posts with loyal yet unqualified fellow Cyrenaicans and armed it lightly—but he generally showed very little interest in the organisation and did not understand that his anti-national (and pro-regional as well as pro-tribal) political sentiment was out of step with an emerging class of young officers which saw Libya as a national entity, surfing on a national sentiment of modernisation and from which the king was entirely disconnected. When the military removed him in 1969, not even units loyal to him reacted.

Too much separation from the military also played a role in the tragic end of Iraq's royal family and political elite, which was collectively wiped out by the putschists in 1958. Although the civilians were aware of the risks of military coups (Iraq's armed forces had by then established a reputation for political involvement), they nevertheless did not see their own demise coming—this although the Iraqi Free Officers organisation (inspired by their Egyptian counterparts) had existed since at least 1952. Granted, the organisation swore itself to secrecy towards the civilians, and benefited from the fact that it had managed to infiltrate the Directorate for Military Intelligence. Nevertheless, especially coup leader Qasim began to reach out to the Communist Party as well as the National Democratic Party; contacts also existed with the Istiqlal Party. The grievances of the officers related mainly to Iraq's foreign policy, in particular its relations with Great Britain and the Baghdad Pact more generally, a military alliance which had been formed in 1955 and con-sisted of Iran, Iraq, Pakistan, Turkey and the United Kingdom. Neither these grievances nor the military's capacity to strike were unknown to Iraq's civilian leaders—but they underestimated both, thanks to a degree of separation bordering on lack of interest.

A counter-example is King Hussein's relation with his officer corps during his crucial year of 1957, when his closeness to the corps made him detect two issues which irked them in particular: the proposal for Jordan to join the Baghdad Pact as well as the presence of British offi-cers who commanded most regiments and all higher formations in addition to sensitive staff appointments.

In the first instance, adherence to the Baghdad Pact implied rejecting the alternative, which was a defence pact including Syria and Egypt—and therefore the strong pan-Arabist tide that was prevalent in the region. This irked in particular the nationalist officers in the military, in spite of generous British promises in exchange for Jordan joining the pact (ten vampire jets in addition to a substantial increase in financial aid). Worse, public opinion broadly opposed the pact, from the conservative to the radical sections of society. After demonstrations and riots across the country, Hussein decided that Jordan would not join the pact after all.

This incident played into a second issue which divided the majority of the officer corps and the civilian leaders: the presence of British officers in the armed forces. Its commander, John Bagot Glubb, represented continuous British influence in Jordan's security sector. The Arab Legion—as the Jordanian military was then called—had been created in 1920 by the United Kingdom and therefore had from the start been dominated by British officers. In 1948, when the force stood at approximately 8,000, 37 of its officers were British—a modest number, but strategically placed in the most important positions. A secret organisation of officers, using the same name as the Free Officers in Egypt, began to circulate leaflets demanding the removal of British officers from the legion. While the British Foreign Office began to fear a coup, Hussein listened closely to what these officers had to say. Although they implicitly posed a threat to his rule, he had developed friendship ties with them. The similar age and the nationalism that drove them were things he could relate to. In a surprise decision, Hussein announced the dismissal of Glubb and the phasing out of the British officers, and eventually appointed the representative of the Free Officers, Ali Abu Nuwar, to become the new commander.

Disagreement had existed also over the operational defence plan on Jordan's western border with Israel. Glubb's plan foresaw a defence of only the key points on the demarcation line with Israel, as a complete deployment along the demarcation line was too hard to achieve. This, however, was judged by Hussein a cowardly move.

All three of Hussein's decisions—dismissal of Glubb, giving up on joining the Baghdad Pact and keeping a defence posture which involved the fortification of the demarcation line—were ultimately the result of his understanding of the Jordanian officers', and by extension the Jordanian population's, mindset. This understanding was the outcome of, amongst other influences, his close relations with the Jordanian officers. Although these decisions strained the monarchy's relationship with Great Britain considerably (which it relied on extensively for funding), Hussein understood that discarding the prevalent strategic trend in his armed forces could cost him much more. This is not to say that he acted under threat; in the end, civil–military relations are about a balanced relationship of agreements, and there was no reason for Hussein to prefer British officers in his military. On the contrary, his agreeing with what he rightfully read as a majority opinion protected and consolidated his position.

## Civilian failure number 3: pulling the army in

Civilians can politicise the military in two ways: from the top down (i.e. the civilian leadership)[10] or the bottom up (i.e. groups in society). In both cases, the attempt to draw the armed forces into politics is a sign of political weakness: civilians call on the military when political institutions fail and there is no constitutional room for expressing discontent.

In the case of civilian leadership, it might be the result of civilian dependence on the military (say, as a result of war or domestic crises) or lack of legitimacy; in the case of civil society it is because they see no other way to change the system by itself. This can happen in systems which are not participatory at all (such as Iraq under Saddam Hussein) or where authoritarianism is so entrenched that token elections alone are likely not to generate change (such as Syria under Bashar al-Assad). In these cases, civilians will seek to bring about change through revolutions. In the Arab world, both civilian leaders and civil society have actively sought to drag the armed forces into politics.

Most recently, the Egyptian military intervention in politics was preceded by open calls from civil society for it to do so. The protest movement Tamarod, along with the secular National Salvation Front, openly called on the armed forces to intervene following weeks of demonstrations. Consequently, both groups rejected the term "coup" for the military intervention, as they deemed it mandated by civilian forces. More discreetly, several leaders of the business community either abstained from investing in the economy under President Morsi, used the media that they owned to express discontent with his leadership, or went as far as supporting the demonstrations financially. While this peaked in the summer of 2013, civilian demands for military interference had begun to proliferate since Morsi's election.

While this was an expression of civilian discontent with his performance and indeed his granting of supra-constitutional rights, it was also the result of the events of 2011. Then, civilians had called on the armed forces not to act against the ongoing demonstrations—which arguably was what forced President Mubarak to stop down. Unsurprisingly, citizens had learned that extra-constitutional regime change requires the armed forces.

Then again, Egypt's history has been full of civilian attempts to draw the armed forces onto its side. Both the Muslim Brotherhood and the communist Democratic Movement for National Liberation (DMNL) aimed for regime change in the 1940s by instrumentalising the military. The Muslim Brotherhood, for instance, actively sought to build a network amongst junior officers—not so much for ideological but more for tactical reasons, as it considered that it would eventually require at least sympathy from the military ranks. Of the Free Officers who later staged the coup in 1952, a significant portion were either sympathisers or outright members of the organisation. In fact, the Officers informed the Brotherhood of their intention to strike the night before they did, and cooperation continued for several months after the coup. Cooperation between the DMNL and the Free Officers was extensive as well; as with the Brotherhood, membership partly overlapped. The party helped the plotters draft and print their post-coup leaflet and generally assisted in the spread of propaganda; as the Brotherhood, they were informed of the plan to strike the night before. Of course, once in power the armed forces do not necessarily see eye to eye with the civilians who helped politicise them. Both the DMNL and the Brotherhood were ultimately jailed by the force they pushed into power. Similarly, elements of the Egyptian Tamarod disagreed with the military's manoeuvring after Morsi's fall, ultimately leading to its own disintegration.

But not just Egyptian civilians have sought to use the armed forces for their own agenda; even when the military regime developed rivalries itself—one side turning to the civilian executive under Nasser, the other to military head and one-time Nasser confidant Abdel Hakim Amer—civil–military relations soured because both sides attempted to use the military as their power base. As a result, they weakened key ingredients of military effectiveness, which contributed significantly to the defeat of 1967 and the largely unsuccessful five-year involvement in Yemen's civil war.[11] The rivalry between Nasser and Amer distorted hierarchies, meddled with appointments and muddled strategic assessments to an extent that military effectiveness was severely damaged.

Nasser had undercut Amer's military authority by creating a presidential council in charge of military appointments and promotions, and pushed for the appointment of General Mohammed Fawzi as chief of the general staff against Amer's will. Although Amer officially bowed to the president's wishes, he simply created a parallel command structure bypassing Fawzi and used the Yemeni war to consolidate his power base in the military, and the military's power base in society.[12] Although the Yemeni war was in part intended to train junior officers in combat, it had a detrimental effect on the forces: discipline deteriorated, equipment was neglected and combat simply avoided. These and other manoeuvrings hurt the armed forces significantly in terms of effectiveness.

Civilians equally hurt the armed forces in both Iraq and Syria, where Baath regimes had deliberately used the military to come to power. In Iraq, the Baath used the military on two occasions to topple the government; ultimately, it knocked down the boundaries between the two organisations in order to control it. One way of doing this was the Baathification of the military—infiltration of the armed forces was part of the Baath's strategy before, during and after the coup. In Syria, the Baath proceeded very similarly: from a political plural organisation, it turned the armed forces quickly into a Baath force.[13]

Iraq's Prime Minister Maliki proceeded in pretty much the same, albeit less extensive way: he bypassed regular recruitment and promotion procedures to appoint officers (often without any military experience) into the corps; their function was to maintain a network of informers within the institution. Officers who had taken aggressive action against Shia militias were dismissed by Maliki without any respect for formal chains of command and procedures, whereas others close to the prime minister's office were not held accountable for failures, such as botched investigations into leads on terrorist attacks. The prime minister also began to use the Special Forces as his personal security agency, soon gaining the nickname "Fedayyen Maliki", echoing the "Fedayyen Saddam"; in 2007, he moved their operational headquarters out of the ministry of defence into his office, and used them without any oversight or accountability to target individuals. While Maliki took these steps to control the Iraqi military, he inadvertently politicised and thereby weakened it.

As a precaution against politicisation of the armed forces, military personnel are not allowed to vote or be members of a political party in several Arab countries. In Egypt, this has been the case since 1971, but it was declared potentially unconstitutional in 2013; however, given the precarious security situation, the upper house of parliament decided to postpone the military vote to 2020. The armed forces have equally not been allowed to vote in Tunisia ever since independence in 1956, as in Lebanon. At the time of writing, the ban has remained in place in both countries, whereas it was lifted in Iraq after 2003. It is worth noting that most European countries ban political party membership and electoral campaigning for its military personnel, while allowing the right to vote.

There are also cases where civilian attempts to draw the military into the political sphere fail, such as in Lebanon. There, several politicians sought to use the military to quell domestic unrest—ranging from President Bishara al-Khouri in 1952, to Camille Chamoun in 1958, or indeed Emile Lahoud in 2005—but in every case, the armed forces refused.

The reason for this refusal is the fact that Lebanon's military is subjected not only to objective civilian control (i.e. parliamentary oversight etc.) but also to what is called subjective civilian control, which is in many ways stronger than the former. In fact, civilian attempts to pull the armed forces into the political sphere will fail when the military is subjected to subjective civilian control: essentially a state where military and society are one in terms of values and identity. The armed forces therefore reflect the dominant social forces and political ideologies of its society, and its leadership is closely linked to the political leadership. Consequently, there is little room for disagreement between civilian and military leaders. In this model, the military "obeys orders because it agrees with the orders".[14]

This does not imply that society is in lockstep on every issue; rather, the military reflects whatever divisions there might be. In the three cases described above, Lebanon's presidents were the object of popular criticism—which some parts of the population agreed with, whereas others did not. These divisions were reflected in the ranks of the Lebanese military. Consequently, the army command decided not to deploy the military in a situation of internal disagreement. Whereas this aspect is often considered the Lebanese military's weakness, it is also what gives it strength in a time of power vacuum at the executive level. Following the failed presidential elections of 2014 (and the vacancy at the head of state level that ensued), the armed forces were nevertheless able not only to develop a comprehensive doctrine to face the new strategic environment, but also to conduct extensive operations—essentially because its plural officer corps mirrors the strategic realities of the Lebanese population.

For the same reason, the military of Lebanon has never been successfully taken over through a coup; in 1949 and 1961, officers affiliated with the Syrian Social Nationalist Party (SSNP) tried to stage coups, although intra-corps jealousy was probably more the motivation than politics.[15] A few months into the civil war, a handful of mini-coups failed to seize the organisation as a whole. A Sunni lieutenant, Ahmed Khatib, attempted the creation of the Arab Army of Lebanon and called on his Sunni colleagues to join him, whereas Colonel Antoine Barakat, a Christian Maronite, created the Army of Free Lebanon in response. He was supported in this by Major Saad Haddad, who created the South Lebanon Army. While the military suffered from these desertions, this did not lead to the complete disintegration of the Lebanese army and certainly not a coup.

It is debatable whether conscription has the same effect of political dilution on the armed forces; Egypt's military staged a coup in 2013 as a conscription force, whereas elsewhere in the region the introduction of conscription coincided with a lull in coups (Iraq, Syria and Algeria introduced conscription only after the military took power). In this context, the officer corps is, however, more important than the enlisted ranks; where a regime will staff the officer corps with members from a social group it deems trustworthy, the mirror nature of the corps will be broken, as it is no longer recruited from all sectors of society. This happens particularly when political leaders feel that their legitimacy is not bolstered by horizontal integration and therefore perceive the armed forces as an extension of potentially threatening groups in society.[16] Two such examples are Iraq under Saddam Hussein or Syria under the Assad family: in both cases, the officer corps was overwhelmingly staffed with representatives from groups deemed loyal: Sunni Tikritis in the case of Iraq and Alawites more generally in Syria. Due to these measures, the military leadership therefore did not accurately reflect society as a whole, and no subjective civilian control was in place.

## Civilian failure number 4: lacking legitimacy

Legitimacy—essentially the consent of the ruled to be ruled by the ruler—is what allows leaders to rule in the first place; it is also required to control the military, which is in itself a necessary ingredient of political authority. With the security agents, civilian leaders maintain order, resolve disputes and protect the polity against outsiders as well as their own government. Civilians therefore need to control the armed forces not only for their own security, but also to assert their authority over the polity.

Effective political authority is therefore always the combination of legitimacy as well as control over the armed forces; however, ultimately legitimacy trumps control of the armed forces. Although several Arab leaders have succeeded in suppressing dissent with the assistance of the security forces, in the long run lack of legitimacy cannot be redeemed by force. On the flipside, as long as the majority of the citizenry perceive the leader to be the legitimate one, the room for civilian manoeuvring is rather large. In the Arab world, it was legitimacy which protected those leaders who survived military coup attempts—and it was lack thereof which brought others down.

Governments can acquire legitimacy in different ways: whereas traditional legitimacy evolves over time (for example, long-term rule by dictators or inherited rule in monarchic systems), legal legitimacy is derived from rules and laws, that is, the ruler is elected or appointed according to a transparent system. Charismatic legitimacy is based on an individual's virtues recognised by the population as qualities that qualify him or her to lead.[17] Legitimacy is therefore independent from the political system, and can exist in authoritarian systems as well as in democratic ones. What matters more than how the leader has acquired the popular consent for his rule is the extent of this consensus in society.

Where such a consensus exists, it will be more difficult if not outright impossible for the armed forces to remove the regime, as they will be acting against popular will. It is important to note that legitimacy is not a given but a process; leaders have to deliver on needs such as security, representation or welfare, or else their legitimacy will be questioned by their institutions or indeed their citizenry.

Where legitimacy is damaged, the armed forces will have room for manoeuvring in order to remove the civilian leaders without facing active opposition from the population—indeed, as seen earlier, citizens might even call on the armed forces to do so. Where legitimacy is intact, the civilians, or parts of the armed forces, will continue to support the leadership and make such a military move difficult.

One such example is the public reaction to the Egyptian military's removal of President Morsi from power in the summer of 2013. His legitimacy was legal, thanks to his electoral success. However, it continued to be questioned by parts of the population ever since he came to power. Having won the election with a narrow majority of 51.7 per cent and a voter turnout of 52 per cent in the second round, the argument quickly arose that his legitimacy effectively rested on only a quarter of the population. Unpopular decisions, such as the declaration which granted him supra-constitutional powers, worsening security conditions and an ailing economy all added to the popular erosion of his legitimacy. In their joint declaration, two civilian protest movements which called for the military to intervene against him repeatedly pointed to Morsi's lost legitimacy as the main reason—legitimacy he had lost because he "violated the laws, the constitution, the judiciary and the freedom of the media".

Two squares in greater Cairo, Nahda Square and Rabaa al-Adawiya Square, were occupied by protesters for over six weeks following the coup, holding signs reading "the people against the coup". In total 85,000 protesters joined the protests, which were dissolved brutally by the armed forces, leading to up to 900 deaths. Protest marches continued over weeks thereafter—but were equally met by counter protests called for by General Sisi. Although pro-Morsi demonstrations did not alter the course of events, they do show that legitimacy was not a clear-cut matter in Egypt. Morsi's fate shows that the legitimacy of the ballot box has clear limits: opposition to rule can be expressed outside the electoral process, and might be seized by the armed forces.

Like Morsi, King Hussein of Jordan was defended by parts of the population in 1957—but in contrast to Morsi, also by parts of the military. His legitimacy was largely a traditional one, embedded in Bedouin legal concepts. Hussein was aware of the political threat potential of the military—his own ascent to the throne was the result of military meddling, as his grandfather's assassination had been allegedly plotted by a disgruntled army officer—but he had neither the intelligence system nor the political maturity for active prevention of coup attempts. His only protection against possible military incursion was the support of the population and, by extension, the personal loyalty of the troops—loyalty based on Hussein's largely traditional legitimacy. Opposed to this was a leftist government based on legal legitimacy—a government which resented the strength of the monarchy, its cooperation with Great Britain and its posture towards Israel. These leftists, supported by a pan-Arabist alliance of army officers (led by army chief of staff Ali Abu Nuwar and his deputy Ali Hiyyari) began to confront the king on crucial issues. Most notably, they demanded the appointment of a leftist prime minister and threatened a coup should the king fail to do so. However, Bedouin units loyal to the king got wind of the conspiracy and began to rampage through the main military camp, threatening anyone they suspected of involvement in the coup attempt. Hussein, who later showed up at the camp to confront the putschists, was met with enthusiasm by these units, which reaffirmed his rule and the loyalty of the military to the crown.

Although Hussein still had a few crises to settle—another coup attempt was uncovered two years later and led to the arrest of thirteen officers (deputy chief of staff Major General Sadek Shara was suspected of being involved)—the public display of public support for his rule was at worst a show of force and at best what protected him from potential military interference. It also confirmed that the Bedouin-tribal-East-Bank dimension of Jordan's population considered Hussein's legitimacy as intact—an alliance which extended into the military, which had been claimed as a possession of the tribes since its early days. In 1956 seven out of thirteen regiments of the 25,000 troops were dominated by Bedouins, who were almost fanatically loyal to the king. These were mostly combat units of the infantry; the monarchy had hence managed to extend its power base into the armed forces—ultimately it was this which protected Hussein from the coup.

A similar example is the aborted coup of Hafez al-Assad's brother Rifaat in 1983; although in contrast to Jordan there was no spontaneous public reaction to the coup attempt, crucial units of the armed forces remained loyal to Hafez. This was at least in part thanks to his legitimacy, in spite of his undemocratic ascent to power; through economic reforms Hafez had managed to secure considerable popular support, especially amongst the Damascene capitalists. As the twelfth Syrian military putschist, he was the first to understand the intricacies of the consolidation of power. What is particularly intriguing about his rule is that he managed to extend his legitimacy to his son and successor Bashar; after Hafez' passing in 2000, not only did the interim president announce the promotion of Bashar to general commander, but senior officers came to swear personal allegiance to him. This was surprising because Bashar had only returned to Syria in 1994, after his older brother Bassil, who had been groomed to become the next president, died in a car accident. Bashar had only a short time to undergo military training and build his support base, yet managed to extend his father's legitimacy towards himself, at least in the military.

Counter-examples of Arab leaders whose removal by the military was met either with silence or approval by the general public are numerous: the end of the Iraqi monarchy in 1958 was celebrated on Baghdad's streets, whereas the overthrow of Egypt's King Farouk in 1952 triggered no reaction by the public, as Nasser noted with disappointment. In 2011, the public took the lead and protested against President Mubarak until the military finally removed him. In all these cases, the public actively or passively acquiesced with the military interference because the regime's legitimacy had expired.

It is important to note that the military origin of civilian leadership does not protect it from the armed forces' questioning of its legitimacy. Even though presidents such as Mubarak, Sadat, Nasser, Hafez al-Assad, and Gaddafi had all seized power with the assistance of the military, they eventually faced opposition from elements of the armed forces. This is because once these officers had assumed office, they had to take on the civilian role in the relationship and monitor, guide and control the military.[18] In that sense, they had changed sides.

Arab civil–military relations are not only a set of relationships; as the analysis shows, they are also always embedded in the wider social and political context. Where civilian leaders are uncertain of their legitimacy, they will resort to punitive measures in order to protect themselves; where civilian control over the armed force is reduced to only one office on the civilian side (as is often the case in autocratic systems), it is even easier to topple. The broader the civilian involvement in overseeing the military, the less likely coups and other political interferences will become. On the flipside, political systems which allow for little civilian expression of discontent will invite politicisation of the armed forces, and virtually draw them into an arena for which they were not intended. Consequently, the key to civil–military relations lies not only in the two components which constitute the relationship; it lies more basically in the way that society as a whole is organised, manages discontent, and the role and rule of the civilian leadership. When civil–civil relations are upset, civil–military ones are likely to be frayed as well.

## Social capital: because they're allowed to

January 2011 marked an important milestone in the military history of the Arab world: two armed forces believed to be part and parcel of their respective regimes fraternised with protesters instead of cracking down on them. Moving pictures of citizens hugging and kissing soldiers, handing them flowers and dancing on tanks marked the beginning of the Arab Spring. In Sanaa, soldiers formed cordons to shield protesters. In Egypt, tanks arriving in Cairo's Tahrir Square were initially greeted with chants of "Are you with us, or are you with them?"[19] Later, protesters began to climb on the vehicles without being met with reprisal. Three days into the unrest, demonstrators began to chant "The army and the people are one hand!" The next day, army vehicles standing by were summoned by the protesters as internal security forces began to approach; the crowd chanted "One, Two, Where is the Egyptian Army?", after which the vehicles were rearranged to protect the civilians from the police forces. A few days later, army captain Maged Boules earned himself the title "Lion of Tahrir" when he confronted pro-regime thugs nearing the main square; he started shooting in the air, soon supported by other soldiers. The onlooking crowd began to chant, "The army and the people are one hand" again, followed by cheers and hugs for Boules. The same chants were used during the so-called Battle of the Camels a few days later, when pro-regime elements attacked protesters on Tahrir Square. A week into the unrest, the Egyptian military issued a statement declaring that "the armed forces will not resort to use of force against our great people. The armed forces are aware of the legitimacy of your demands and are keen to assume their responsibility in protecting the nation and the citizens, affirms that freedom of expression through peaceful means is guaranteed to everybody."[20] It had officially taken sides—and facilitated the departure of President Mubarak.

In Tunisia, the refusal to use force against civilians preceded fraternisation; when President Ben Ali deployed the armed forces, he reportedly requested use of live ammunition against the protesters (just as the police was already using). When Chief of Staff Ammar was put under house arrest for refusing to do so, the armed forces withdrew from the streets of Tunis, returning only when Ben Ali had left for Saudi Arabia. When a second wave of riots shook the country, rejecting the interim government seen as a mere prolongation of the previous regime, Ammar paid protesters an immediate visit, declaring by megaphone: "Our revolution is your revolution (...) The army will protect the revolution."[21] Tunisian media ran articles on Ammar titled "the man who said no",[22] and in an outpouring of affection, citizens began to decorate tanks with flowers and to hug soldiers.

In 2011, Tunisia and Egypt were the only two cases of large-scale display of affection between the armed forces and their respective populations (neither in Libya nor Syria did similar fraternisations occur), but this was not the first time that Arab populations had expressed sympathy for their military and its men. Several hundred thousand Egyptians demonstrated after President Nasser's resignation speech following the 1967 defeat against Israel, forcing him to return to office; the 2013 coup was preceded not only by large-scale demonstrations but also by calls for military intervention; two months after the event, a campaign dedicated to the presidential election of army chief Sisi claimed to have gathered 964,000 signatures. In 2005, Lebanese President Emile Lahoud ordered the armed forces to act forcefully against the protesters calling for Syrian withdrawal from Lebanon following the assassination of former prime minister Rafik

Hariri; when the military decided to stand by rather than shoot, soldiers were handed roses and "long live the Lebanese army" was sprayed on walls surrounding Martyrs' Square, where the demonstration took place.[23] Such expressions of sympathy are not only rare for other state institutions, they express a bond that can indeed exist between the military and the population from which it originates.

While it goes without saying that expressions of support like this are not democratic mandates, they are popular mandates regardless: mandates which capitalise on a certain image the armed forces have amongst their respective citizens. This social capital determines in large part how far an armed force can go beyond its original defence mandate, and how much it can get involved in domestic politics. Where an armed force has no positive link with its population, fraternisations as in 2011 are not even an option. Without explicit or implicit civilian permission, the military's room for political manoeuvring is very much restricted. So the main question is perhaps not what motivated Egypt's and Tunisia's forces to act the way they did, but why did the population even allow the armed forces to take on a political role?

## A positive image

The main reason why civilians may greet the arrival of the armed forces in the political arena is that the institution has a positive image. In spite of their often dismal performance in battle, Arab armed forces are, by and large, seen positively by their particular citizens. Repeated defeats against Israel might have shaped how outsiders judge Arab militaries, but they do not alter the fact that most Arabs have a positive relationship with their armed forces.

According to one survey conducted in Lebanon, Egypt, Jordan, Saudi Arabia, Egypt, Tunisia, Mauritania, Iraq and Yemen (Fig. 3.1), 77 per cent of citizens expressed a great deal or some trust in the armed forces.[24] Numbers were lower in Iraq and Yemen, but elsewhere, a near consensus existed amongst Arab citizens.

This is particularly salient when compared to other institutions, such as parliament or political parties (Fig. 3.2).

Interestingly, military performance plays no noticeable role in the positive image of a force; in fact, the reverse seems to be true: the less

Figure 3.1: Trends in public opinion of respondents' confidence in their con-
tries' armies

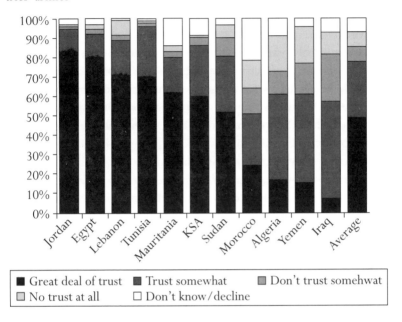

Figure 3.2: The level of citizens' confidence in their main public institutions
(the overall average of the surveyed communities)

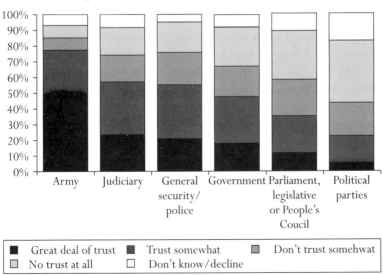

active an armed force is, the more positive its image. Those armed forces most active in recent times—such as in Iraq or Algeria—have in fact lower approval rates than armed forces which had not seen combat in a while.

These regional findings are confirmed by other, national surveys. Even before the Egyptian military's instrumental role in 2011, 70 per cent of citizens believed it to have a positive influence on the country. In the months after Mubarak's toppling, 88 per cent (some surveys go as high as 94 per cent)[25] thought the armed forces were playing a benevolent role. In comparison, views of the police were more balanced with only 39 per cent approval rates, whereas the judiciary received 67 per cent. Even after its somewhat controversial interlude in power via the Supreme Council of the Armed Forces (SCAF), the military still had higher approval rates than most political parties, with 73 per cent seeing it as a "good influence" shortly before the coup in 2013 (again, some surveys rank it as high as 94 per cent).[26]

Arguably, the Egyptian armed forces played an actual military role, having seen combat in conventional war against Israel, guerrilla war in the Yemen and counter-terrorism in the Sinai; but even an armed force largely passive in military terms, such as the Lebanese, has high approval rates. In 2002, 75.3 per cent of Lebanese declared to trust their armed forces, even though parts of the country were still under control of the Syrian military. More importantly, this approval was evenly distributed across all confessions of Lebanon—and clashed significantly with how Lebanese judged the state in general terms. In 2014, a poll found it to rank highest in Lebanese approval with 70 per cent, compared to 4 per cent for parliament.[27] However, Lebanon's armed forces had not engaged in combat with Israel since 1948—although its performance was noteworthy—and had split in 1984 during the civil war.[28] Even then, the Lebanese military was described across the media with words such as "legitimate", "unitary", "heroic", and "trustworthy" (Table 3.1).[29]

Similarly, the Iraqi armed forces had suffered a defeat in the war of 2003 and, more humiliatingly, had been disbanded. In a 2009 survey, only 46 per cent of Iraqis saw it as an effective security provider; but 70 per cent said in the same survey they felt secure when seeing the Iraqi army in their neighbourhood. When asked which of the security forces they trusted most (militias, tribes, US forces or Iraqi army), 85 per cent named the Iraqi army.[30]

In Tunisia, as concerns over the political course of the country emerged in the summer of 2013, only 1 per cent believed the army to be the biggest threat to the revolution;[31] at the same time, while the army was entangled in a bloody counter-terrorist operation, demonstrations in Tunis expressed popular sympathy for the institution. Posters with slogans such as "I love the army", "We support security and the army", "The army is the protector of the nation", "Security is a shared responsibility" and "We honour our army with our blood and our souls"[32] were carried by the demonstrators. As in Lebanon, the Tunisian armed forces had not been engaged in combat since a short clash with the French forces in 1961 over the evacuation of a naval base in Bizerte. In Jordan, 90 per cent of citizens declared themselves to be "satisfied with the performance of the Jordan Armed Forces",[33] which at the time of the survey was mainly busy with guarding its border with Syria and managing the refugee influx.

Table 3.1: Confidence in state and army

| | Percentage of Lebanese who trust State and its institutions | Percentage of Lebanese who trust their Army |
|---|---|---|
| Druze | 62.5% | 75.1% |
| Shi'a | 43.7% | 80.6% |
| Sunni | 53.1% | 83.1% |
| Catholic | 46.9% | 73.0% |
| Maronite | 15.5% | 65.4% |
| Orthodox | 26.7% | 75.1% |
| Lebanese total | 41.7% | 75.3% |

Source: Fabiola Azar and Etienne Mullet, 'Muslims and Christians in Lebanon: Common Views on Political Issues', *Journal of Peace Research* 11 (2002)

Even though surveys might not be an exact science, they still confirm a general trend when it comes to the public image of Arab military forces. Graffiti, chants and genuine demonstrations in their support, such as in Lebanon, Egypt or Tunisia, back the perception that Arab military forces, by and large, have a positive image and a positive relationship with their respective societies. It is this social capital that they rely on to venture out into the political arena.

But this image needs to be nuanced in several ways. Firstly, what is it that nurtures this affectionate relationship, if not battle performance? Secondly, does the affection concern the institution as a whole, or does it extend to those with military background or indeed military rulers? And thirdly, if social capital propels the armed forces into power, how does governing affect it?

## Drivers of a positive image

There are several reasons why armed forces have a positive image. First of all, military values such as discipline, bravery, obedience, honesty, political impartiality are generally valued in society. The armed forces claim to represent, and are seen to represent, the nation and the state as a whole. Nationalism is what feeds this relationship, and it drives on the symbolic character of an institution often called the cradle of the state. In part this is because by design the armed forces are, of course, the defender of the state; and by their staff, they are part of the people whom they are supposed to serve. The narrative is therefore there to be taken.

Military conscription is only an extension of this: aside from its purely tactical aspects, the draft is thought to instil military, and therefore nationalist, values in young people. In plural societies such as Syria, Lebanon and Iraq, the armed forces were hoped to create a national sentiment transcending communal identities, and have been in part successful in doing so. A Lebanese survey showed that 57 per cent of recruits believed that military service favours national cohesion, and 67 per cent said they considered the service a positive experience.[34]

While this has led some to the conclusion that conscription therefore serves as a legitimising tool of military rule (military regimes in Iraq, Syria and Algeria introduced conscription after taking power), most civilian regimes in the Arab world used to rely on military service too.[35] While some have abolished it since (such as Jordan in 1999, Iraq in 2003, Morocco in 2006, and Lebanon in 2007), Qatar and the UAE have done the opposite and only introduced it in 2014. At the time of writing, compulsory military service still existed in Algeria, Tunisia, Syria, Egypt,

Sudan (although compulsory in Mauritania, the law is not enforced); Yemen, which had suspended conscription, reinstated the practice in 2001, as did Kuwait in 2015. The only Arab states never to have had conscription are Saudi Arabia, Bahrain and Oman—but even there, calls for the service regularly appear, most recently even by the Grand Mufti and former military officers.[36] The link between nationalism, armed forces and conscription is therefore still existent in the Arab world, although military service has not had the impact as a national cohesion-builder or moderniser that many had hoped for; more importantly, the symbolic character of the military remains intact.

In addition to their symbolic nature, the armed forces came to represent modernity, progress, technological innovation in the years following independence—notions which mattered in societies then still largely influenced by feudal structures. This has worn off with modernisation and economic development, but it did matter in the 1940s and 1950s. Modernisation theory posited that the military was a quasi 'natural' moderniser of backward societies, simply because modern military technology would make its leaders sensitive to the underdevelopment of the surrounding societies—or as Huntington put it, "in these early stages of political modernisation, the military officers play a highly modernising and progressive role. They challenge the oligarchy, and they promote social and economic reform, national integration (…), they assail waste, backwardness, and corruption, and they introduce into society highly middle-class ideas of efficiency, honesty, and national loyalty."[37]

While history has proved Huntington wrong, it is true that at the time when the armed forces arrived in power on these assumptions, they were indeed shared by parts of the population. As societies were undergoing rapid social change, reformist ideologies such as socialism began to emerge and became part of the military's rhetoric. Egypt's Free Officers made land reform their flagship project; on the political agenda since the 1940s, it became the symbol for everything that was wrong with Egypt's social make-up (more than 65 per cent of the land in Egypt was owned by less than 6 per cent of the population, and less than 0.5 per cent of Egyptians owned more than one-third of all fertile land).[30] The social reform agenda which many Arab militaries proposed made them popular in particular in those societies which had a strong peasant component;

coincidentally, military rule has been more frequent in Arab states with a strong agricultural dimension than in tribal societies.[39]

Although the modernising impact of the armed forces in power is debatable, the military did have a certain effect as a social vehicle for disenfranchised sections of society, in particular the middle class excluded from elite circles in the years after independence. Where the armed forces are close to or in power, they become even more attractive in social terms. In Libya, the post-coup armed forces became a prime vehicle for social advancement, until they attempted a coup against Gaddafi and became subject to severe coup-proofing measures.[40]

## The antithesis of politics

Perhaps more important than the armed forces' image as an efficient moderniser and symbol of the state, military values clash particularly hard with the negative image which political leaders and political institutions notoriously have—particularly with those institutions generally held responsible for political crises in the first place: political parties and parliament. Where politics are polarised and divisive, an institution seen as neutral and unbiased will be a positive counter-example. Coups therefore take place more often than not in a crisis context.

In contrast to the armed forces, parties and parliaments have a particularly bad image in the Arab world: 23 per cent declared to trust parties (as opposed to 61 per cent who declared not to trust them), and 36 per cent parliament (as opposed to 44 per cent who had no confidence in it) in a survey.[41] It is worth noting here that Arab coups occur more often in republican than in monarchic systems; mainly this is because coups take place more often in states in which they have already occurred. Monarchies such as Jordan, Morocco, Libya (until 1969) and Iraq (until 1958) have indeed experienced such attempts, too. But whereas the first two managed to contain the threat, the latter two did not. In contrast to this, the Gulf States have by and large not seen any military interference with their politics. It is imaginable that coups occur more often in systems that allow for highly polarising party politics than in those systems which have a more consensual system.

Where political parties are perceived as serving their own interests, the armed forces are often seen as serving the state; where parliaments are seen as endless talking shops, the military is seen as a body of action; where both are seen as elitist, the military is seen as a middle- to lower-middle-class institution—which explains, in part, why the military is especially popular among poorer Egyptians, for instance; 69 per cent of lower-income respondents characterised the military's influence as very good, compared with 48 per cent of those in the middle-income category, and 46 per cent of high-income Egyptians.[42]

Coups occur therefore often in situations where politics in general and parties in particular are in crisis. Where a regime is lacking legitimacy, and where regime change through the ballot boxes is either not possible or not trusted, civilians will support a military coup passively or actively as a way of influencing politics. This is what occurred in Egypt throughout the first half of 2013, when the opposition to President Morsi openly called for the armed forces to intervene amidst rising unemployment and increasing bread prices. But even where the military is not called openly, party politics in crisis has served more often than not as the necessary impetus for it to act.

Egypt's 1952 coup is one such example. Peasants and workers had risen up several times to demand the ownership of their estates in the years before the coup.[43] In January of that year, large-scale riots broke out in Cairo after British forces had clashed with, and killed, fifty Egyptians in the Suez Canal zone. Spontaneous unrest targeted institutions associated with Westerners, ranging from cinemas to cafes and the opera house, expressing popular anger over British presence in Egypt. The Free Officers then released a statement declaring:

> The presence of the army in the streets of Cairo is for the purpose of foiling the conspiracies of traitors who seek destruction and devastation. We will not accept a blow against the people. We will not fire one bullet against the people or arrest sincere nationalists… Everyone must understand that we are with the people now and forever, and will answer only the call of the nation… The nation is in danger. Take note of the conspiracies which surround it. Rally around the Free Officers! Victory will come to you and to the people, of which you are an indivisible part.[44]

Shortly thereafter, the editor of *Ruz al-Yusuf*, a political weekly, noted that "Egypt is in temporary need of a dictator (…) for the people, not against them, for and not against freedom; a dictator who will push Egypt forward and not hold her back."[45] Incidentally, this was the same magazine in which General Naguib, later co-opted by the Free Offices, had written a series of anonymous columns accusing senior officers of corruption.[46]

Party politics had "become synonymous with personal corruption and patronage"[47] before the Free Officers struck; in the years between formal independence and the coup, Egypt's pro-forma democracy was dominated by an ongoing power struggle between Great Britain, the crown, the main party Wafd (and some smaller parties). The ensuing instability meant constant elections and government reshuffling, and endlessly postponed negotiations over British troop presence in Egypt. In an increasingly acerbic atmosphere, rival parties to the Wafd emerged without ever being able to match it. Locked in internecine battles and destructive rhetoric, parties failed to pose a real challenge to either Britain or the palace, and soon turned into one of the most hated bodies in Egypt. Perhaps not surprisingly, one of the Free Officers' first moves was to abolish political parties.

Syria too was in a state of crisis shortly before its first coup; although by then independent and free from foreign troops, it faced severe challenges. Cost of living had risen by 500 per cent since before World War II, unemployment and corruption were rampant, while the cost of building newly independent institutions skyrocketed.[48] In an increasingly repressive political environment, a doctor noted in his diary three days before the coup of 1949: "I write these lines so that the officers and men may know that in these bitter days the thoughts of many Syrian citizens turn to the army, some of whose feelings we share."[49]

In Iraq, riots had been prevalent throughout the country ever since its inception in 1921; Baghdad had trouble asserting its authority in the Kurdish north and the Shiite south, and political ideologies struggled with each other for the country's direction. Like Egypt, Iraq emerged into independence with a constitutional monarchy as a system; but under a seemingly stable surface, instability was looming. While urban elites, the upper army echelons and the landowners had settled into the new power structures, new social groups with different demands, ideals and values began to form new political parties. In the aftermath of the correctional coup in 1945, the prince regent signed licences for five new political parties, amongst them the Istiqlal (Independence) Party and the National Democratic Party. While Istiqlal promoted a very pan-Arab (rather than Iraqi) rhetoric and had backing mainly amongst Iraqi Arab Sunnis, the National Democratic Party emphasised Iraqi over Arab identity and was more appealing to Shias and minorities. The Communist Party, although unlicensed, operated successfully especially amongst urban intellectuals. In a climate of increasing polarisation, riots, demonstrations and strikes expressed an increasing divide in Iraq's society. In 1948, mass demonstrations against the British presence in Iraq resulted in several hundred casualties; anti-Jewish riots led to the departure of over 100,000, almost the entire community. In 1952, a strike by port workers in Basra escalated under the leadership of the Communists; King Faisal II acceded to the throne, and the elections of 1954 resulted in a fragmented parliament.[50] It was at this time that the Iraqi Free Officers formed, and then seized power in 1958.

Libya was somewhat different from Egypt and Iraq in that political parties played no role since they simply did not exist under the monarchy; but the kingdom was lacking legitimacy regardless. When declared an independent country by the United Nations in 1951, Libya was a largely traditional society with few institutions and little income. Its independence was an accidental by-product of the end of World War II, and not the outcome of an ideology or a popular fight for independence. Instead of parties, traditional networks of tribes and patronages represented citizens' interests. Oil reserves were discovered in 1959, and the rapid inflow of substantial revenues only led to large-scale corruption; King Idris' conservative policies in a region swept away by Arab nationalism only emphasised the gulf that existed between the ruler and a population entirely divorced from its leadership.[51] So high was the level of frustration that rumours of a military takeover had circulated months before it happened, forcing King Idris to move army units around the country in an effort to prevent their strike.

In Sudan, civilian governmental failure in the first two years of independence led to the total discrediting of parliament; when the armed forces struck in 1958, it was therefore welcomed. Unsurprisingly, political parties were banned immediately. In Algeria, the success of the Islamic Salvation Front in the country's first multi-party elections (winning 54 per cent of the votes in local and 48 per cent in the first round of parliamentary elections) gave way to military intervention as the result revealed a highly polarised society in crisis. The military move might have been criticised by parts of society; those fearful of Islamist rule certainly welcomed it as the only way to protect themselves against social change which they resisted.

Sometimes, abstention from politics will actually feed the military's positive image: the case of the Lebanese military, which abstained from action against demonstrators in 1952, 1958 or indeed 2005, is a good example of a force valued for staying above politics. On each of the three occasions the government faced an intense crisis and called on the military to protect it from civilian demonstrations. In 1952, mass demonstrations called on President Bechara El Khoury to resign in the context of a deteriorating economy; in 1958, President Camille Chamoun was widely criticised for siding with France and the United Kingdom during their attack on Egypt; in 2005, President Emile Lahoud was seen as an agent of Syria, which was held responsible for the assassination of former Prime Minister Hariri. In all three cases the president, as formal commander in chief, requested the armed forces to put an end to the demonstrations, in vain. Even their passivity during the country's civil war was hailed by some as the only option for the armed forces, if they wanted to be seen as unbiased towards all Lebanese groups. The Tunisian military, which facilitated regime change by abstaining from internal politics, is a similar example.

## Liking the army, not military rule

An important distinction has to be made when it comes to the armed forces' role in power; while the military as a whole might have a positive image for all the reasons explained above (which provide the armed forces with the necessary leeway to become a political actor in the first place), this does not necessarily translate to military politicians, nor is it extended to the armed forces in power. High approval rates of the armed forces are the result of symbolic attributes and a specific political context rather than constituting an invitation to rule. Recent polls show that only 35 per cent of Tunisians, 25 per cent of Iraqis and 19 per cent of Lebanese support the armed forces in power.[52] A majority of Tunisians (53 per cent) and a near totality of supporters of the Ennahda party (96 per cent) judged the ousting of President Morsi as "not correct",[53] and even Egyptians were divided, in spite of open calls for a coup which preceded the move. Shortly before the coup, 44 per cent said they were in favour of a military takeover; a year later, this had increased to 54 per cent. Immediately after the coup, the military still had 93 per cent approval ratings; but within two months, this had dropped to 70 per cent. According to a different survey, these rates had dropped to 56 per cent in mid-2014, still way ahead of other institutions such as the judiciary or political parties. In an increasingly polarised society, the armed forces were nevertheless not seen as the main obstacle to political reconciliation: only 23 per cent thought this overall, but 49 per cent of supporters of the Muslim Brotherhood did so, and 28 per cent of the Salafi Nour party.[54]

Individuals with a military background do not by default have a more positive image than their civilian colleagues: in Egypt, a survey asked people what they would like their next president to be like; although two military men ranked first (35 per cent named Anwar Sadat, 26 per cent Nasser), these numbers are still comparatively low.[55] They also clash somewhat with the emotional image of Nasser, whose resignation triggered large-scale demonstrations in 1967. In spite of his somewhat mythical standing, Nasser is not seen unequivocally as a great leader. In Tunisia, former chief of staff Rachid Ammar received 50 per cent approval rates, the same amount the former secretary general of Ennahda, Hamad Jebali, received after stepping down.[56] In Lebanon, President Emile Lahoud, former head of the armed forces, witnessed a series of demonstrations calling for his resignation, especially after the assassination of Hariri. He had arrived in power straight from his time in the armed forces, where he had overseen the reunification of a fragmented and disintegrated military following the civil war, which gave him the image of a strong nationalist dedicated to the reconstruction of Lebanon.[57] Michel Aoun, Lahoud's predecessor as the armed forces' chief, held the presidency controversially during the civil war and has suffered equally from public disapproval. In contrast, both Michel Suleiman, whose term ended in 2014, and Fouad Chehab are seen in a positive light—by and large because they embody the Lebanese military's strictly unbiased and centrist attitude. Shortly before the end of Suleiman's mandate, he was viewed positively by 54 per cent of Lebanese—approval which was particularly strong amongst Druze and particularly weak (30 per cent) amongst Shiites. "The relatively strong support for President Suleiman's term across most religious communities suggests his comparatively centrist policies and stances—most notably his vocal opposition to Lebanese involvement in the Syrian war—were broadly in tune with the public at large."[58] Chehab, who was Lebanon's first president with a military background from 1958 to 1964, is credited with establishing the armed forces as the neutral arbiter of the country's many religious groups; his refusal of an extension of his term against the constitution, as well as his balanced and moderate approach, are still remembered positively—so much so that when Druze leader Walid Jumblatt wanted to pay Suleiman a compliment, he compared him to Shehab: "I want to do this man who has refused extending his presidential term justice. He has proven to resemble one of Lebanon's iconic presidents, Fouad Shehab."[59]

Individuals with a military background do not take the positive image of the armed forces with them into power; only where they extend what the military stands for in office (such as being unbiased, nationalist, honest) will they be able to maintain that popular capital. Egypt's President Sisi, whose campaign as well as first 100 days in office have capitalised on his image as a military man, received between 61 per cent and 82 per cent approval rates in different polls in September 2014—but it was widely uneven depending on age group, with rates of 71 per cent amongst the elderly and 41 per cent amongst the youth.[60] Most notably, those surveyed felt that security and stability had improved under Sisi, but not the economy—hence playing into a typical military stereotype.

While the armed forces might end up in power because of social capital, society will judge them depending on their performance in power. Exercising governance is a challenging endeavour and has left military forces bruised across the board, as it depletes the popular capital the organisation had before coming to power. The distinction between the positive image the armed forces have as an institution and the negative image when governing has an important impact. It means that a) venturing into politics is a risky endeavour if the armed forces want to maintain their positive image; and b) that once armed forces are in power, they need to stress the social mandate they were given.

## The challenges of governance

One example of this are the highs and lows of Egypt's Supreme Council of the Armed Forces (SCAF) during its year-and-a-half rule following Mubarak's ousting. The body, originally created by then President Nasser, was never intended to assume political power; instead, its roughly twenty members (all of them senior military officers, including the defence minister and chief of staff) were to coordinate strategy and operations during wartime. Largely dormant during the Mubarak years, the council appeared on the political scene in February 2011, when it issued several declarations ultimately cementing Mubarak's departure.

Almost overnight, the SCAF took on the role of transition manager, assumed political control for six months and suspended the 1971 constitution. In a nod to history, state-owned media played patriotic songs reminiscent of Nasser's era, and talk shows emphasised the benevolent actions of the armed forces.[61] But the SCAF had no clear vision for where this transition would lead; it stalled on the issue of upcoming elections, postponed the handover of its power, refused the ban on former regime-affiliates running for parliament, and cracked down harshly on protesters. In no time, demonstrators chanted "down with the SCAF". When presidential elections finally put an end to military care-taking, the SCAF quickly issued a constitutional declaration granting itself autonomy from civilian oversight (which was later revoked by Morsi).[62] As a result, many Egyptians began to doubt the benevolent actions of the SCAF.

More importantly, it was seen indeed as a body distinct from the armed forces as a whole. While the military had unequivocally high approval rates in the beginning of 2011, the SCAF itself had rates of 67 per cent.[63] Amidst protest and unrest, 44 per cent of Egyptians thought the SCAF to be neutral, 38 per cent against the revolution and 18 per cent for the revolution  while the armed forces as a whole maintained positive rates.[64] The short governing experience left senior military officers bruised. When calls for military intervention began to emerge following President Morsi's constitutional declaration (granting himself sweeping powers) in late 2012, the armed forces' leadership hesitated, not eager to repeat the unhappy experience of governance. As demonstrations continued and mediation attempts failed, the military eventually stepped in after six months of unrest—only this time, it chose to hand the business of governing to civilians. It appointed a civilian interim president, Chief Justice Adly Mansour, and immediately called for elections legitimising the action. In a televised speech, Sisi repeatedly stressed the apolitical role of the armed forces:

> The Egyptian Armed Forces first declared, is still declaring and will always declare that it stands distant from political forces. The Armed Forces, based on its insightfulness, has been called by the Egyptian people for help, not to hold the reins of power, yet to discharge its civil responsibility and answer demands of responsibility. (…) Since the past, the army has called for national dialogue, yet it was rejected by the presidency in the last moment. (…) As a result, it was necessary for the army to act on its patriotic and historic responsibility.

In a similar televised speech given to army officers ten days later, Sisi declared that "The SCAF never sought out this mission and it never asked for it. (…) The place of the armed forces is now known and clear in the modern world and no party has the right to drag into complications, which might prove to be too much to handle."[65] This echoes the finding that the military taking power hurts first and foremost the armed forces: on the inside because it politicises an institution built on meritocracy rather than politics, and on the outside because it throws the organisation into a business for which it is not designed, that is, politics. It also explains the high prevalence of counter-coups.

In spite of modernisation theorists' grand statements of the military's natural leadership in "backward" societies, the armed forces in power have not fared better than their civilian counterparts. In a comparative study looking at the evolution of GDP, energy consumption and school enrolment under military regimes, findings showed that "officer-politicians do not make any efforts or contributions to economic change".[66] The Egyptian land reform on which the Free Officers embarked ended up redistributing only 15 per cent of the land.

There are several explanations for why armed forces generally fail at governance: one of them is most certainly the fact that the military transposes its own hierarchical structure and decision-making procedure on civil society. But a directive style in choosing policy options and implementing them rarely yields the best result in politics; in fact, ignoring how the population views a given situation and potential solutions for it affects how they can make decisions legitimate. From a military point of view, political problems can be solved with managerial and technical answers; societies are administered, not governed. As a result, the connection between society and regime is then weak, decisions are out of touch with the population's demands, and in times of crisis the people will be less inclined to make necessary sacrifices.

An example of this is Iraq's Colonel Qassem, who came to power in 1958. Although the coup was welcomed by several groups in society, he began to lose support as early as four weeks into his governance. He was eventually overthrown in 1963 because his "views of an independent, non-aligned, indivisible, socially progressive, secular state, authoritarian under his rule, took no account of the realities of the Iraqi condition and, in sum, were incompatible with the aims of any one of the political forces which had given the revolution its initial welcome".[67] In Sudan, civilian opposition to the dismal results of military rule under Ibrahim Abbud led to popular demonstrations and ultimately its ousting in 1964. When armed forces do not deliver what society wants, they will be challenged just like civilian regimes.

### Different types of military rule

As a result, armed forces in power have experimented with different types of governance—but all are determined by the relationship the military has, or seeks to have, with society: the penetration of society can be limited or extensive; the military regime can be open or closed to civilian influence; it can seek to change or maintain society as it is. Depending on this, the military becomes either a moderator, staying disengaged from politics but retaining an important veto over important decisions; or a guardian, watching over only the crucial areas but seeking status quo preservation; or a ruler, seeking real societal transformation. The ruler is the least frequent model; only 15 per cent of military regimes seek to transform society in an actively engaged manner. The other two models are both equally common.[68]

Ruler regimes are less frequent because in order to achieve large-scale social change, regimes need to attain a high level of mobilisation and social penetration. This is particularly difficult in non-democratic systems, and requires a high degree of governmental delivery. Guardians and moderators do not require either, and can maintain a certain level of distance from a civilian regime in order not to be blamed for lack of delivery. Although ruler regimes might seem appealing at first, as they guarantee the military's extensive control over governmental affairs, experience has taught Arab forces that absolute military rule is a heavy burden. With time, military rulers have therefore become much less frequent.

Change between the different types of government is possible: Egypt's military government, for instance, went from an initial period in the 1950s as a guardian to a ruler in the 1960s, and to a moderator in the 1980s and 1990s. Its brief guardian role in 2012 left it bruised, returning it to moderator after 2013. The Free Officers, for instance, seized power in 1952 with a series of transformative objectives in mind: some of them (removing the king, putting an end to imperialism) were easier to achieve, but others (eradication of monopoly capitalism, establishment of social justice) proved to be more complex. From an initial interlude as a guardian regime, the Free Officers therefore soon moved to a larger societal project called scientific socialism, and therefore became rulers. As transformative processes require mass mobilisation, the regime created first the National Liberation Rally in 1953, the National Union in 1957 and later the Arab Socialist Union in 1961; its objective was the mobilisation of Egyptian society for a political goal. But all three parties failed to deliver:

> Created by officers who visualised Egypt in managerial terms, as an organisation instead of a polity, led and staffed by officers and civil servants with minimal political skills who were quite removed from their local "constituents", distributing no political, economic, or symbolic rewards to the membership, it is not surprising that these three parties had little attraction for the masses and little value for those who did join.[69]

While Egyptians approved of Nasser's politics—raising the standard of living, introducing a welfare system and extending education—they did not seek to engage actively with the regime. The necessary link between ruler and ruled therefore broke down when the regime began to fail: first in economic and later in military terms. As the regime did not trust civilians and began to post military officers in national administration jobs for which they were ill-equipped, policies were not sustainable.[70] By the mid-1960s, Egypt was facing a payment crisis, university graduates could not find jobs, and the armed forces were run more by rivalling networks than by meritocratic principles. This culminated in the defeat of 1967 against Israel, and created pressure for real civilianisation of government. So deep was the crisis between the armed forces and the people it claimed to represent that the verdict against officers deemed responsible for the military fiasco was met with large-scale demonstrations, beginning amongst the workers who were joined by the students—the first in Egypt since the coup of 1952, and the first to openly challenge the regime. The demonstrations as much as the defeat led Sadat, who succeeded Nasser in 1970, to the conclusion that the armed forces needed to return to barracks: not only to improve Egypt's economy, but to improve its fighting capacity. Military officers venturing out too much into the political sphere were punished with early retirement: Generals Sadiq, Saadeddin Shazli and Gamassi had all criticised Sadat in one way or another, although they had also been very instrumental at some point. Crucially, Sadat liberalised Egypt's economy albeit in a controlled manner, and therefore moved from a ruler to a guardian role. The shedding of military uniform and donning civilian clothes was only one way to claim civilian rather than military credentials.[71]

The return of Egypt's military to politics in the summer of 2013 was very much informed by the SCAF's difficult experience in power after Mubarak's ousting. Although the first appointment was a civilian technocratic government, a combination of public pressure and internal acquiescence at last led to the nomination of former army head Abdel Fattah Sisi to the presidency in May 2014. His election with 96.91 per cent of the votes—against one other candidate—might echo Nasser's election in 1956 with 99.9 per cent (as the only candidate), but it was arguably more transparent. In the months leading up to his nomination, Sisi had to repeatedly deny any political intentions. Campaigns collecting signatures to pressure Sisi into running began as early as August 2013, the month following the coup. "Military spokesperson Ahmed Mohamed Ali reiterated that the Armed Forces does not intend to field or endorse a candidate for the presidential elections, adding that collecting signatures for General Abdel Fattah Sisi's nomination is a public sentiment that cannot be prevented."[72] It also occurred in a general context of increased insecurity following months of riots and overstretched security forces: crime rates had gone up, homicide rates had tripled since the 2011 uprising, kidnappings and car thefts had quadrupled, armed robberies had increased twelvefold.[73] Under these circumstances, Egyptian police had gone on strike protesting against their working conditions and the politicisation of their work.[74] Unsurprisingly, Egyptians felt that a military representative would be best suited to rein in the chaos. Once this was done, however, he would be judged on his economic performance—and he would still need to build a popular power base.

Sudan's military leaders underwent a similar learning experience as Egypt's leaders between 2011 and 2013. Its first military ruler, Ibrahim Abbud, sought to solve Sudan's problems without much civilian input, therefore had little political following outside the armed forces and was toppled by mass protests. But his successor, Gaafar Nimeiry, recognised the necessity of mass mobilisation; he created a single party akin to the Egyptian model, the Sudanese Socialist Union, and had himself elected in order to create a veneer of legitimacy—only to be overthrown by fellow officers in 1985.

Elsewhere in the Arab world armed forces had similar experiences with the challenging business of governance; direct military rule was indeed the case in Iraq under Qassem and his successors, Abdel Salam and Abdel Rahmen Arif, but the armed forces were moved first to a guardian role under the Baath regime of Ahmed Hassan al-Bakr, and eventually lost their political role under Saddam Hussein. In Syria, the three coups led to direct military rule first under Husni al-Zaim, later Sami al-Hinnawi and Adib Shishakli, and lastly Fawzi Selu; under the Baath regime which came to power in 1963, the armed forces shared power with the party and eventually experienced the same fate as its Iraqi counterpart. In Algeria, the armed forces' close link with the National Liberation Front led to a guardian role often moving towards covert ruler role; more often than not, however, the Algerian military has sought the preservation of a status quo rather than social transformation.[75]

## A war of words: "coup" versus "revolution"

Whenever armed forces decide to act, they do so at least in part because they believe they have a civilian mandate to resolve whatever crisis is occurring. This does not imply that riots and widespread discontent justify the military's interference in politics; but it does explain why the armed forces might feel compelled to act in accordance with the public mood.

It also explains why Arab military forces quickly move to use the word *thawra* (revolution) rather than *inquilab* (coup) for their actions. While both events have the same outcome—a change in government—their crucial difference is the number of people involved, and therefore the question of legitimacy arises. In the case of a coup, usually only a portion of the armed forces (and an even smaller element of society) takes part; in the case of a revolution, the notion is one of a mass event. The use of the word 'revolution' therefore suggests that the armed forces acted on behalf of the population rather than only for themselves. Or as Abdel Nasser himself wrote:

> Had the Army Officers attempted the revolt in their own account because they were inveigled in the Palestine War, or because they had been shocked by the defective weapons scandal, or because of the attack on their honour in the club elections, it could not have been called a revolution—mutiny would have been a more appropriate name.[76]

Interestingly, the Free Officers did not call their removal of King Farouk a revolution right away; in their communiqués, expressions such as *nahda* (awakening) or "blessed movement of the army"[77] were employed; only in 1953 did the word appear in the context of the "revolutionary command council" mentioned in the provisional constitution. From then onwards, the term *thawra* (revolution) became the standard expression, echoed in Nasser's book *Philosophy of the Revolution*, in which he nevertheless lamented the absence of revolutionary fervour which followed the coup:

> For a long time it waited. Crowds did eventually come, and they came in endless droves—but how different is the reality from the dream! The masses that came were disunited, divided groups of stragglers. (…) At this moment I felt, with sorrow and bitterness, that the task of the vanguard far from being completed, had only begun.[78]

Stressing the popular mandate for a coup is crucial for any armed force involved in politics; it is the necessary justification. In Syria, the 1963 coup is commemorated every year as the 8 March revolution; the

Iraqi coup of 1958 is remembered as the 14 July revolution, and his leader, Abdelkarim Qasim, was toppled in the 1963 Ramadan revolution. The coup which returned the Baath party to power in 1968 became known as the 17 July revolution, and the 2013 toppling of Morsi, although labelled a coup by most Western media, is commonly called a revolution in Egypt.[79]

Armed forces use other methods, too, to emphasise the link between themselves and the population. One way is to stress the origin of the forces: in Algeria, the military's official title is "popular national army"; in Egypt, the armed forces are most commonly referred to as the "People's Army". Abdelkarim Qassim, Iraq's first military leader in power, declared that "the army and the people had merged into a single entity after the Revolution";[80] General Naguib, the first head of Egypt's Revolutionary Command Council, declared that "the army is the nation and every Egyptian is a soldier".[81] Following Morsi's ousting, General Sisi went on record as saying that the differences between the Egyptian military and the Muslim Brotherhood were ideological as the "loyalty of the armed forces is to the state, whist the Brotherhood's loyalty is to the organisation and the Umma".[82]

The notion of the defender of the nation, the cradle of the state, the protector of the people recurs in these themes. The tomb of the Unknown Soldier, common in many Western states since the end of World War I, embodies the link between the population and the military organisation. The monument spread to Arab countries as well, although it sometimes uses the term "martyr" to include non-military victims as well. Egypt has seven such monuments across the country commemorating the wars of 1948, 1956, 1973, as well as four abroad in Israel, Kuwait and Yemen honouring Egyptian soldiers fallen there. Iraq has two tombs of Unknown Soldiers commemorating the war with Iran; another memorialising the soldiers fallen during the 1958 coup was later removed by Saddam Hussein. Syria erected one in 1986 commemorating five battles from antiquity to the twentieth century; Algeria erected a tomb in 1982 to celebrate its twenty years of independence. Tunisia's tomb, located in Tunis, was vandalised in 2013 by Salafi extremists; a separate memorial in Sejoumi was built in 1982 to commemorate those executed by French colonial authorities; Lebanon's Martyrs' statue was originally dedicated to nationalists executed in 1916 by the Ottoman representative, but it came to include all victims of the civil war in 1990; there are also numerous smaller memorials scattered across the country, dedicated to both military and civilian victims. Kuwait's memorial commemorating the victims of the Iraqi occupation was unveiled only in 2014; the United Arab Emirates dedicated a square in Sharjah City to its fallen soldiers from the summer of 2015. Only Qatar, Saudi Arabia, Bahrain and Oman currently do not have such a monument linking personal sacrifice to statehood.[83]

To underline the link between the armed forces and its people, convoys of tanks drove around Cairo a year after the 2011 demonstrations bearing the slogan "The army and the people are one hand" inscribed on the side, and billboards were put up around town proclaiming "The 25th January Revolution—the army protected it. The army and the people are one hand." A photo taken in 2011 on Tahrir Square, showing a soldier smiling at a toddler on top of his tank, featured heavily, too (Fig. 3.3).

Figure 3.3: Arab forces certainly require the capacity, the will and the lack of an opponent to become political actors—but the veneer of approval is also popular, and much more difficult to engineer than the other elements.

4

# MODELS OF NON-POLITICAL ARMIES

Political intervention of Arab forces depends on four criteria: whether a force has the capacity to act, whether it has the will to act, whether it encounters no civilian opposition to act, and lastly, whether it has the popular support to act. Consequently, there are broadly four types of Arab forces when it comes to politics—it being understood that forces can change category over time and have done so in the past. Institutional and historical dynamics of war, conflict, financing or lack thereof alter not only the organisation itself but also its relation with the populace as well as the leadership.

The first two categories in this model do not become political for military–intrinsic reasons: they either simply do not have the capacity, or they do not have the interest to act. In both cases, external forces play a minor role in the decision *not* to be a political actor.

*The failed force who couldn't: Iraq, Libya, Yemen*

A failed military organisation is one which fails to fulfil its core mission, defence. Where an organisation is not capable of acting cohesively to accomplish its *raison d'être*, it will be even less capable of acting politically. It might disintegrate and see individuals from the ranks becoming politically active, but it will not be able to act as one, and consequently have little to no political effect. The failure of a military organisation on a large scale is generally rare, and as such a nearly traumatic national event as it implies the failure of the state.

Nevertheless, there are today three such examples in the Arab world: Iraq, Yemen and Libya. The main reason for this proliferation of failed forces is the fraught relationship that civilians have had in the region with their armed forces, leading to distrust and coup-proofing measures as well as politicisation, rather than professionalisation of military forces. The sorry state of these three forces is consequently a side effect of Arab politics since the 1970s more than anything else: it is not a coincidence that those forces in the worst state today were also, at one point, highly political ones which then became the object of restricting measures.

## The tired phoenix: Iraq's armed forces

Iraq's military has spent its first seven decades of existence as either a political or checked force—in any case one to be reckoned with. "The spinal column"[1] of Iraq, as King Faisal called it, staged four failed and six successful coups and counter-coups until Saddam Hussein arrived in power in 1979; and even though he did everything he possibly could to prevent it from happening again, at least three coup attempts were made under his regime, too.

However, the military's disbandment and somewhat flawed reconstruction since 2003 have turned it into an organisation incapable of executing its main mandate, and consequently of developing any political ambitions. This culminated, in 2014, in four divisions, or 30,000 troops, abandoning their posts in the face of IS in Mosul, leaving sophisticated weapons behind for the jihadi militia to collect and incorporate into its arsenal.[2]

The confrontation with IS in Mosul was not the first of the Iraqi military's failures: when confronting Muqtada Sadr's Mahdi Army in Basra in 2008, more than 1,000 troops abandoned their post during the offensive, and it also saw large-scale desertion in Anbar province earlier in 2014;[3] but this provides useful insights into the Iraqi military's current state. From a tactical point of view, units deserted after three days of fighting a hybrid type of war: concrete reasons included IS' extreme violence, lack of equipment and unclear orders, but these are, by themselves, not sufficient explanations for a desertion on that scale.[4]

True, manpower was low in those units thanks to rampant absenteeism (some numbers indicate only 10,000 out of 30,000 troops were present), but IS had a maximum of 2,000 men, and did not even plan on taking the whole city. At best, it hoped to conquer a neighbourhood and hold it for a few days. Also true is that the units were low on weapons and ammunition; logistical disarray aside, Iraqi decision-makers have kept their military units notoriously low on ammunition, to avoid a military takeover. Training sometimes took place shouting "bang bang" to simulate firing.[5] But on day two of the battle, artillery, which had previously been moved to Anbar, returned and pounded the city; air support arrived, too, in the shape of helicopter gunships.[6] True, IS employed gruesome violence, torching and crucifying soldiers—but fighting violent insurgencies was not new to these units and most certainly not to the operation's head, General Abboud Qanbar. Nevertheless, when Qanbar (then the defence ministry's deputy chief of staff) and commander of the ground forces General Ali Ghaidan retreated to the city's eastern edge on day four of the battle, the soldiers thought that their senior officers had abandoned them, and deserted either spontaneously or because they were told by their commanding officers to do so.

While IS had the advantage of surprise, the Iraqi military, in theory, had experience, heavy weapons and superior manpower. What they did not have—and what IS possessed—was a flexible command structure, cohesion, leadership skills and something worth fighting for. Desertion and disintegration are, in military terms, the worst mishaps an organisation can experience; an institution properly trained for war should not simply fall apart in the face of any enemy, no matter how gruesome. Both phenomena are, in fact, always the product of the institution, not of the adversary.

Desertion is first and foremost an individual's expression of discontent, and is the loudest form of questioning an army and its legitimacy; it is also always more the product of the military institution rather than the society in which it is embedded.[7] Variables in desertion motivation are accommodation, violence within the army, and the military's relationship with society. Sometimes, desertion indicates how soldiers perceive the likely outcome of a conflict and take sides in time.[8] Generally, the rank and file rather than the officers desert.[9] Disintegration, however, is on a totally different scale from desertion. Disintegration is the disengagement of a whole unit, expressing something beyond the individual's discontent with his circumstances. It is for this reason that disintegration automatically has a far more political twist to it than desertion, and is therefore much more damaging. "Disintegration may be considered so damaging to the army, the government, to that most delicate fabric, the national psyche, that the event's documentation is put under lock and key for generations."[10]

Four reasons can be identified for disintegration: the first is failure of leadership; the second is collapse of primary groups, meaning cohesion. As research has shown, it is the primary group, the "buddies", that makes or breaks cohesion. Whenever these groups collapse, no political ideology can uphold fighting morale.[11] During the war of 2003, for instance, Iraqi "surrender decisions (…) were usually made at very low levels, often among small groups of soldiers".[12] The third reason for disintegration is alienation: when "individuals within primary groups are suddenly confused as to what they ought to believe", a shifting of values takes place and makes the individual reconsider. If the whole group follows in this reconsideration, disintegration may soon follow. The fourth reason is desperation over a hopeless situation.[13] In the case of Mosul, several factors all led to the implosion of the Iraqi units—but they all point to a broader problem of cohesion, leadership, command-and-control structures, rather than logistical aspects such as weapons and ammunition. General Martin E. Dempsey, chairman of the US Joint Chiefs of Staff, assessed that around half of the Iraqi military brigades were deemed to be "reputable partners. They seem to have a *certain* cohesion and a commitment to the central government." The rest, he assessed, had problems with "infiltration and leadership and sectarianism".[14]

But cohesion, leadership and nationalism are not purely tactical military issues; they are strategic and therefore political. Mosul therefore points to a root cause larger than the Iraqi armed forces alone—distorted civil–military relations, all leading to a malfunctioning of the military to the inside.

Three aspects of the immediate post-Saddam phase played into the distortion of civil–military relations: 1) inconsistent American planning meant that the Iraqi forces were not rebuilt in a coherent fashion; 2) insecurity, as well as 3) American desires to withdraw substantially from

Iraq by 2007 meant that the Iraqi military had to grow much faster than any armed force should grow, regardless of professional standards.

To begin with, pre-invasion American plans foresaw a recall of the armed forces (almost half a million troops at the time), but the civilian Coalition Provisional Authority (CPA) under Paul Bremer disbanded it—although recall programmes were already operating.[15] And while the decision was controversial enough, it was not followed by a thorough plan to create "an entirely new Iraqi army" as Bremer had announced.[16] The very small force of 44,000, focused entirely on external not internal security, lacking an air force, tanks or artillery, took remarkably long to take off. Almost a year after the invasion, barely 10,000 troops had been recalled although security was rapidly imploding. When the file was moved from the CPA to the American military, recruitment and recall programmes increased eight times within a year. Plans for a small force were quickly abandoned; by 2005, the forces' size was to be 130,000; by 2008, this had grown to 200,000 (180,000 of them enlisted personnel and 20,000 officers). The idea of external security tasks only was given up, too, as the military had to tune in quickly to counter-terrorism and counter-insurgency efforts. The Iraqi forces had to grow not only much quicker than anticipated, but also to a much bigger size than originally planned. Every five weeks, 14,000 personnel entered the new Iraqi Army. Within six years, the Iraqi military thus quadrupled in size—a number five times what was originally anticipated by the United States.

There are several problems with any force growing this quickly. The first is the issue of training: while it is true that in pure numerical terms, almost all troops received basic training, including 68 per cent of the officers, there is a huge variety in terms of length, content and type of training.[17] Returnees from the old Iraqi Army, for instance, received three weeks training, whereas newcomers had to undergo between five and thirteen weeks; in some instances, training from the Saddam era was counted, too. "Iraqi soldiers make do with 3 to 5 weeks of basic training before entering the battlespace. (…) from initial soldier reception to independent operations with Coalition support in a mere 10 months."[18]

But more importantly, training alone does not make an armed force, especially not one built from scratch. It is usually most effective in units with existing structures and experienced officers, NCOs and teams. The rushed creation of whole new units is always difficult, and requires time and, most importantly, officers. The Iraqi military was (and is) lacking officers, who in turn need time and training to grow into the crucial role they play. As General Dempsey stated in 2007, "we've been growing young second lieutenants through the military academies for about three years, but it's really difficult to grow majors, lieutenant colonels and brigadier generals. It simply can't be done overnight. So we've had to rely heavily on officer recalls and retraining programmes. However, the pool of qualified recalls is beginning to thin out."[19] Rebuilding an armed force, especially an officer corps, requires tremendous amounts of time rather than just training and weapons. As a former US trainer to the Iraqi army said, following the Mosul debacle, "no matter how many billions of dollars you spend you cannot buy experience. You cannot buy legacy. You cannot just manufacture that out of nowhere (...) They've been set up for failure from the beginning."[20] In 2014, the Iraqi air force was still virtually non-existent, with only three combat aircraft. Air support for Mosul was therefore by default limited.

That the Iraqi military was going to need decades to get to the necessary level, however, was never a secret: in 2008, Defence Minister Abdul Qadir Obeidi calculated that the military would not be ready before 2020, an estimate shared by both General James Dubik, former Multi-National Security Transition Command Iraq, and chief of staff Lieutenant General Zebari; the commander of the Special Forces' first brigade put the target date somewhere between 2020 and 2030.[21] Iraqi military, and indeed civilian, leaders were therefore crucially aware of the need for more time if they wanted to build a functional armed force. On the eve of the American troop withdrawal, former foreign minister Adnan Pachachi said that American officials shouldn't "delude themselves"[22] about the readiness of Iraq's security forces.

But not only time was working against the reconstruction of the Iraqi military as a cohesive and professional force: the civilian leadership, particularly Prime Minister Maliki, was working against it too. Distrusting the institution and operating in a highly volatile security environment, Maliki concentrated overseeing the military in his own hands. He did this mainly by altering the purpose of the office of the commander-in-chief; originally designed as a coordinating body chaired by the prime minister, the office turned into his own coup-proofing body headed by an ally, Farouk al-Araji, who had left the Saddam military with the rank of lieutenant colonel and was promoted to general, formally holding the title of "Adjutant General of the Armed Forces".[23] The office was given increased staff and moved physically into the prime minister's office. Later, when Maliki combined the portfolios of minister of defence and interior, it became the de facto executing body of the whole security sector, sidelining the relevant ministries. He began to appoint and promote officers without parliamentary approval, as required, by making these decisions "temporary", and thereby shut out the legislative from the security sector. Later, he created regional command centres attached to his office which concentrated power in the office even further; technically designed to bring military and police efforts under one command, the centres were used to appoint loyal generals, and to bypass other decision-making bodies such as the ministries of interior and defence (whose leadership was by majority Sunni).[24] With this body in place, Maliki began systematically to circumvent command structures and undermine leadership by issuing direct orders to officers via mobile phones, upsetting battle plans by moving troops around directly and requesting the arrest of individuals.[25] The personal appointment and promotion of officers not only threatened meritocratic principles but ignored military procedures and authority. Frequent rotations of even loyal officers was designed to prevent relationships between officers and their subordinates—a technique that Saddam Hussein also used.[26]

Echoing Saddam-era political commissars, so-called *dimaj* (integration) officers were inserted into the military's senior ranks; without formal or military experience, their function was to maintain a network of informers within the institution. Experienced senior commanders had to step aside or were overruled in their decisions; officers who had taken aggressive action against Shia militias, for example, were dismissed by the office without any respect for formal chains of command and procedures. Kurdish officers were purged from Mosul's two army divisions and replaced by Maliki loyalists. Officers close to the prime minister's office were not held accountable for failures, such as botched investigations into leads on terrorist attacks.[27] In addition, the civilian leadership fast-track promoted Shia officers in order to create a sectarian balance at the highest military echelons, creating frustration amongst peers.[28] As one army colonel put it, "We have even seen Sunni officers pretending to be Shiites."[29]

None of this was helped by the fact that the officer corps was fragmented and in parts distrustful of the new political and indeed military system. Of the current officers, 70 per cent served in the old Iraqi armed forces, and virtually every general officer, and more are still needed. Six years into the reconstruction, only 82 per cent of its officer posts were manned (as opposed to 157 per cent of enlisted personnel), and it was estimated that it would take a decade to close that gap.[30] The recall of former officers had several implications, positive and negative. On the positive side, it saved time, finance and efforts, as it returned men with decades of (war) experience into an institution lacking leadership entirely.

On the negative side, however, it clustered in the senior ranks representatives of precisely that section of Iraqi society which felt antagonised by the new political system (ranging from the humiliating disbandment of the armed forces to debaathification measures), namely Sunni Arabs. As the old Iraqi military's officer corps was estimated at 80 per cent Sunni Arab (almost half of which were allegedly from Mosul; the remaining 20 per cent, after a large-scale purge of Kurdish officers in the 1990s, were mostly Arab Shia), this translated into a new officer corps where the upper ranks are dominated by Sunni Arabs (although Shias are beginning to rise through the ranks);[31] the lower ranks, however, are more diverse. As a result, divisions and distrust exist not only between the corps and civilian leadership which is dominated by Shia, but also between the upper and lower officer ranks. These run along at least three lines: ethnic make-up, military culture and political context of recruitment. Whereas the upper ranks are Sunni, trained in a Baathi military culture and recruited under a dictatorship, lower ranks are at last 50 per cent Shia, American-trained and recruited after the invasion. This ethnic 'sandwich' with several layers affects cohesion as it leads to distrust, issues of authority and communication. Efforts to create new links between these layers have resulted in new forms of internal organisation and relationships, which were, however, rejected by the senior officers, who saw them as it odds with their military tradition—one that observers have described as a "Baathist–Soviet"[32] military culture.

The reconstruction efforts launched after the failure of Mosul focus on tactical training (such as battlefield tactics, land navigation and infantry skills), but they also include lessons in leadership. However, what the Iraqi armed forces need more than training is to repair their sorry state of cohesion and their relationship with the civilian leadership. Both will require decades—and will stop the Iraqi military from playing a political role.

## From revolutionary to write-off: the Libyan armed forces

Like its Iraqi counterpart, the Libyan military moved through stages first as a political and later a checked force, only to collapse during the war of 2011. Since then, it has not re-emerged as an institution and even less so as a capable force. Whatever was left of the Libyan military was outmatched by rebel militias, sidelined by political bickering and hampered by a lack of access to equipment or manpower. The Libyan forces have therefore gradually moved from having a role in politics to being entirely dysfunctional.

Three dynamics led to the situation of today: the first is the state of the Libyan forces under Gaddafi, particularly the two decades preceding the war; the second is the conflict itself; and third are the botched attempts to rebuild the force since then.

The years under the *Jamahiriya* (the pseudo-democratic system that Gaddafi created) were no good for the military. Although it was the armed forces and its Free Officers under the leadership of Gaddafi which ousted King Idris in 1969, the institution spent most of its existence under the new regime feeling powerless. Originally the backbone of the system and showered with funds, Gaddafi soon turned on the institution when two of his Revolutionary Command Council colleagues, Bashir Hawadi and Umar al-Muhayshi, attempted to use the military to block his political reform plans.[33] The coup attempt was carried out by about twenty to thirty army officers who allegedly hailed mostly from Misrata, but failed when the plotters were discovered, subsequently arrested and executed two years later.[34] The event changed fundamentally how Gaddafi and the regime viewed the armed forces: no longer as a pillar of the regime, but as a potential threat.

In the following years, Gaddafi retained direct control over the armed forces, along with Abu Bakr Yunes Jabr, by excluding the military (along with other crucial policy areas such as foreign relations and the oil sector) from the "popular rule" of the political system he had created. But critical moves against the regime continued to emerge from the military: in 1983, five officers were executed for plotting a coup; in 1984, fighting broke out in barracks over a similar plan, leading to the arrest of several thousand soldiers; in 1985, sixty officers were arrested for a similar reason; again in 1985, Colonel Hassan Ishkal, the military governor of Surt, was executed for disagreeing over the role of the revolutionary guards within the armed forces; in 1993, another coup attempt failed.[35]

Consequently, Gaddafi employed typical coup-proofing measures to weaken the armed forces' political potential: he personalised recruitments, appointments and promotions, balanced the military in tribal terms to counter a potential cluster of interests, while placing sensitive positions in the hands of officers from his own Gadadfa tribe (such as responsibility for the Cyrenaica region, military security, responsibility for the Benghazi sector, ordering armaments and munitions, and domestic security). His tribe similarly dominated the highly prestigious air force. The Warfalla and Maqarha were loyal tribes that also received preferential treatment. Gaddafi then sought to undermine the crucial relationship between officers and soldiers by regularly rotating officers through the seven military regions.

These policies all hurt the Libyan military tactically: its performance during the war with Chad from 1978 to 1987 was marred by lack of leadership, cohesion and training; since the military was never allowed to train above the level of company, it had serious difficulties in coordinating efforts of artillery, armour and infantry.[36] It consequently suffered high rates of desertion. But while Gaddafi had succeeded in effectively handicapping the effectiveness of the armed forces, this still did not protect him entirely from the potential threat: the coup attempt of 1993 was staged mainly by officers from the nominally loyal Warfalla tribe, so doubts about the "true loyalty" of the military persisted.[37]

When the 2011 uprising broke out, the Libyan armed forces were both weakened, but also had very little experience with civilian conflict. Distrusting the military, Gaddafi had used Revolutionary Committees to suppress discontent throughout his years in power. The result was that the institution dispersed in three directions: the majority deserted, a second smaller section supported the regime and the third section the rebels.

In the first month of the conflict alone, 8,000 soldiers reportedly defected in the east; by four months later, the Libyan military had allegedly shrunk to somewhere between 10,000 and 20,000 (from its original 51,000).[38] Desertions depended essentially on three aspects: the actual location of the unit, which could or could not offer the individual safety; the individual's opinion of the conflict and/or the regime; and the cohesion of the unit in question.

Desertion occurred particularly in liberated areas and those the deserting soldier originated from—in part because this provided personal safety, but also because the task of suppressing citizens from the same tribe or area posed a problem for many. On the flipside, areas where regime support was traditionally stronger (in Sirte, in tribal areas of the Gadadfa, Warfalla and Maqarha), desertions were less frequent; whereas they were higher in areas of the east traditionally considered pockets of resistance against Gaddafi. Considerable numbers of officers also deserted as early as March in Zintan, located in the west, while other officers based in the west collaborated with the rebels while remaining in their posts.

The longer the conflict lasted, the more the regime's circles of support eroded to the point where formerly loyal tribes (such as the Warfalla) switched sides and triggered even more desertions.

But most importantly, unit cohesion was weak throughout most of the Libyan military and provided very little motivational and identity protection against the political onslaught of the conflict. Civil wars challenge military cohesion generally; however, other forces have held out much longer than Libya's, which literally melted away within weeks—a testimony to the low degree of professionalism, cohesion and effectiveness which Gaddafi had instilled in his alleged fighting force.

Only a handful of units were an exception to this rule. Several entire units defected (approximately 1,000 troops),[39] to the rebels, such as the Special Forces. Crucial to this outcome was the leadership of the unit commander in question, although Major General Abdel Fattah Younis' appeal to the Libyan military to "join the people and respond to their legitimate demands"[40] certainly played a role, too. Younis later became the commander of the rebels' National Liberation Army, only to be murdered a few months later—probably by rebel units. The units which had defected from the Libyan military proved to be better trained and organised than the rebel forces, but, like Younis, they struggled with rebel distrust.

With the bulk of the Libyan military manpower gone, Gaddafi relied essentially on one brigade to fight his war (in addition to mercenaries he acquired from sub-Saharan Africa): the 32nd brigade of about 10,000 troops, under the command of his son Khamis (called the Khamis brigade), fought until the very end of the conflict and proved surprisingly cohesive. Staffed mostly with men from the Gadadfa tribe, it was—in contrast to the rest of the Libyan military—well-equipped, well-trained and coup-proofing measures were spared.[41] It was consequently the first brigade to be sent into Benghazi when the uprising began, and is credited with the assault on Misrata and the defence of Tripoli.[42] Thanks to its privileged training, this brigade was capable of doing anything to save the regime, such as deliberately targeting civilians, torturing and executing captives, and using indiscriminate weaponry such as cluster bombs and land mines.[43]

When Libya's civil war ended, little was left on which the new authorities could build a new military force. The previous armed force had had so little cohesion, tradition and popular symbolism that—in contrast to the Iraqi military—it had few institutional remnants to be made use of. All that was left was several thousand middle-rank officers with dubious professional and political credentials.[44] They were outmatched by numerous militias running on revolutionary rhetoric and weapons delivered during the conflict. Meanwhile, the civilian leadership was not experienced enough to drive a security sector reconstruction process, and instead oscillated between giving into militia and popular demands and making weak attempts at getting both police and armed forces in order. Ultimately the process turned into a competition over the title of national armed force—which both the militias and the rump military claimed.

First glimpses of this rivalry became apparent when the National Transitional Council announced the plan to integrate former rebel fighters into the military. As Libya needed both to dismantle its militias and to create a new security structure, this proposal sought to solve both problems in one go. However, the plan was doomed from the beginning: neither the militias nor what was left of the armed forces supported it.

Of the 140,000 militiamen who had been cleared by the Warrior Affairs Commission for professional reintegration, only 6,000 expressed an interest in working in the military; the vast majority instead desired to become civil servants with desk jobs.[45] This feeling was indeed mutual: the remnants of the armed forces were very reluctant to integrate militiamen, whom the officers saw as undisciplined and politicised.[46] The military's demands for retraining and individual integration was rejected by the militias, who deemed their war experience enough and sought integration as whole units.[47] It is worth noting that the integration of whole units into an existing military structure is indeed problematic, as it poses problems of command structure, cohesion, authority, hierarchy and discipline.[48] Most successful post-conflict reintegration programmes have consequently proceeded at the individual rather than collective level.

Instead of integrating a new military structure, the militias began to style themselves as rivals to the armed forces—not only in name but also in style. The militias openly rejected the newly appointed chief of staff Youssef al-Mangoush (whom the civilian leadership took three months to appoint),[49] and self-declared military units popped up all across Libya. Adding a veneer of legitimacy, militias were nominally drafted into the security sector as the Supreme Security Committee (SSC), a body in charge of internal security, or the Libya Shield Forces (LSF), a parallel military force formally reporting to the army chief of staff. But only on paper was the LSF part of the military: it did not take orders, did not follow military training standards and was involved in several violent incidents. Its lethal clash with Benghazi civilians led to the chief of staff's resignation in the summer of 2013, and highlighted the reality of Libya's security sector. The militias were a law unto themselves, and the remnants of the Libyan military were neither in charge nor in control. As then chief of staff Obeidi told parliament: "We have no ability to reformulate the Shield Force, nor to change its leadership."[50]

It was a mess at the civilian level, too. As Libya was governed on a provisional declaration, there was no blueprint for responsibilities in the defence sector. While Law 11 of February 2012 sought to define the roles of defence minister as well as chief of staff, it empowered the latter, turning the minister into a supervisory rather than policy-shaping position. It also declared the supreme authority over the armed forces to be the head of state—a position the constitutional declaration had not included. In August 2013, the president of the interim parliament, the General National Congress (GNC), Nuri Abu Sahmain, decided that given the absence of a formal head of state, he should be the commander-in-chief—a power grab revoked by the assembly and later bestowed upon him for one month only. But civilian hold over the militias was virtually non-existent: the GNC has announced several times the disbandment, disarmament and reintegration of the militias without any impact; several training attempts in Jordan and the United Kingdom had to be cut short due to severe issues with discipline.

Tensions also existed between civilians and the formal military structure: defence minister Osama al-Juwaili did not get along with chief of staff Youssef al-Mangoush, who he felt excluded him from key policy decisions; Prime Minister Ali Zeidan complained about al-Mangoush's successor, General Abdul Salaam Jadallah al-Obeidi, for being disobedient. The military simply ignored orders to intervene in Sabha and later in Sirte—a claim which the army spokesman rejected publicly, stating that "if we receive any orders, the matter will be studied at that time".[51] Defence Minister and later Prime Minister Abdullah al-Thini equally struggled with authority over a military institution unwilling to submit to civilian supervision: chief of staff Salim al-Qinaydi publicly blamed the GNC's constant interference and politicisation of the officer corps for the sorry state of the armed forces.[52]

Lastly, the remnants of the Libyan officer corps were not cohesive either. As early as November 2011, fissures appeared in the ranks as 150 officers and non-commissioned ranks decided publicly to reject Youssef al-Manqoush as chief of staff, instead electing former general Lieutenant General Khalifa Haftar in a ceremony without consequence.[53] In 2013, officers again went on record as calling for al-Mangoush's resignation, because of his incapacity to rebuild the armed forces; and later, the general chief of staff office as well as the staff of Mu'aytiqah airbase rejected the new chief of staff al-Nazuri on television.[54]

In 2014, the remnant that was left of the Libyan military fell apart over Haftar's announcement of a coup and military campaign against the

Islamist militias: certain units, such as the air force or those in al-Jufrah, publicly declared their support, whereas others, such as the army command, rejected it. Just as the Libyan government was now torn between two parliaments (the Tobruk-based House of Representatives [HoR] and the Tripoli-based General National Congress), what was left of an already hollow institution was ripped in two.[55] A looming lustration law, adopted earlier in 2013 but about to hit the officer corps, perhaps played a role in this decision. According to the law, anyone in the armed forces who held a command position would be banned from employment in several sectors, including government. The law would consequently apply to a rather large group of individuals in the armed forces.

Since that point, Libya has descended into chaos, and with it what was left of its military forces. Certain pockets are now under control of General Haftar, whose status was formalised by the House of Representatives in early 2015 as commander of the armed forces.[56] At the same time, the House decided to create the post of commander-in-chief as a three-month rotating title, expressing the desire to retain control over a force increasingly dominated by Haftar.[57] But relations between the assembly and the military wing soured over the year: Haftar's forces twice imposed a travel ban on Prime Minister al-Thinni (whose relationship with Haftar is a difficult one—al-Thinni has openly called Haftar a putschist), fired senior officials appointed by the HoR and were accused of corruption by the legislative.[58] Haftar has equally struggled with maintaining cohesion in his troops, particularly after falling out with one his closest aides, Faraj al-Barasi. His future role in a unity government was not clear at the time of writing—but his goal, as minister of defence or at least commander of the armed forces, seemed to be in jeopardy.

While especially Haftar and certain elements of the HoR would like to project the image of a cohesive fighting force, it is clear that there is no Libyan military in that sense today—and certainly not one playing a political role.

## Yemen's armed forces: from state force to tribal force

The trajectory of Yemen's military has been similar to that of Iraq and Libya: from kingmaker to regime-changer, the force was to be reckoned with—until recently, that is. After it ousted the imamate and then the first two presidents in what was then North Yemen, in 1978 it finally brought former President Saleh to power, who had first been an officer, then a military governor. Saleh was, like Gaddafi, first a friend of the Yemeni forces: he increased their number from a tiny 3,000 to 66,700 and initiated significant modernisation drives. He used the force also in the civil war preventing southern secession, and let it fight six campaigns against a Houthi insurgency from 2004 onwards and several counter-terrorism operations against al-Qaeda in the Arabian Peninsula.

But the Yemeni military was far from cohesive or professional; rather, it was held together by personal and tribal loyalties, and accordingly fell apart when it had to endure political pressure. In large part, this was Saleh's own doing, especially after 2000: distrustful of the military on whose tails he had come to power, he put family members in charge of key units, appointed and promoted officers on the basis of personal ties or tribal affiliations, thereby undermining the official command structure and creating a shadow one directly tied to him. As Gaddafi did with the Khamis brigade, units loyal to him received better training and equipment than the rest of the armed forces.[59] Elsewhere in the military, corruption and smuggling spread, directly encouraged by Saleh. Whether in trading weapons or food, or supporting the existence of ghost soldiers (fictional staff whose salaries were doled out to officers), the armed forces were engaged in institutional malpractice. Tribes used the military to bolster their positions and secure patronage; military ranks conferred no authority unless bolstered by membership of an influential tribe; and communication ran along tribal lines, not command structures.

But because the overall deal still held up, the forces were more or less operational; those deployed on multidivisional campaigns, such as those under General Ali Mohsen, were the most cohesive. This fragile cohesiveness was endangered once Saleh and Mohsen fell out over the former's succession. According to the 1978 tribal agreement which had brought Saleh to power, Mohsen would become his eventual successor; but in 2000, Saleh began to groom his son Ahmed Ali to become his political heir, making him the head of the Republican Guard, which he transformed into a highly-trained and well-equipped eight-brigade force.

The Yemeni military began to split into three separate entities: a highly effective force under Ali, a reasonably capable 1st armoured division under General Mohsen, and a tired and depleted regular army caught somewhere between. When protests struck Yemen in early 2011, the armed forces consequently fell apart along these three lines: units followed Major General Ali Mohsen who announced on television that "according to what I'm feeling, and according to the feelings of my partner commanders and soldiers ... I announce our support and our peaceful backing to the youth revolution. We are going to fulfil our duties in preserving security and stability."[60] Others stayed loyal to Saleh, or simply went home. Overall, however, the military units avoided open confrontation with each other.[61]

Once Saleh was ousted, rebuilding and reforming the Yemeni military became one of the key priorities. Alas, the process unfolded along the lines of historical antecedents: control of the armed forces became synonymous with political power and access to resources. Rather than reform and professionalise the institution, efforts focused on sidelining political opponents from within the institution, and placing supporters inside. Saleh-successor President Abdu Rabbu Mansour Hadi (himself a former general of the Southern Yemen army) set up two committees charged with elaborating a reform plan; but his own actions targeted first and foremost the de-Salehisation of the officer corps. He dismissed several of Saleh's family members from key posts in the armed forces, encountering disobedience and resistance. Air force chief Mohammed Saleh, half-brother of the former president, threatened to shoot down aircraft landing at Sana'a airport should he not be reinstated. Elsewhere, new commanding officers were physically prevented from joining their units. Although Hadi removed a substantial number of Saleh supporters, he could not remove them all—doing so would have crippled the armed forces, and in any case the negotiated departure of Saleh did not warrant an all-out purge. To several of Saleh's opponents, Hadi did not go far enough, as there were still some of his family members in the military. But more importantly, his moves were not part of a larger reform strategy, and were not transparent. Rather than being technical in focus on issues such as the retirement law, rotation of generals, the ghost soldier issue and balancing units in terms of both size and equipment, the reforms became highly politicised.

In late 2012, Hadi announced a restructuring of the armed forces based on the recommendations of a committee charged with developing the reform programme. Although theoretically technical, the restructuring placed the inner-military power struggle between Ahmed Ali and Mohsen at its heart, disbanding the Republican Guard as well as the 1st Armoured Division. Both men were sent into retirement but continued to play a role in Yemen's politico-military landscape: Mohsen returned from retirement in contravention of presidential orders to command the remnants of his units against the Houthi assault on Sana'a, while Ahmed Ali has been accused of being actively involved with those army units allied to the Houthis. The reform also streamlined the military into services (army, navy, air force, border guards).[62] At the same time, the armed forces began to expand—opening the door to the accusation of trying to staff them with loyalists.

As security began to implode all over the country and the political power struggle between Saleh and Mohsen supporters continued, increasing the military became a request from all sides in the expanding political conflict. Whether Houthis, southerners or tribes from the strategically important Marib region, the integration of men—sometimes as many as 85,000—was a key demand.[63] Hadi, at least nominally, gave in to them, reinstating over 8,000 southern officers and soldiers, and voicing support for even Houthi integration.

At this point, security in Yemen was no longer in state hands. Marib tribes raided military equipment, tribal forces were formally tasked by Hadi to act against al-Qaeda in the Arab Peninsula, and the Houthi militias took Sana'a—posing as the country's new army. It was no coincidence that, in Sana'a, they first seized the armed forces general command, the ministry of defence, and the headquarters of military region VI. Equipped with dozens of tanks and masses of heavy weaponry seized from the Yemeni army, they also began to dress in regular uniforms.[64] The armed forces meanwhile had essentially fallen apart and joined sides in the conflict; mutinies and disobedience had become the norm.[65] Defence Minister Mahmud al-Subaihi expressed his grievances over the slow reform efforts, publicly accusing senior officers of "betrayal and collusion with armed militias".[66] In March 2015, the Houthis captured a military base in Yemen's North of Aden and took the defence minister hostage. Saudi Arabia decided to intervene, a battle that was still ongoing at the time of writing, and Mohsen was brought back first as the deputy commander of the military and later appointed vice president.

Meanwhile, plans to reform the armed forces continue to be developed—ranging from an all-out disbandment, to integration of militia fighters, to the creation of a separate southern army, and of course the purge of disloyal troops.[67] But instead of being a political actor in its own right, Yemen's military is merely the battle ground for political conflict, and plays no role itself.

## *The professional force that won't: Lebanon, Tunisia*

A professional force who will not act politically is one which, while capable of fulfilling its defence role, does not have the ambition and will to get involved in politics. While the institutional capacity might be there, the political interest is not. This type of force is not necessarily checked by strong civilians, but mainly by its own lack of desire to intervene. It is consequently one which, under different circumstances, might become a political actor one day.

This type of force is comparatively rare in the Middle East and North Africa; the main reason for its rarity is that the difficult political and economic circumstances of the region give several forces an incentive to act politically. Three forces that are exceptions to this rule are the militaries of Lebanon, Tunisia and Morocco, though all three have different reasons to abstain from political meddling.

## The aloof national symbol: the Lebanese armed forces

In the Middle Eastern military landscape, the Lebanese armed forces are often portrayed as an exception: rarely involved in politics, plural in nature, operationally passive, yet universally adored by virtually all groups that make up Lebanon's society. The reality is somewhat more complex, but when it comes to involvement in politics, the Lebanese military has indeed never prompted a successful coup. Even its three failed coups were more declaratory than effective in nature. Two of these failed because the armed forces themselves did not follow the call of the plotters: in 1976, almost a year into the civil war, Lieutenant Ahmed Khatib called not only for more Muslims in the officer corps, but also announced the creation of Lebanon's Arab Army with his 40-odd company as the founding nucleus. A few hundred soldiers and

119

a low-ranking non-commissioned officer heeded the call, ransacked a few barracks and looted equipment—but the armed forces as a whole remained intact. Two months later, General Aziz Ahdab appeared on television announcing a coup designed to save country and army, which triggered no reaction from the armed forces and rejection from the general public.[68] This lack of institutional support expresses the military's lack of interest in such political adventures. But even the third attempt in 1961, which was foiled by the intelligence services, was not the result of intra-corps plotting: instead, an extra-military entity, the Syrian Social Nationalist Party, had recruited three officers into its grander coup scheme. The trigger for the coup thus came, as in the case of Iraq with the Baath party, from outside the military.

But the absence of military involvement in Lebanese politics is not, as in the cases of Libya or Iraq today, the result of lack of capacity. Indeed, the Lebanese military has intra-corps cohesion, leadership and a sufficient degree of professionalism shielding it from extensive political meddling. Instead, what has prevented the officer corps from taking the institution into politics has been, and still is, a combination of five factors: absence of political consensus in the officer corps, a strong and historically rooted depoliticisation policy of the armed forces, high levels of professionalism, the trauma of civil conflict, as well as a rewarding popular image. Thanks to this somewhat aloof attitude, all have played into the Lebanese armed forces remaining outside the often difficult politics of the country.

Without these five elements, the Lebanese Armed Forces would indeed have the required coup-capacity, although its image has not been one of a particularly powerful fighting force. This is mainly because it has been held against measures of military success: when coups require less capacity than a war, and indeed are often inspired by military defeat or passivity. But the institutional shape of the armed forces should be measured not only against their operational effectiveness; after all, the Lebanese military, in spite of its severe shortcomings in equipment, has proved on several occasions that it can get a job done: in 1948, when the a battalion of the armed forces defeated Israeli units in Malikiyya on the southern border; in 2000, during its battle against the Islamist group Takfir wa al-Hijra in the Dinnieh region; in 2007, when it confronted another Islamist militia in the Palestinian refugee camp Nahr al-Bared; and more recently, in its battle against the

Nusra Front and IS near the border town of Arsal.[69] All of these operations are however held against those moments when the armed forces abstained from action: such as during the civil unrest in 1952 against President Bishara Khury; that of 1958 against President Camille Chamoun's pro-Western policy, during the 15-year civil war (1975–90); the 2005 demonstrations leading to the ousting of Syria; the war with Israel in 2006; and the clashes between supporters and antagonists of Hezbollah in 2008; and of course those events with other forces, such as the Syrian and Israeli military, both of which took control of parts of the country for several years.

But these moments of abstention for the Lebanese military had broadly three causes, which do not include lack of capacity. In the first instance, the armed forces simply had no civilian mandate, crucially during the civil war years or the war of 2006. In the second case, the Lebanese military had no illusions about the superior fire power of both Syria and Israel; parts of it nevertheless engaged, in 1989, in a bloody and ultimately futile operation against the Syrian forces. But thirdly and most importantly, the Lebanese military has repeatedly displayed the capacity for collective disobedience—which in itself requires corps cohesion.

In 2005, President Emile Lahoud ordered the armed forces to break up demonstrations against Syria—an order which the military leadership ignored, although Lahoud had been its chief until 1998, responsible for rebuilding an institution shattered by civil conflict.[70] Similarly, it ignored orders by presidents Khury and Chamoun in 1952 and 1958 to act during the civil unrest sparked by disagreement with their administration. To conclude that the military simply cannot be deployed against Lebanese protesters would be plain wrong, however; on several occasions, most recently during the "You Stink" campaign concerning rubbish disposal, but also during demonstrations by Free Patriotic Movement supporters or Bashar al-Assad opponents, it did act—indeed with too much rather than too little force.[71] However, when the military leadership concludes that deployment during a civil conflict would be seen as sectarian, it has shown a preference for abstention even at the price of disobedience—which in any case has never gone punished.

Given that the Lebanese military has the capacity for collective military action, reasons other than those from the previous chapter disqualifying the forces from politics must be at play.

The first is the fact that although the Lebanese officer corps might display some institutional cohesion, it is still not one politically cohesive bloc. As seen in the second section of Chapter 2, collective action is in part the result of shared interests. While the Lebanese military does have institutional collective interests which bind it together, its corps does not share one political or social vision for the country. This is largely the result of its plural origins. The Lebanese military is, like the society it stems from, composed of several religious denominations. Following the introduction of a quota system for the officer corps in 1978, it has achieved near-parity with 49 per cent Christians and 51 per cent Muslims. But these are broken down further into denominations: 29 per cent Maronites, 22 per cent Shiite, 22 per cent Sunni, 11 per cent Greek Orthodox, 8 per cent Greek Catholic, 7 per cent Druze and other, smaller sects. The quota does not apply to enlisted personnel and non-commissioned officers, giving it a slightly more Muslim outlook in total, with 35 per cent Sunni, 27 per cent Shia, 13 per cent Maronites, 6 per cent Druze, 6 per cent Greek Orthodox, 4 per cent Greek Catholics.[72]

But beyond the religious divide, politics in Lebanon are and have been highly sectarian. The political system, although somewhat altered since the end of the civil war, shares power amongst the country's groups according to denomination. In the same way as the key political posts are earmarked for certain groups, posts in the armed forces are earmarked, too. The commander is usually a Maronite, the chief of staff traditionally a Druze, deputy chiefs of staff for personnel a Sunni, for operations a Shia, for logistics a Christian and so forth. Although this goes against typical meritocratic principles, the system has two advantages: it is clear from the start and therefore transparent, and it maintains (at least in theory) meritocracy within a certain denomination. For instance, while a Maronite officer's aspirations might go as high as commander of the Lebanese armed forces, a Druze's will aim for chief of staff. In any case, every batch of an officer generation will reach the rank of general, as the corps is not pyramid but rather chimney in shape. The main reason for this lack of early retirement is that it is necessary to maintain the denominational balance of the corps.

But the Lebanese military is not only pluralistic when it comes to religion; it also stems from different parts of the country and different economic backgrounds. Although a somewhat elitist organisation right after independence, Lebanon's armed forces are today representative of a highly pluralistic society: 35 per cent of its officers are from villages, 45 per cent from towns and 19 per cent from cities; 26.4 per cent are from Mount Lebanon (which used to be the main region for officer recruitment in the early days following independence), 20.7 per cent from South Lebanon, 23.3 per cent from North Lebanon, 12.5 per cent from Beirut and 17 per cent from the Bekaa valley (up from 10 per cent in the years between 1945 and 1975).[73] Its officer corps can be further broken down into roughly three military generations: those recruited into the armed forces in the 1950s under the then commander Fuad Chehab; those who were shaped by the civil war of 1975–90; and those who joined under Syrian tutelage, 1990–2005. The newest, post-Syrian generation is just now reaching junior officer ranks of captain and major. Depending on time of recruitment, these generations not only hold certain views of the armed forces, but also have had to position themselves politically. Lastly, the Lebanese officer corps is of course equally lacking cohesion in political terms. Military cohesion in this plural setting is preserved because:

> no group of officers—whether defined by sectarian identity or political allegiance—has felt isolated in the LAF (Lebanese Armed Forces) since 2005. The overlapping of different types of affiliations (sectarian, political, or generational) and the crosscutting ties among officer groups have so far preserved the LAF's unity.[74]

For the armed forces, especially the officer corps, to take over power in such a setting, it would have had to develop a collective interest overriding all these regional, religious-denominational and socio-economic interests. While it is often argued that plural forces do not stage coups because no group could ever control the whole force, this is in fact not the decisive factor. Whereas mono-ethnic plotters can struggle with controlling a whole force, multi-ethnic forces such as those in Nigeria and Ghana for instance can witness coups by minorities, regardless of the numerical realities. Officers from a minority did not encounter any issues with obedience of soldiers from the majority; the notion that enlisted Shia men would not take orders from Sunni or Maronite officers paints an extreme situation which is unlikely to occur in an armed force which is trained to function according to military principles.

Pluralism in an armed force can be used for political purposes, of course, and lead to severe problems in command structure, cohesion and leadership once individuals put more emphasis on their particular identity than on the military profession. This is, however, a process driven from outside the armed forces: where the regime displays ethnic motives, the military—as a collective or as an individual serving in it—is more likely to begin identifying with particular identities as well. Consequently, it is the ethno-sectarian context which serves as a pull-factor for the military, rather than the plural nature itself which pushes the forces either into political action or implosion.[75]

Coups with openly sectarian motives have taken place, although mostly in Africa; they usually occur when the regime's ethno-sectarian politics go against the military's collective interests, rather than an ethnic group using the armed forces to consolidate its position in the state. In the Arab world, there are no coups which have openly claimed to be ethno-sectarian in nature; often, these motives are read into the event only after the fact. The two examples here would be the Moroccan coup of 1972, later portrayed as a Berber coup; and the 1971 arrival of Hafez al-Assad in power, which has given way to a narrative of Alewitisation of the Syrian military. But neither event claimed itself to be an ethnic one.

But beyond the question of ethnicity and pluralism, such forces only feel compelled to act against a system which jeopardises the interests of either the armed forces or the different groups living in the country. The Lebanese system, however, carefully balances sectarian interests. Although often criticised, it ultimately serves enough collective (but not individual) interests to remain in place.

In general, approaches looking solely at the military's plural nature as the explanatory variable overstate the sectarian dimension in officer identity. Of course, sectarian identities do matter in the Lebanese military: in recruitment, promotion and appointment, sectarian affiliation are crucial. Consequently, sectarian ties have transcended ranks; but they have crossed other ties which are generational, political and of military nature (e.g. service-identity such as in the navy or special forces).

Rather than a sectarian force, the Lebanese military considers itself, and is considered by outsiders, to be not only professional but having a distinct policy of political abstention. *Chehabisme*, a strong conviction of military professionalism that attempts to be blind to religious sectionalism, stands at the centre of Lebanese army officer professional identity. It stresses their distance from sectarianism and politics, and focuses on the special, supra-ethnic position of the armed forces in Lebanese society. Inspired by its first commander Fuad Chehab, it has become an almost doctrinal school of thought (in spite of the fact that Chehab's policies as a president later included extensive use of military intelligence). Chehab is often called the 'father of the Lebanese army', and was tasked with the construction of the military following independence. In his many exchanges with Lebanese politicians, for example, concerning equipment purchases or the integration of Palestinian fighters—he requested and got autonomy in the management of military matters.[76] Later, he extended his autonomy to the point of sometimes hidden, sometimes open disobedience towards the civilian leadership when he thought the military as an institution were being threatened.

It was this ideology which helped the armed forces' reconstruction efforts, and allegedly played a role in the choice of Emile Lahoud as their commander in 1989. His Chehabist convictions were thought to ease the reintegration of renegade officers who had fought with former commander Michel Aoun against the Syrian military.[77] Although this school of thought is particularly strong in the oldest generation which joined the armed forces in the 1950s and 1960s, it is still highly present as an ideology in the corps world view.

It echoes, of course, with the general ethic of professionalism. Lebanese officers have drawn a contrast with the Iraqi scenario in 2014 in Mosul by pointing to the fact that "the Lebanese army is and always was professional, the Iraqi one never was".[78] To repeat, professionalism in the military is characterised by institutional values, a purpose which transcends self-interest and serves the greater good. Corporate identity, expertise, certain standards are all part of military professionalism in the larger sense; the "military mind" as a set of values is the result of military professionalism and encompasses discipline, nationalism, rationality, logic and much more.[79] Professionalism is a way of being, rather than a set of rules; it is somewhat difficult to measure, but not so difficult to notice. Whether an institution adheres to training and education standards, the pride its members feel to serve in it, the extra mile they will go to fulfil their mission are all indicators that professionalism is strong. Even an institution paralysed by disintegration and civil war, such as the Lebanese army, could maintain traces of professionalism: most deserting units remained in regular contact with the military leadership, even when they were in territories outside governmental control; soldiers and officers, whether they had deserted or not, continued to received their salaries and were even promoted; training, as well as army command publications continued in spite of ongoing fighting. More importantly, those who had deserted the armed forces continued to operate along military lines, continuing their training, sentry duty, maintenance of equipment and communication with command.[80] Indeed, even the coup attempt of 1961 demonstrated some features of corporate military frustration stemming from professional values: the commander's decisions not to suppress tribal revolts in 1954, or interfere in the civil unrest of 1958, his alleged turning of a blind eye towards weapon flows from Syria were seen as actions not worthy of Lebanese professionalism. Perhaps in recognition of this, the military leadership allowed an extra month's salary to all security forces staff, "in appreciation of the efforts made by these forces"[81] in crushing the coup.

Military professionalism also comes with the a certain preference for distance from civilian and political decision-making; in part, this is because certain features of civilian politics, such as disagreement, consensus-based decision-making, particular interests seem to be at odds with values the military cherishes, such as nationalism, unity, hierarchies and effectiveness as the main criteria for decision-making. Chehabist officers see political leaders as corrupt and inefficient; a monograph published by a general in the 1970s was aptly entitled *al jaych houwa al hall* ("the army is the solution"), and another book by a Lebanese general was titled "The army remains the solution". As one Lebanese general put it, "we just need civilian money to operate, but we want nothing to do with them—and we want them to leave us alone".[82] Although Chehabism plays an important role in this, Lebanese military professionalism goes further than that: it cherishes standards, efficiency and nationalism—and sees itself as the symbol of Lebanon as a whole.

This aspect is the result of two historical dynamics: the first is the impact of the civil war on the Lebanese military, and more importantly its recovery afterwards; the second is its traditionally positive image in

Lebanese public opinion. Both aspects act as deterrents when it comes to military meddling with politics.

Although the Lebanese military was not an active player in the civil war of 1975–90, it suffered significantly from it. Once violence had broken out, it saw desertion rates of 5–10 per cent—comparatively low, as the internal security forces experienced 24 per cent. There were also incidents of mutiny and disobedience, with the departure of not only Lieutenant Khatib and General Ahdab, but also others such as Majors Saad Haddad (to form the South Lebanon Army) and Fuad Malek (to form the Army of Free Lebanon). Neither Haddad nor Malek called for a coup, however, and did not explain their motivations in military ways as did Khatib and Ahdab: Malek advocated an ethnically segregated military and later joined the Christian militia *Forces Libanaises* as their chief of staff; whereas Haddad allied himself to Israel, with curiously his own forces being ethnically mixed, too—40 per cent Christians and 60 per cent Shia and Druze. Both men were dismissed in 1978, along with 192 other officers who had compromised themselves during the early days of the conflict. Although the Lebanese military was then only deployed in smaller units, usually with the task of maintaining ceasefires between warring militias, it performed well on these occasions and played no decisive role in the fighting.

True disintegration along ethnic lines occurred much later, however, facilitated by the fact that most of the Lebanese military's brigades were highly homogenous in denominational terms (a system abandoned in 1991). In 1984, first about 1,000 Druze left the Lebanese military (almost their entirety in the force, a move which did not harm it structurally due to their 6 per cent share in manpower); later, the predominantly Shia 6th brigade of roughly 1,500 men refused to take orders from command.[83] Both departures were due to a larger political context: in the first instance, the Lebanese military had crushed the Druze militia on the battlefield; in the second case, it had to fight the Shia militia Amal in west Beirut. These incidents have been seen as proof that the Lebanese military cannot be used against armed groups of a certain denomination, but the situation is more complex. Disintegration usually occurs within institutions that have been damaged in terms of manpower, morale, cohesion and professionalism—which was the case with the Lebanese military nearly a decade into the conflict. Its remnants managed to confront the *Forces Libanaises* five years later, in spite of the high Christian share in the officer corps (although this operation turned out to be the most traumatic episode of the war for the military in terms of both desertion and casualties). Since then, the Lebanese military, with its 35 per cent Sunnis, has managed repeatedly to confront Sunni extremist groups.

The civil war has taught the Lebanese officers an important lesson in line with Chehabism, however: politicisation spells disaster for a force which is too pluralistic to absorb such shocks. Since the end of the war, the force consequently sought to establish itself as the only legitimate force in the country; it achieved this by integrating a limited amount of militia fighters into its ranks and by reforming its brigade system.[84] It has also embarked on a rather remarkable advertising campaign across billboards, videos and magazines, stressing the link between Lebanon and its people. One video, published in 2012, features popular pop singers such as Nancy Ajram, Assi Helani, Wael Kfoury, Samir Saffir and Nawal Zoghbi.[85] 1 August, the founding day of the military, is celebrated annually not only with parades, but also with political leaders expressing their support for the armed forces.

In its songs and publications, Lebanon as a nation is synonymous with the armed forces. The military almost appears to bypass its civilian masters and communicate directly with the population—and rightly so, since its own reputation is significantly more positive than that of the civilian leadership. In a 2001 opinion poll, at a time when Syrian forces were still in the country, 41.7 per cent of Lebanese said they trusted their state and its institutions; 75.3 per cent said they trusted the Lebanese armed forces. In 2011, the numbers were roughly the same for the military, with 71 per cent trusting the armed forces and 5 per cent the state.[86] This affection for the armed forces is visible elsewhere: during the 2005 demonstrations, graffiti sprayed around downtown Beirut declared "Long live the Lebanese army" or "We want no other army in Lebanon than the Lebanese one". When passing by an army checkpoint, Lebanese citizens often say *"Marhaba ya watan"* ("Hello, nation"). This does not necessarily imply that the Lebanese are oblivious to their military's shortcomings—after all, it coexists with Hezbollah and has no control over all of Lebanon's borders—but this does suggest acceptance of coexistence. It is at least in part due to this positive image that former presidents Chehab, Lahoud and Suleiman were elected to the presidency, and it plays a role in the public appreciation—even by protesters—of former Special Forces commander Chamel Roukoz.[87] But as a whole, the Lebanese military has nothing to gain and everything to lose should it venture into politics.

## *La grande muette?* The Tunisian military

Tunisia's military last rose to political prominence in 2011, when it famously (and allegedly) refused to use force against civilian demonstrators—ultimately triggering the fall of Ben Ali, and hence paving the way for the country's democratisation. Although it was previously thought to be an armed force under tight civilian control and therefore not a potential political threat, it was the events of 2011 which moved it into the current category of a capable force largely restrained by its own decisions. Disobedience on such a large scale expresses two elements crucial for this type of force: capacity for collective action (which neither the Libyan nor the Yemeni forces had), as well as breakdown of civilian supervision (which restrains another type of force explained in the next chapter).

Forces which could but do not act politically may choose this path for a host of reasons, in the same way that they may choose to act politically for a number of reasons, too. In the Tunisian as in the Lebanese case, disobedience to an unpopular government is a possibility, because the military can tap into a more or less positive relationship with the civilian population. It is this link which gives it room for manoeuvring to distance itself from the regime; but this does not necessarily imply that the force either has the appetite for more assertive political action, or that it chooses disobedience for entirely altruistic reasons.

What allowed the Tunisian military to act the way it did in 2011 was its decade-long relative aloofness from politics. Often described as "*la grande muette*" (the big silent one), Tunisia's armed forces corresponded even more to the original meaning of the term than its originator. Coined during the French Third Republic, the phrase came to express the exclusion of military personnel (both professionals and conscripts) from politics, particularly from the right to vote; the idea being that the armed forces should abstain from politics, and hence be silent. But whereas French military personnel were eventually granted the right to vote, as well as become candidates in 1945, their Tunisian counterparts never had this right. The 2014 constitution echoed this French influence not only by emphasising the "republican" character of the armed forces, but equally by stipulating in its article 18 that the armed forces are "required to remain completely impartial"—which opponents of the right for military staff to vote considered cannot be achieved if they are allowed to vote or indeed stand as candidates. The electoral law adopted a few months later, after intense debates between supporters and opponents, maintained the exclusion of security personnel from the political process. It was not clear whether the exclusion would apply also to conscripts, as stipulated in Presidential Decree 35 in 2011.[88]

The reality of the Tunisian military's silence on political matters was, and is, of course somewhat more complex than the myth of the *grande muette*.

In 1962, some of its officers and non-commissioned officers took part in a plot designed to assassinate President Habib Bourguiba; betrayed by one of the NCOs, the conspiracy was uncovered before it could strike. Here as elsewhere, institutional interest played into the plotters' motivations, in spite of the Tunisian media's portrayal at the time of them being self-interested, uneducated agents of outside forces. The plotters, a collection of broadly three groups, each had their own concerns—but where political considerations mattered for the civilians (mostly political opponents of Bourguiba and former resistance fighters), the officers were aggrieved about Bourguiba's handling of the 1961 Bizerte crisis.

Then, the president had rather abruptly announced that Tunisia would retake the French military base in Bizerte by force, without the armed forces being prepared—for combat generally, and certainly not for a significantly stronger and experienced opponent. In the ensuing battle, which unfolded in parts in the streets of Bizerte, several hundred to thousands of Tunisians, both military and civilians, died. The young Tunisian military was then barely four years operational: although several of its officers had served either in the French-colonial Armée d'Afrique or the largely ceremonial Beylical Guards, they were ill-equipped and received no political guidance on how to fight such a conflict.[89] The officers involved in the battle held Bourguiba and his defence minister, a civilian, accountable for the debacle.

In the subsequent trial of twenty-six people related to the failed coup, all eight military officers (as well as one *in absentia*) received the death penalty, along with five civilians. At the last minute, President Bourguiba changed this to a life sentence for two of the officers and one of the civilians; ten were executed in total.

Although death penalties were common in the region and had, by 1962, become the normal response to foiled coups, this was a new and unexpectedly punitive reaction by Tunisian standards. After the 2011 revolution, this led to the creation of an association formed to redeem the plotters, asking for them to be included in the process of transitional justice as martyrs. But while the defence ministry assisted in the recovery of five of the bodies, it refused their burial in the martyrs' cemetery of Sijoumi.[90] As one media commentary noted wryly:

> can you consider the 10 individuals executed after their trial for the 1962 coup against President Habib Bourguiba as 'martyrs'? … Had they succeeded with their coup, would these plotters not have dragged Tunisia into a cycle of violence difficult to recover? … The title of martyr cannot be seriously attributed to them. This would sully the remembrance of all the martyrs of the nation who sacrificed their lives for the national cause and the liberation of the people. And not for… power.[91]

A symbolic funeral was organised by the families and attended by several hundred people regardless—the coffins covered with the Tunisian flag.

The strong reaction of Bourguiba to the plot was certainly indicative of how he intended to handle the armed forces as a political agent. Although the armed forces as a whole were not involved in the coup attempt—indeed, the number of officers involved was negligible, although more than the convicted eight were said to be involved—it cost the Tunisian military dear. Already excluded from their voting rights, military personnel were equally denied membership in political associations—not even in the only existing Destour party of Bourguiba. Like some of his colleagues, Bourguiba proceeded to subject the armed forces to coup-proofing measures: he moved the National Guard from the Ministry of Defence to the Ministry of Interior in order to prevent collusion, reduced the military budget and made sure that only loyal officers were in charge. The military was used only twice to crush civilians during the bread riots of 1978 and 1984, supporting internal security rather than taking a lead role.[92] Tunisia's defence ministry remained firmly in civilian hands—breaking with the regional tradition of officers in charge of the file—and when Ben Ali became interior minister in 1986, he was the first career officer to become a member of the cabinet.

Things changed somewhat under Ben Ali, a former military officer who had moved towards internal security in the 1970s. He arrived to power in a bloodless coup in 1987, with the help of two fellow graduates from the French military academy Saint-Cyr: commander of the presidential guard Ben Ammar and chief of staff es-Cheikh. Shortly after, Ben Ali began to tie the military leadership closer to him.

He appointed senior officers as ministers of the interior, justice and foreign affairs and other high-ranking security posts. The chief of staff as well as the director general of military security were now included in the National Security Council; but the post of defence minister remained civilian. As Bourguiba before him, Ben Ali rotated defence ministers regularly after a maximum of three years in office: in the sixty years since Tunisian independence, only two out of twenty-seven defence ministers—Slaheddine Baly and Bahi Ladgham—have served significantly longer than that, with nine and eight years in office respectively.

The interior forces, empowered since Bourguiba, eyed the military-strengthening developments with suspicion. In 1991, they announced the discovery of an alleged plot uniting military officers as well as the Islamist party Ennahda. A total of 244 military members (113 of whom were officers) were arrested and tortured, and later tried and expelled from the armed forces for allegedly meeting secretly with the party's leadership in Barraket Essahel.[93] The corps, already small, was seriously depleted. In 2011, the concocters of the fake coup went on trial and received several years of sentences for torture. In the following years, all military pension, health insurance and rank rights were restored to the wrongly accused, and President Moncef Marzouki officially apologised on behalf of the Tunisian state.[94]

The incident led to the complete removal of military staff from Ben Ali's environment. The officers in ministerial posts were deposed and the armed forces' budget cut: the 12,000 National Guard of the Ministry of Interior received double the budget of the 30,000 armed forces. At $70 million, the Tunisian military's budget was even lower than Lebanon's, and the Arab world's lowest. Ben Ali also moved to tighten his control over the force; he left the joint chief of staff post empty after General el-Kateb retired, filling it himself and regularly bypassing the minister of defence's decisions. By appointing officers based on loyalty rather than merit, Ben Ali frustrated the corps further and further; in the meantime, the armed forces had no task other than occasional missions with the United Nations in the Congo, Rwanda and the Ivory Coast. The military began to feel "imprisoned" in their barracks.[95] In 2002, when army chief of staff Abdelaziz Skik died in an air crash along with twelve officers, rumours were ripe that this constituted another regime attempt at weakening the military leadership. In contrast to the fake coup of 1991, this incident was never tried after the revolution. Nevertheless, when the time came to desert Ben Ali, the officers felt no loyalty towards a regime which had consistently mistreated them.

In contrast to other forces in the region—such as Egypt—the Tunisian military has, however, stayed out of politics since 2011, in spite of occasional nudges in a political direction by the political opposition. The main reason for this is that it is not in the interests of the institution to embark on such a tricky adventure: not only are its interests met under the new political regime, but it could gamble its highly valued positive image in society. While Tunisia's new democrats are only just beginning to learn benign civilian supervision of the armed forces (in contrast to Ben Ali's malign version), the armed forces are being restrained mostly by themselves, in two particular aspects: that their interests are now being met, and their positive relationship with the population which they seek to preserve.

Previously excluded from decision-making in matters pertaining to national security, the Tunisian military is fully included in the post-Ben Ali system. The tone for this was set during the transitional period under the troika of 2011–13, when responsibility for military matters became increasingly dispersed in an ultimately constructive way amongst not only the executive but also parliament and civil society. A post for a military adviser was created (for the first time) in the president's office, and the number of officers in the revived National Security Council increased. In contrast to Ben Ali's times, eleven officers have been appointed governors of border and interior regions where security is toughest. More challenges remain ahead: since the jihadi threat is an internal one, it requires cooperation with the internal security forces which, so far, have not been institutionalised. Naturally, the deployment of forces within Tunisian territory has raised concerns about their political ambitions.

Matters were further helped by the accidental balancing of the officer corps by then President Marzouki. Distrustful of Ben Ali-era officers (and particularly joint chief of staff Rachid Ammar), Marzouki used the crisis of 2013 to make some important changes: not only did Ammar resign for mishandling the jihadi threat in the Chaambi mountains, but also the chief of staff of the air force, the director general of military security and the inspector general of the armed forces were replaced—all of them with officers from the traditionally sidelined inner regions.[96] As former presidential chief of staff Imed Daimi noted:

> the promotion of the generals from the regions was like transitional justice in the army. The goal was not to make a gap between the regions, but rather because the officers from the interior regions were deprived of or banned from the higher ranks. Marzouki gave them their deserved ranks, and when Hamdi was appointed [chief of army staff], all of the mid-level officers from the interior regions said finally, the end of the privileging of the Sahel![97]

With the corps already content and empowered, the government equally substantially increased its previously modest defence budget. Not only had the military been severely underfunded by the previous regime for decades, it now faced a serious Islamist insurgency. Although its share is still 25 per cent smaller than the interior ministry's, the defence ministry's budget has grown faster than anyone else's since 2011 and stands in 2016 at $1 billion (up from $400 million in 2011). The military received much-needed armoured vehicles, and more contracts with American companies were signed to acquire armoured helicopters, missiles and transport planes. The United States tripled its military aid to Tunisia in 2015, paving the way for more equipment.

Lastly, the injustices done to the Tunisian armed forces under the previous regime have been addressed comprehensively and indeed faster and more extensively than those committed elsewhere. The many associations of former military officers—such as the Association of Justice for Military Veterans and the Association of Former Officers of the National Armed Forces—have played important roles in branding the armed forces first and foremost as victims of the Ben Ali regime. The judicial rulings, along with financial and statutory compensations, have only tightened the bond the armed forces already have with the civilian population. The associations act almost like effective unions, transmitting military concerns to the wider public, which is, after all, their main audience.[98]

As a collective, the Tunisian armed forces have learned from Egypt that venturing into politics puts this important relationship at risk. In 2014, a survey found that four out of five young Tunisians declared trust in their armed forces more than any other state institution—as much as in their own families. In fact, the Tunisian support for its military regularly turns into demonstrations, such as when eight soldiers were killed during an operation against militants in 2013. Carrying banners reading "I love the army", "the army is the protector of the nation", "we are honouring our army with our blood and our souls", demonstrators expressed their support for the armed forces.[99] The revitalised conscription programme (Tunisia has had one since, but only 10 per cent of any cohort are effectively drafted), backed by a flashy recruitment campaign, is now designed not only to ease the pressure on Tunisia's labour market, but also to strengthen the bond between Tunisians and their military force.[100]

The Tunisian armed forces proved in 2011 that they were capable of collective action. While they are still learning the details of counter-insurgency, they have shown that as an institution they have the cohesiveness and structural strength to act as one. But the political climate in Tunisia since that date has not given it any reason to venture further into politics: its needs, unmet under Ben Ali, are recognised by the government; it is involved in decision-making pertaining to its operations, enjoys increasing funds and equipment, and is appreciated by its population. It has no reason to venture into politics—for the time being.

5

# MODELS OF POTENTIALLY POLITICAL ARMIES

An armed force capable and perhaps willing to venture into politics will not necessarily end up doing so. Civilians, whether in government or the population at large, play a determining factor here. Where the armed forces are embedded in the government–regime nexus, they will have their needs met and not have the interest to act; elsewhere, the civilian component of the regime is simply too strong an actor for the military to take over. Whatever the reasons, they are, in contrast to Chapter 4, military-extrinsic: meaning that the political fate of the armed forces is decided outside its realm.

## *The capable force that is checked: Jordan, Syria, Saudi Arabia*

The ideal scenario for a state is a military force which is technically capable but successfully checked by civilians. A state which relies on military self-restraint to avoid a coup (as described in the previous chapter) will have to live with a lingering coup potential; a state which has no capable force is already a failure in itself. The political ambitions of an armed force can be checked in several ways: in benign ways, by cooperating with, rather than merely controlling, the military; and in more aggressive ways, by coup-proofing it. Both methods can achieve the desired effect, although the latter may ultimately produce the weakened force described in the first section of Chapter 4.

As aggressive coup-proofing has had disastrous results, the constructively checked force is now on the rise in the region—although the traditionally controlled force, such as in Syria, still exists. Actors involved in civilian supervision elsewhere, such as parliamentary committees and civil society, might be less present; but forces as in Jordan, Morocco or the Gulf have found their place within the state system. Although they might have the capacity and occasionally even the interest to act politically, they are firmly embedded in a larger civilian system which is difficult to outmanoeuvre.

### The Jordanian military: from tribal to royal

The Jordanian military is an example of a generally subordinate force. It was born at the same time as Jordan itself[1] with the somewhat ambitious name of *al-Jaysh al-Arabi* (usually translated as Arab Legion), in what was then a depopulated desert area sandwiched between Mandate Palestine and Iraq. "There wasn't much of note in the desert kingdom of Transjordan except the king and his army", wrote a *New York Times* correspondent in 1948.[2] But the army did not create Jordan singlehandedly, as one scholar noted.[3] Rather, it was the simultaneous birth of the Hashemite monarchy and the military which consolidated the state; the civilian component has thus played a crucial role in how the Jordanian military did, or did not, interfere successfully in politics.

From a purely tactical point of view, the military could have staged coups. Battle-hardened in several conflicts—against Israel in 1948, 1967, 1968 and 1973, against Syria and the Palestinian Liberation Organisation during the violent events now known as Black September in 1970 and more recently against IS—the Jordanian military has displayed a capacity for collective kinetic action, although it was defeated repeatedly on the battlefield. It is precisely because of these defeats that it has undergone reform and important tactical as well as structural changes.[4] A volunteer force (only 15 per cent of the Jordanian military are conscripts), the force is highly professional and well-trained; its emphasis on military skill, discipline and maintenance of weaponry are better than elsewhere in the region. Although not without its tactical shortcomings, the Jordanian military would certainly have the necessary cohesion to stage a coup if they so wished. But the Jordanian military rarely had an interest to do so; and on the few occasions when institutional discontent grew, the civilian leadership knew how to react before a coup could strike.

Three dynamics played into the one tricky moment King Hussein had to manage in his relationship with the armed forces: the military's increased intake of West Bankers and urban officers, the presence of British officers in the Jordanian military and the looming joining of the Baghdad Pact. The three infused the force with a restlessness it had not seen before, nor indeed has seen since.

In the first instance, the Jordanian military had grown substantially in the years since its inception. From a force of 1,300 in 1941, it grew to 8,000 in only five years, and tripled to 25,000 by 1955. Over the course of a decade, the Jordanian armed forces had grown 15 times in size—a speed and volume difficult for any institution to adjust to. One consequence was moving away from the largely tribal and Bedouin-based recruitment of the 1930s: not only had the available pool of healthy young men of the Bedouin and non-Bedouin tribes been depleted, but new posts in technical and administrative units now required higher educational standards.[5] Bedouins (who were "almost fanatically loyal to the king")[6] remained concentrated in seven out of thirteen regiments, mostly in combat units of the infantry. But opposition or discontent with the monarchy began to grow in the technical and administrative units and at the highest levels of the officer corps.

There were several reasons for this discontent: the presence of British officers in the corps blocked access to the highest ranking posts in the force for these officers; strategically they disagreed with the idea of joining the Baghdad Pact and Jordan's relation with Great Britain; tactically they disagreed with the defence posture towards Israel. Politically, the Free Officers of Jordan were a loose conglomeration of pan-Arabist and leftist officers, very much inspired by their Egyptian counterparts who had ousted King Farouk only five years earlier; in contrast to them, however, the Jordanian Free Officers were rather transparent with the king concerning their most pressing objective: the removal of British officers.

The number of British officers in the Arab Legion was small—in 1948, there were 37 in the corps–but they blocked the highest ranking posts for Jordanian officers. *Ta'rib* (arabisation) of the corps became synonymous with full Jordanian independence from Great Britain, focusing on the commander John Bagot Glubb—who himself claimed that the armed forces would not be ready for a fully Jordanian officer corps before 1985.[7] The officers lobbied the king—who had a rather paternal relationship with Glubb—to the point where they succeeded. On the evening of 28 February 1956, the removal of Glubb was executed much like a coup: his house as well as the airport were surrounded by armoured vehicles, the telephone lines to the residences of other British officers cut and those present in barracks confined to quarters.

Once the remaining British officers were phased out of the Jordanian military, the officers from the East Bank, the cities and the Free Officers benefited most from the newly available posts; especially Ali Abu Nuwar, who moved first to commander of the 1st brigade of the West Bank, to assistant chief of staff and then chief of staff, and began to advise the king regularly on strategic and political matters. Bedouin officers were slower to realise the empowering side effects of the officer corps' Arabisation.[8] But the removal of the British officers did not bring stability to the ranks: it empowered already highly political officers whose ambitions seemed to aim further than attaining a certain rank.

A year after Glubb's departure, a highly tense political situation came to the boil. A leftist coalition in parliament, supported by the Free Officers, resented not only the monarchy but also its cooperation with Great Britain and its posture towards Israel. The end of the monarchy suddenly became a real possibility.[9] The first flexing of the military–political muscle occurred in April that year, when units of the 1st Armoured Car Regiment surrounded Amman and set up road blocks without any explanation; a few days later, chief of staff Abu Nuwar allegedly insisted on the appointment of a leftist prime minister and threatened military intervention should the king not fulfil this demand.

In the official version of events, the king received the ultimatum at the same time as two separate officer delegations came to warn him of a potential coup. What is undisputed is that in the meantime Bedouin units loyal to the king began to suspect a conspiracy, and rampaged through the main army camp at Zerka threatening anyone they suspected of involvement in the coup. Rumours of King Hussein's death began to spread, and popular unrest threatened the cities.

King Hussein meanwhile summoned Abu Nuwar, so that they could go together to Zerka base to demonstrate that the king was alive and in control, with his chief of staff there to stress the latter point. On the way, they came across several army units who enthusiastically received him, demonstrating their loyalty to the monarchy, and demanding the death penalty for Abu Nuwar.

> When Hussein arrived in Zerka, the camp was in total confusion. There was still some firing going on, and in the darkness men were running to and fro, many of them only half-dressed, desperate to find out what was happening. No one was in command. The royal car was stopped a number of times, and as soon as Hussein was recognised, he was cheered and his car mobbed. The news that he was alive and in Zerka spread quickly through the camp, and deterred any further resistance by officers and units that were disaffected. (...) By midnight, the opposition had melted away.[10]

In another version, the king wandered among the troops shouting "I am your king. If you don't want me, I will go!"[11]

The following day, a delegation of army officers declared the military's allegiance to the throne, and Hussein made a radio broadcast in which he hailed the unity of the nation and the army—although perhaps really he meant the unity of king and army. The public display of support for his rule was at worst a show of force and at best what protected him from potential military interference. In any case, it showed that especially the Bedouin–tribal–East Bank dimension of Jordan's population considered Hussein's legitimacy intact.[12]

King Hussein still had a few crises to settle: two more coups were uncovered in 1958 and 1959. The first, a small conspiracy led by Lieutenant Colonel Mahmud al-Rusan, was allegedly financed by Syria, although this was never proven. Fingers were equally pointed at deputy chief of staff Major General Sadek Shara, who was suspected of being involved, although he was absent at the time. Ironically, Hussein's request for military support against the coup from his Hashemite cousins in Baghdad served as the pretext for their demise: as the Iraqi Prime Minister decided to send the 20th Infantry Brigade to Amman to prevent a coup, the units moved, undetected, into Baghdad and toppled the Iraqi monarchy.

A year later, another coup attempt was uncovered and led to the arrest of thirteen officers, including deputy chief of staff Shara.[13] Both plots were in their early planning stages; their discovery was most likely the result of two rival factions in the officer corps cancelling each other out. One faction, led by chief of staff Habis al-Majali, was considered pro-British, in favour of a strong regional role for Jordan and a hard line towards the revolutionary United Arab Republic (the merger of Syria and Egypt). The Shara faction under the deputy chief of staff was considered pro-American and inclined to be more accommodating towards the radical Arab states. Both factions vied for direct access to Hussein, and the easiest way to achieve this was by discrediting the loyalty of others. Intra-military jealousies seem to have played into Hussein's hands.

Ultimately, Hussein succeeded as the civilian head of state because he had the capacity not only to remove potential rivals from the armed forces, but also to mediate between rival factions in the corps. A few years after the Shara "coup", the al-Majali faction itself split in two along lines of tribal interests. Al-Majali and his supporters were facing opposition from defence minister 'Akif al-Fayiz and his allies—both factions extending their support into the political landscape. When actual fighting broke out between these two groups in the barracks, Hussein—who, again, had rushed to the scene–sided with al-Majali and purged the military of his opponents.

The aftermath of these two crucial years for Jordan's armed forces can still be felt today. The date of Glubb's removal, 28 February, is still celebrated by the king as the Arabisation day of the military.[14] The full control of the Jordanian officer corps and hence the military has thus become a symbol of national independence.

Perhaps more importantly, they defined the relationship between armed forces and monarchy for the coming decades. For while King Hussein was aware of the political threat potential of the military—in fact his own ascent to the throne was the result of military meddling, as his grandfather's assassination had been allegedly plotted by a disgruntled army officer[15]–he had neither the intelligence system nor, in the beginning, the political maturity for active prevention of coup attempts. His only protection against possible military incursion was the support of the population and, by extension, the personal loyalty of the troops. He consequently continued to pay close attention to the concerns of the armed forces.

Both he and his successor King Abdallah did this in four main ways: ensuring that the collective interests of the force are met both in manpower and in budget; ascertaining the political loyalty of the highest ranking officers; developing and maintaining close personal ties with the corps; and establishing a continuous narrative in which the military, the court and Jordan are one.

While both force size and spending grew under Hussein, both developments need to be qualified: firstly, Jordan's military posture was largely determined by an actual conflict with Israel until 1994; secondly, while Jordan spent a considerable 14 per cent of its GDP in 1965 on defence, it did so in a very resource-constrained environment. In absolute terms, the Jordanian military was therefore not lavishly supported and had to rely on outside supplies for crucial equipment. This was a fight the king was willing to join: when both the United States and Great Britain were concerned about the rise of the military's influence, he told them that he would have to form a military government if he did not receive "something which would enable him to show his Army that he was getting tangible support" from his allies.[16] In 1989, Hussein silenced public criticism of the economic crisis by explaining the problem as the result of military procurement needs.[17]

Meanwhile, the forces continued to grow exponentially—from 25,000 in 1956, to 65,000 in 1967, and 70,000 in 1980—and Hussein launched a professionalisation of the corps in 1962. Ageing officers were retired and recruitment, appointment and promotion of officers was formalised. The British ambassador at the time noted: "responsibility for security has been taken out of the amateur, blundering and dangerously inefficient hands of the Army".[18]

By 1970, Hussein and the military were entering another turbulent period of Jordanian politics. The war of 1967 had led not only to the arrival of 300,000 Palestinian refugees, but also the newly created Palestinian Liberation Organisation (PLO). Implicitly mandated by the Arab League's Khartoum summit to wage war against Israel from Jordanian territory, it was soon at odds with the Jordanian government: not only on the end state to be achieved, but also on the means to be used—and particularly to what extent Jordan was willing to pay a price for the Palestinian struggle. Within no time, Jordan saw the Palestinian guerrilla as a state within a state. In September 1970 began a showdown between the Jordanian military and the guerrilla forces which lasted for nearly a year, ending with the expulsion of the PLO from Jordan.

Soldiers of Palestinian origin in the Jordanian military then numbered 25,000, or nearly 40 per cent of the corps; despite the loyalty conflict they felt during the operations, only 25 per cent of them deserted. Nevertheless, the monarchy proceeded to 'Jordanise' the armed forces in subsequent years: not so much in the rank and file, where those Jordanians of Palestinian/West Bank origin still make up 30–40 per cent, but more so in the officer corps where, while present in the lower echelon positions (with the exception of first-line combat units), they hold only 10 per cent of the upper echelons.[19] Although Palestinians had largely remained in the armed forces during the confrontation, King Hussein could not afford to doubt his corps; he needed to be able to trust them fully, and he no longer trusted Palestinians. Black September therefore gave him the opportunity to consolidate his relationship with the officers further.

King Hussein, as all of his sons, made a point of having actual military experience. Perhaps because Jordan was the result of a Hashemite armed struggle against the Ottomans, every male royal has served in the armed forces. Hussein pushed his British Sandhurst education further by training to become a pilot (an experience which encouraged the build-up of the Jordanian air force). His son Abdallah, trained at Sandhurst as his father and four brothers, had a military career in the Jordanian forces before ascending the throne in 1999: first in the 40th Armoured Brigade, later as the commander of a tank company in the 91st Armoured Brigade. He also trained to fly Cobra attack helicopters in the Royal Jordanian Air Force's anti-tank wing. His son, crown prince Hussein, is similarly enrolled in the Jordanian officer corps.

Prince Hamzah, another of Hussein's sons and previously crown prince, is also a career officer and was deployed with the Jordanian military in peacekeeping operations in former Yugoslavia; he is a trained rotor and fixed wing aircraft pilot. Prince Faisal, King Abdallah's brother from the same mother, is a trained pilot and became deputy supreme commander of the Jordanian Armed Forces. Prince Ali served in the special forces and was in charge of the king's special security in the royal guards until 2008. Lastly, Prince Hashim served as a captain in the Jordanian Armed Forces 3rd Royal Ranger Battalion. All male members of the family are regularly seen wearing their uniforms, particularly to their own weddings.

King Abdallah, as his father, became particularly involved in the force. He assumed command of the special operations in 1993, significantly improving its capacities. Nicknamed the "warrior king', he can frequently be seen amongst his troops and participating in training—to the point where he was rumoured to fly personal sorties against IS in 2015.[20] But the throne's links with the armed forces go beyond mere personal ties: structurally, supervision of the military was and is very much handled by the king himself. Beyond his title as supreme commander of the armed forces, a constitutional amendment of 2014 granted the king sole authority to appoint the head of the armed forces; previously, the government would recommend appointees to be approved by the king by decree. Although the military is still under the supervision of the executive and legislative, both arms have been rather weak: until summer 2014, Jordan had no defence ministry (the file was traditionally handled by the prime minister who de facto relegated it to the chief of staff, himself responsible only to the king), and the relevant committee in parliament has very little overseeing powers. While it approves the military budget, for instance, it does not see a detailed spending sheet.[21] The king's hold over the armed forces is therefore unrivalled, but not destructive as in other Arab cases. The Jordanian armed forces are still capable—in contrast to Iraq's or Libya's, for instance—of formulating collective demands. More recently, its association of veterans—said to be 140,000 strong—has become a politically active voice against privatisation, corruption and the neoliberal domination by Jordanian business.[22]

Both kings have used their speeches to push the notion of the armed forces being one not only with Jordan, but specifically with the monarchy, Arabism and Islam. The military was and is therefore repeatedly depicted as a defender of not only the country but the entire Arab nation, Arab sovereignty and Arab civilisation.[23] The esteem in which Jordanians hold their armed forces can be measured particularly in the public reaction to the fate of pilot Moaz al-Kasasbeh, shot down by IS over Syria and subsequently burned and stoned to death. Demonstrators held not only the flag of Jordan but also pictures of the pilot reading "We are all Moaz". Previously somewhat critical of Jordan's participation in the campaign against the militia, the popular response called for revenge.

While the Jordanian military is a capable force and indeed has collective interests, the civilian government—and especially the royal palace—is ultimately the more powerful political player.

## The Syrian Armed Forces: from coup frontrunners to regime henchmen

The armed forces of Syria used to be the most politicised of all the forces in the Arab world: not only in terms of quantity—seventeen attempted coups between 1949 and 1982—but also in terms of effectiveness, as thirteen of these succeeded in toppling the regime. Even the once very political Iraqi armed forces come a distant second with 'only' eleven coup attempts, of which more than half failed.

Somewhat ironically, Syria's first coup in 1949 was not highly political in motivation; military-intrinsic concerns such as salaries, promotions, budget and civilian support during the Palestine war were what drove the plotters first.[24] But as two more coups struck Syria the same year, the concept became not only more political, but also more established as not only the quickest but also easiest way to attain power in Syria—a concept which grew ever more attractive as the Syrian political landscape fragmented further and further, and ever more radical parties at odds with each other emerged.

Just as the more established Nationalist and People's Parties lost power to smaller and more radical ones like the Baath and the Communist Parties, so did the officer corps become increasingly politicised and vulnerable to political penetration from the outside. At the same time, coups became a particularly interesting method for small constituencies with little leeway otherwise. The 1954 coup, for instance, was engineered by Baathist, Communist and Druze officers in collusion with civilian counterparts. The series of coups and coup attempts which followed the first one of 1949 were consequently less the result of institutional concerns (although elements of these were found in every coup, especially the one putting an end to the union with Egypt in 1961) and more of a highly fragmented and polarised political landscape which instrumentalised the armed forces as a tool to come to power.

The turning point came with the elections of 1954: already quite polarised on foreign policy questions, Syria's political landscape fragmented and radicalised at the same time. The previously strongest People's Party (which advocated a union with the Hashemites) fell from 71 per cent in 1949 to 21 per cent; the Baath, previously at 5 per cent, now stood at 15 per cent and became parliament's second strongest party; the Nationalist Party, in favour of Syrian independence, had 13.5 per cent. Together, these three parties had barely half of parliament's seats; the rest were scattered over six smaller parties and independents. Parliamentary democracy, it seemed, was not working to the advantage of anyone.

As Syrian politics grew ever more antagonistic, equally belligerent officers from different political inclinations came to the conclusion that a political union with Egypt would solve the country's problems—and more importantly, chase away prospects of an alleged Communist landslide in the upcoming elections of 1958. A delegation of twelve officers, headed by Chief of Staff Bizri (oddly known for both his Nasserist and Communist tendencies) flew to Cairo to convince President Nasser of the idea, which he reluctantly accepted. The brief union was not a happy one—especially not for the Syrian military, which was politically sidelined by the explicit demand of Nasser. Not only were Communists, Baathists and other dissident officers purged from the corps or moved to Egypt (1,000 officers in total), along with the Aleppo Air Academy and Homs military college; worse, decision-making moved entirely to Cairo. Syrian politics was suddenly out of the military's hands.

After only three years of union, the United Arab Republic (as the construct was called) was abolished by a coup led by Colonel Abdelkarim Nahlawi. Syrian troops supported the move against Egyptian paratroopers sent from Cairo. A few days later, sixteen leading Syrian politicians issued a statement thanking the army for their "blessed deliverance".[25] But the break-up with Egypt polarised Syrian society only further, particularly within the Baath party. The elections of 1961 gave way to a dysfunctional parliament: the People's Party had 19 per cent, the National Party 12 per cent, the Baath 11.6 per cent, and over half of parliament's seats were attributed to small parties and independents.

Over the next five years, Syrian society along with the armed forces drifted politically in very different directions. Foiled coup attempts occurred in 1962 and 1963, either to oust the secessionists or the Nasserists. Within the Baath, fissures became apparent as the party's leadership had split over the union with Egypt. The February 1963 Baath coup in Iraq, which ousted the military regime of Abdel Karim Qassem, certainly added inspiration: on 8 March 1963, the so-called military committee of the Baath party, as well as sympathetic senior officers, staged a successful coup against the government of Nazim al-Qudsi from the People's Party and installed a Baath regime. This type of coup was not a guardian coup, as it did not merely remove a government: it removed a whole system and therefore qualifies as a breakthrough coup.

The military committee of the Baath had formed in Egypt around a nucleus of five Syrian junior officers sent there as part of Nasser's military de-politicisation programme. Three years later, inner-Baath struggles led to an overthrow of the traditional Baathists such as Michel Aflaq and Salah al-Din Bitar by this younger generation—the generation of Hafez al-Assad, as well as Salah Jadid. As the new regime began to purge the Baath, as well as the military, it was met with resistance: at least four foiled attempts occurred between March 1963 and 1970, when al-Assad finally toppled Jadid in his "corrective revolution".

Although highly involved in politics in the first three decades of Syrian independence, the armed forces were, however, not a political actor in their own right. Instead, the officer corps was neither cohesive nor professional enough to withstand the constant politicisation by civilians in a highly polarised environment—a feature that was visible also in its poor tactical performances during its operations against Israel or Jordan. The more politicised the armed forces became, the worse their performance.[26] Some officers recognised the danger which politicisation can bring to the armed forces and advocated neutrality; but "there was fear that the army was losing prestige and influence by its withdrawal from the political scene."[27] The dangerously apolitical officers were sent abroad as military attachés.

Whenever the army did act politically, it did so in collusion with civilians seeking to take advantage of its military power. This lack of political military agency is also reflected in the fact that more often than not, Syrian coups were guardian coups designed to remove a certain government rather than to change the political system as a whole, or indeed to establish the armed forces in power. With the exception of Adib Shihakli's 1951 coup, Syria's first four coups maintained the political system including parliament and political parties, and three other attempts (1966, 1970, 1982) were inner-Baath coups equally preserving the system. It was consequently not the armed forces as a whole which staged coups, but certain factions therein in cooperation with civilians.

Things changed to some extent with the consolidation of power by Hafez al-Assad: the Syrian military, in spite of the at least three coup attempts, was by and large firmly under his control. It also regained its military strength, which had been damaged by political infighting: after all, the war with Israel in 1973, the crushing of an Islamist uprising in the late 1970s to early 1980s, and the occupation of Lebanon all required a force maintaining cohesion in battle. To achieve both the protection of the military as an institution and his own regime, al-Assad relied on a combination of traditional coup-proofing techniques—but implemented in a constructive rather than destructive manner. These were mechanisms to gloss over the Syrian military's increasingly ethnic factor, the creation of parallel forces, the appointments of loyal officers to strategic posts as well as the doling out of benefits to the officer corps. Taken together, these measures created the illusion of a united, cohesive and national force; in reality, however, the Syrian armed forces consisted of two intertwined militaries in one. What remained unchanged, however, was the traditional infusion and control of the Syrian military by the civilian politicians—and this was brought to the test with the Syrian civil war.

The first aspect al-Assad had to address was the ethno-religious dynamic which had come to the forefront after the 1963 coup. Although Baathist in outlook, the ousting was interpreted very much as a minority action: of the five founding members of the military committee, three were Alewites and two were from the Ismaili sect, both minorities in Syria. Until then, neither Syrian politics nor the military had been ruled by primarily ethnic or religious considerations.

Yet several dynamics had released the sectarian genie from the bottle. Firstly, political inclinations somewhat overlapped with ethno-religious affiliation, which played to the advantage of the more cohesive Alewite community. Small (10–20 per cent of the population), disenfranchised, and rural, the Alewites very much sympathised with the socialist tone of Baathism; whereas Sunnis were, as a larger community, more diverse and consequently took to different political streams. Consequently, in the military:

> Sunnis of one persuasion ended up purging Sunnis of another persuasion, or low or middle class Sunnis joined Alewites or Druzes in purging upper class Sunnis, or rural-oriented Sunnis joined with Alewites and Druzes in purging city-based Sunnis. In political terms, the Secessionists, the Huranists, the Nasserists, the group of the independent Ziyad Hariri, and the supporters of the Baathi Amin al-Hafez were successively purged between March 1963 and February 1966, and, with every purge, the Sunnis in the officer corps decreased in significance.[28]

Before 1963, Alewites were not concentrated in the officer corps but in the non-commissioned officers as well as the rank and file; but they survived the purges better than their Sunni counterparts.

Secondly, the constant political bickering of the 1950s within the armed forces led to mistrust, a breakdown of military procedures and hence to a breakdown of professionalism. Command structures, promotions, recruitments and appointments all relied increasingly on shared identities. Rather than sectarianism leading to political turmoil, it was the other way around.[29] In addition, Alewites had incidentally ended up strategically in units relevant to launching a coup, such as air squadrons, the armoured brigades around the capital, as well as intelligence forces.

To the Baath regime, its overly Alewite makeup was a disadvantage. It needed the support from all of Syria's population to stay in power, and as such tone down the notion of sectarianism. This was even more the case when it came to the military: not only was an all-Alewite force numerically not feasible and Sunni troops therefore necessary, but also the symbolism of the armed forces mattered to the regime and its legitimacy. It consequently pursued a policy of "glossing over" the Alewite factor in the armed forces. While the officer corps was purged of non-Baathist officers, who were quickly replaced with Baathi (and often Alewite) supporters, crucial and visible roles were given to Sunnis or other minorities. Of Syria's ten defence ministers since the 1966 coup, six were Sunnis, one Greek Orthodox and three Alewites; more importantly, in the first three decades of the regime, the chief of staff was always a Sunni, flanked by Mustafa Tlas, who served for twenty-eight years as minister of defence, also a Sunni. Sunni officer grievances nevertheless prevailed and were real—yet they were voiced in military professional terms, not sectarian ones.[30]

It is important to note that the regime succeeded, in spite of an Alewite overrepresentation in the officer corps, in largely shielding its troops from sectarianism. This was facilitated by the creation of parallel forces. The so-called Defence Companies under Hafez al-Assad's brother Rifat's command, later replaced by the Republican Guard Division and the Special Forces under Bashar al-Assad's brother Maher, are not only predominantly staffed with Alewites, but their goal is to protect the regime. This freed up the armed forces for their actual business of war, and allowed them to maintain more diverse manpower as well as cohesiveness.

The fact that sectarian aspects did not play into the desertions witnessed since 2011 is testimony to this: low-ranking Sunni soldiers who had deserted stated very clearly that their motivation to leave was largely based on humanitarian concerns, and stressed that religion did not play a significant role in the armed forces. Similarly, desertions have occurred also from the Alewite community—the most notable being former chief of staff and defence minister Ali Habib Mahmud.[31] The ongoing conflict is however likely to reverse this trend, and lead to a re-sectarianisation of the Syrian military.

But while the regime was busy clouding its somewhat lopsided recruitment into the armed forces, it ensured that strategic positions in the armed forces were occupied by loyal inidividuals, whether Alewite or Sunni. Although al-Assad recognised the detrimental impact of politics on the armed forces, this did not imply depoliticisation; instead, it meant Baathification. The corps, while revamped and refocused on meritocratic principles, was at the same time purged of political opposition.[32] While it mattered to give the officer corps at least the illusion of diversity, by the time of Hafez al-Assad's death in 2000, 90 per cent of general officers were trusted Alewites—often tied personally to the president. Even during the 1973 war, Alewite units were deployed less, to avoid their loss as important loyalty pillars in the armed forces; and decision-making remained highly centralised—decisions which made no military sense.[33]

In addition, although officers received notoriously low salaries of between $400 and $800 a month, they received privileged housing and access to luxury cars; they were also allowed to use their positions for enrichment in a variety of ways. Syrians who dodged their military service bribed the officer of the unit in question; within their military sector, officers were allowed to rule as if in a personal fiefdom. Corruption, nepotism and patronage networks became a tool to tie the officers directly to the regime; this is also what damaged it in terms of military professionalism, but not to the point where it broke cohesion.[34]

Interestingly, the transition from Hafez to Bashar al-Assad in 2000 brought little change in the relationship between regime and military, although Bashar did not have the same military pedigree as his father. An ophthalmologist by profession, he was fast-tracked through the ranks when his older brother and heir apparent, Bassil, died in 1994. Nevertheless, the first step in the power transition was Bashar's appointment by the acting vice president to be the Syrian military's commander, and his promotion to *Fariq*, the most senior rank in the armed forces. A few hours later, members of the senior officers' corps went to see Bashar to express not only their condolences but also their loyalty and complete support. Only then was he elected president with 99.7 per cent of the votes.[35] Military subordination seemed ultimately more important than the political process.

When the Syrian civil war erupted in 2011, the armed forces, their cohesiveness and fighting power were put to the test. While numerous predictions foresaw its immediate collapse, the military was still fighting at the time of writing, five years into the conflict.[36] It was consequently still very much intertwined with the regime, rather than a potential independent actor capable of ousting it—which some had called for.[37] While this is in part the result of the pre-war policies of both Bashar and Hafez al-Assad, the regime has handled the conflict in such a way as to protect the armed forces as its ultimate legitimacy-giver. Should the Syrian military collapse, so would the regime's claim to be the legitimacy government.

It has done so in several ways: it has bolstered its depleted ranks with militias and foreign forces, increased the salaries of the troops, hailed the army in virtually every speech, employed a nationalist narrative and relied on politicised tactics.

Desertion has halved the Syrian military in the years since the war started: from 300,000 it probably now stands at 150,000–175,000 troops maximum—a fact even Bashar al-Assad openly recognised in summer 2015 when he mentioned a "lack of human resources" in the military.[38] By the end of 2011, 3,000 Sunni officers were said to have deserted from all ranks. Crucially, however, these officers never defected with their whole units, and since they were not in critical positions, their departure did not affect the effectiveness of the military as a whole. The strategy of loyal appointments to critical posts thus paid off in this situation. Since 2014, desertions have come to a near-halt.

Since the beginning of the conflict, the regime has employed several techniques to refill these empty posts: it has prolonged active service members (the so-called class of 102), granted amnesties to avoiders of military service and deserters who have not joined the ranks of the opposition, and recalled retirees. Its most efficient way, however, was the creation of localised militias as well as the help of foreign forces such as Hezbollah, which are of particular use in infantry operations. This leaves the Syrian military with mostly artillery and air power operations, potentially shielding it from further desertion.

At the same time, the regime repeatedly increased military service—with little effect, however, as inflation in Syria has been rampant since the outbreak of the war. In 2011, every civil servant received a one-time rise of 1,500 Syrian pounds (around $32 at the time), a 30 per cent salary increase for every employee earning less than 10,000 Syrian pounds a month, and a 20 per cent increase for those earning more than 10,000. It increased salaries further in 2013 by 40 per cent on the first 10,000 Syrian pounds earned and 20 per cent on the second, and increased the pensions for military personnel. In early 2015, it awarded a one-time payment of 4,000 Syrian pounds (around $15) to all government employees, and announced further increases in October 2015.[39]

In the numerous speeches Bashar al-Assad has given since the war broke out, his key message has been not to underestimate the armed forces. While his first speech in January 2012 devoted barely two sentences to the armed forces ("Standing hand in hand with the country's institutions, assisting these institutions and the army, and morally supporting the army!"), this changed as the conflict evolved. A year later, he adopted a grander tone:

> Greetings to those who deserve the biggest greetings: the men of the Syrian Arab Army. Greetings to our valiant officers, NCO's and soldiers

(…) who are exerting sweat and blood for the sake of Syria, which they see dearer than themselves and all that they possess. Greetings to our Armed Forces as they wage the fiercest of wars, determined to restore peace and security (…). Our Armed Forces, which have recorded acts of heroism through their cohesion, steadfastness, and national unity, were a reflection of the people's steadfastness and cohesiveness. (…) Glory to every soldier who fell in the battle while defending the national soil. Glory, all glory, to every soldier who carries his arms and blood to continue the mission of those who fell."

Along with defence minister Fahd Jassem al-Freij, al-Assad seized opportunities such as army day on 1 August to hail the military as the saviour of the "cultural identity of the Arab nation and Syria", carrying the "pan-Arab responsibility on its shoulders for decades" as the true embodiment of Syria and patriotism. The longest tribute to the forces came in al-Assad's speech of 2015, when he not only recognised desertion as a problem but also called on the Syrian people to support it more. "If we want the army to offer its best, we must offer for it the most we have. If we want it to operate at its maximum power, we must provide for it all the energy it needs (…) Defeat does not exist in the lexicon of the Syrian Arab Army."[40] In 2016, the Syrian military was allowed to vote for the first time in parliamentary elections—another measure to appease an embattled force.

Of course, in spite of these measures, morale is low in the Syrian forces today. Over 50,000 soldiers have fallen in the conflict; in 2014, IS executed several hundred captured Syrian soldiers in Raqqa and Hasaka province. On social media, recruits regularly complain about conditions, low salaries, outdated equipment and forced conscription.[41] Within the forces, mistrust is rampant: some analysts estimate that only 65,000 to 75,000 of its troops are actually reliable for offensives, whereas the remainder are posted in defensive positions.[42] Nevertheless, as a force, the Syrian military is still standing; as CIA Director Brennan noted: "Syria has a real army (…) a large conventional military force with tremendous firepower."[43] Not only that: it is a force which executes what the civilian government orders it to do. The Syrian regime and its military are as intertwined as they have always been, and the armed forces are not an independent political actor.

## Tribal, royal or professional? The military of Saudi Arabia

The Saudi state-building experience differs from those of other states in the Arab world. It was never colonised by Western powers, and only its western coastal region, the Hijaz, was under Ottoman control. The majority of the Arab peninsula, however, was not controlled continuously by a single force, instead changing hands repeatedly; this, in addition to its desert nature and tribal-Bedouin culture, made the creation of permanent state structures not only difficult but also unnecessary. When Saudi Arabia finally became a unified country in 1932, not only did the establishment of state institutions begin somewhat later than elsewhere, therefore, but it had few existing structures on which to build. In contrast to other countries in the region, its state-building was also an indigenously-driven process (in spite of some outside assistance). Saudi civilians consequently preceded the armed forces by far in state-building terms. The monarchy not only had a power base in the population, it also provided the state with a narrative and political control, and literally created the state institutions which today make Saudi Arabia. It therefore constituted a supremely strong civilian counterpart which the military could never outmatch in political terms, although it tried on a number of occasions.

Four intertwined dynamics led to the military not playing a political role in Saudi history: the profoundly distrustful attitude of the civilian leadership contributed to a slow and inconsistent build-up of the armed forces; the creation of a force from scratch meant that especially the officer corps was neither cohesive nor strong enough to oppose the civilians; this weakness in turn led the civilian leadership to avoid the forces' deployment in conflict for fear of its failure; lastly, because of this passivity, the Saudi military had no emotional meaning for its population and consequently virtually no popular backing for any political action.

Distrust towards the armed forces was an early feature of Saudi politics—largely because King Abdulaziz (also known as Ibn Saud) experienced the mutiny of an allied militia early on. He had conquered Saudi Arabia largely with the help of the Ikhwan, armed sedentarised and religiously zealous Bedouins. But their relationship soured as the state became consolidated and their benefits from raiding and booty subsided. As the Ikhwan revolted, Abdelaziz managed to supress them with the help of a force raised from the Najd region as well as Bedouins, and some British air support by 1930.[44] Once the Ikhwan were suppressed, Saudi security was managed mainly along tribal lines: armed tribes were funded from the state's budget, whereas some remnants of Ottoman troops patrolled the cities in the Hijaz. For his personal and regime security, Abdulaziz had 1,000 royal guards backed by tribal levies, raised from areas he knew to be loyal, Riyadh and towns in the Najd.

The first steps towards an established force began in the 1940s, when the regular forces numbered 1,000–1,500 troops; its officers hailed mostly from the Ottoman troops which had served the Sharif of Mecca before he was expelled in 1924. A defence ministry was created in 1944, a military school founded in Taif and a programme launched with the United Kingdom to create a regular professional force. Nevertheless, the force struggled with recruitment, educational levels of staff (only 1 per cent of recruits were literate) and budget (Saudi Arabia's fiscal base was very small then); promotion of officers occurred randomly and directly by the king, frustrating those without extensive patronage networks such as the former Ottoman officers and those from areas which the king did not trust; pay was low and living conditions dire, leading to high desertion rates, although the troops saw no combat. A second attempt was launched in 1951, this time with American assistance. It foresaw the creation of three to five regimental combat teams within three years, which, however, failed, like the British mission, to achieve its objectives. While the armed forces grew—to 7,500–10,000 troops in 1953, as did its share in budget (53 per cent in 1953)—the general trend was slow and eventually brought to a halt in 1958.[45]

This was the result of four developments: the arrival of the Free Officers in power in Egypt in 1952; the discovery of two plots by senior officers; the death of King Abdelaziz in 1953; and the unleashing of Saudi-internal power struggles.

In the first instance, Riyadh originally sought to find an accommodation with Cairo, leading to the conclusion of a mutual defence agreement and a training programme for the Saudi military, through which 200 Egyptian advisers were sent to Saudi Arabia, and Saudi officers were sent for training in Egypt. By 1958 this changed, however: the overthrow of the Hashemite monarchy in Iraq by Nasser-inspired offi-cers turned the tides of the relationship: from then on, Egypt under Nasser was a threat to be kept in check. The military training pro-gramme was ended—not without encountering protests from the Saudi officers against the decision. This was made worse by the discov-ery of a plot in the Saudi military a few years earlier, equally bearing Nasserist traits. The officers, led by Lieutenant Abdel Rahman al-Sham-rawi who had studied in Egypt, were inspired by the dynamic, modern and revolutionary nature of Nasser himself; they were equally frustrated by the corrupt, nepotistic and discriminatory personnel policy of the Saudi military. As a result of the coup attempt, the already understaffed officer corps was purged and several of them executed. A few months later, when the al-Rith tribe demanded more religious rights, twelve officers from the same tribe supported the rising and were similarly purged. Lastly, power struggles within the family affected the Saudi military. When defence minister Mishal ibn Abd el Aziz was dismissed for corruption and Nasserism in 1956, King Saud, successor of King Abdelaziz, appointed his son Fahd ibn Saud to appease his own concerns regarding the military's loyalty. This in turn created fears amongst other members of the family, such as Crown Prince Faisal. "The double handi-cap under which the regular armed forces laboured, as a suspected source of disloyalty to the regime as a whole and as a source of specific support for Saud against his rivals, made it easier for Faisal to contem-plate freezing them."[46] Between 1958 and 1965, acquisitions for the armed forces virtually came to a halt: no more aircraft or heavy equip-ment were purchased. At the same time, King Saud diverted manpower and financial resources to the White Army of tribal levies and Royal Guard to bolster his personal power.

But both the threat from Egypt as well as the Saudi military came back to the forefront in 1962: a coup, inspired by Cairo, toppled the imamate in North Yemen, leading first to civil war and then the arrival of 40,000 Egyptian troops. Saudi Arabia, supportive of the Imam, sent aircraft with supplies—but four crews instead defected with planes and cargo to Egypt. In response, the entire air force was grounded and air space patrol outsourced to the United States. In November that year, another plot by Saudi air force pilots, all of them from the ruling fam-ily, was uncovered.

At the same time, a Saudi Committee of Free Princes was formed in Cairo along the lines of the Free Officers, calling for political reform. Radio Cairo began openly advocating an overthrow—indeed, assassination–of the Saudi monarchy. While the Egyptian air force continuously bombed Saudi border areas, the Saudi leadership recognised that its military was no match for the Egyptian forces and was not to be trusted politically; even worse, it worried that an Egyptian invasion would highlight this weakness and subsequently lead to an insurgency.[47] In the following years, the Saudi leadership focused its security efforts therefore on the National Guard, mainly in charge of internal security. Another Nasserist plot, discovered in 1969, only confirmed these suspicions of the military: sixty air force officers, as well as the director of the air force academy in Dhahran, allegedly planned to bomb the royal palace and kill the entire royal family. Immediately, 200–300 officers, several of them high-ranking, were arrested and dismissed, dealing another blow to the corps. While this led to a discussion in the royal family as to whether the modernisation of the armed forces should continue, the modernist bloc prevailed—largely thanks to British withdrawal from the Gulf, as well as the Arab–Israeli war of 1973.

Distrust towards the Saudi military lessened from the 1970s onwards: Sultan ibn Abd al-Aziz became defence minister and remained in the post for 48 years, and investments were increasingly made with a long-term vision. Exploding oil sales allowed the Saudi military to receive more comfortable funding. Between 1962 and 1975, defence expenditure rose twentyfold; following the assassination of King Faisal in 1975, salaries in the armed forces increased by 87 per cent and by 137 per cent in the internal security forces.[48] Nevertheless, the Saudi forces remained ill-equipped: most of the budget was spent on air defence, and sophisticated hardware remained dormant due to lack of staff able to operate it. While an American plan foresaw the expansion of the Saudi military from 60,000 to 98,000, it in fact shrank to 52,000 in 1982. Another plot discovered in the air force in 1977 by Jordanian and Egyptian intelligence led not only to the trial of the conspirators (save for three who escaped with their aircraft to Iraq) but also to severe restrictions for the air force: no flights longer than 30 minutes were allowed, nor was ammunition.[49] Generally, neither services (such as air force and army) nor combat units were allowed to communicate directly but always had to go through higher echelons in order to avoid coup attempts.

The seizure of the Grand Mosque in Mecca by insurgents in 1979 was met with a dubious performance by the National Guard (in fact, the leader of the insurgents was a former corporal in the guard and a descendant of an Ikhwan member) and the armed forces which were called to assist. It took the 3,000 forces two weeks and 578 casualties (127 killed) to clear the mosque of 300–600 insurgents. An anti-terror unit was created as a result of this incident, and a brigade of Pakistani origin was added to the military to make up for its shortfall. The armed forces continued to hover around its modest size of 45,000, despite being showered with a defence budget of 27–39 per cent in the 1980s. Most of this expenditure was spent on infrastructure and training rather than weapons, which made up only 5–15 per cent of annual defence spending in that decade.[50]

What changed the Saudi perception of its armed forces, however, was the Iraqi invasion of Kuwait. In spite of $300 billion spent since 1965 and thousands of American, French and British training personnel, the country was practically defenceless in the face of potential Iraqi aggression. The high command admitted that Iraqi forces could have taken al-Ahsa governorate in the country's south-east within six hours.[51] Saudi forces engaged in the war under American command, especially the air force which had seen the most extensive training. The Royal Saudi Air Force flew 6 per cent of the sorties flown by the coalition, although most of these were defensive combat air patrol. One air-to-air combat, however, led to the shooting down of two Iraqi planes by Saudi pilot Captain Ayed Shamrani, still revered today as a national hero.[52] Nevertheless, Saudi Arabia's military performance was in some ways even worse than expected. Kuwait hence drove home the insight that Saudi Arabia was ill-prepared for a war, as King Fahd declared in an address to the nation:

> Regarding the building of the armed forces, the main lesson to be learned from the Gulf War and the experience of our forces, which did extremely well, and out of the reality in which we live today, we in the Kingdom of Saudi Arabia have made a decisive decision to immediately embark on expanding and strengthening of our armed forces, providing them with the most effective and most advanced land, sea, and air weap-

ons the land the world has produced as well as advanced military and technical equipment.[53]

Since then, Saudi Arabia's military has continued to expand both its manpower and equipment, and has seen combat action most notably against IS as well as in Yemen. A lingering feeling of distrust might, however, still exist: after all, it was the National Guard, not the army, which was sent to quell the uprising in Bahrain in 2011.

But the distrust which Saudi Arabia's leadership had and has towards its military is not the only reason for the absence of its military from the political scene. For this to be an option, the forces would require a degree of institutionalisation the Saudi military simply lacked. There was virtually no institutional memory from an existing force, whether colonial, traditional or revolutionary, with any knowledge and experience in modern warfare and military structures. The conquest of Saudi Arabia by the later neutralised Ikhwan constituted desert warfare, which has little in common with modern and urban warfare; the remnants of the Ottoman officer corps, albeit professional, were not Saudi nationals and had difficulty reaching the higher ranks. But without an officer corps, the Saudi military would struggle to establish itself, as training alone does not make an armed force, especially not one built from scratch. Training is usually most effective in units with existing structures and experienced officers, NCOs and team. The rushed creation of whole new units is always difficult, and requires both time and, most importantly, officers. While the Saudi military had time, it did not have officers, nor a continuously committed engagement from the civilian leadership to grow.

In addition, the Saudi officer corps was far from being cohesive. Although in theory staffed from all regions, Hijazi officers have often complained about lack of promotion. In 1965, they made up 52.5 per cent of the officer corps, a share which was not reflected at the level of command positions (it is also likely that their share dropped after the 1969 coup attempt, involving Hijazi elements).[54] In part this was the result of not only patronage networks sidelining meritocratic principles, but also the presence of royal princes in the corps (particularly the air force). Prince Khaled bin Salman, the son of King Salman, flew one of the highly publicised sorties against IS, as one of many examples.[55] Furthermore, regular purges of the corps diluted its cohesion.

Although growing along with the Saudi middle class in the 1970s and 80s, the officer corps never developed either a class or professional identity which could have served as a springboard for successful political action.

While it was this lack of professionalism and cohesion which propelled the Saudi leadership to avoid the deployment of the military, common combat experience is usually the fastest way to acquire both. The Saudi forces were however deployed only rarely. A baptism of fire occurred in 1948, when a small battalion of two companies was sent fighting under Egyptian command against Israel. Like with other armed forces participating in that war, it highlighted the Saudi military's shortcomings, although it saw very little action. In 1969, the outpost of Wadi'ah was taken by forces from Southern Yemen; Saudi troops were sent, along with substantial air support, to recapture it; but they were not allowed to pursue the Yemeni troops, although they stayed in Saudi territory after abandoning the post, and they were accompanied by units from the National Guard.[56] The military was similarly deployed twice for non-combat missions, in Jordan in 1956 and in Kuwait in 1961, both times to show support for the ruling family. Its participation in the war against Iraq delivered perhaps the most important insight for the monarchy that a force not capable of fighting is not worth its money. The deployment against IS in 2014 and particularly in Yemen since 2015 can be considered the real testing ground for the Saudi forces, which were allegedly even considering to field ground operations in Syria in early 2016.[57] Perhaps more importantly, their deployment is a sign that the leadership trusts the forces to be capable enough.

Lastly, the military never featured in the political landscape of Saudi Arabia because it never had the necessary characteristics. It was not involved in decisive national battles, did not represent a particular political message and had no connection with the population as an all-volunteer force. Once a truly national threat manifested itself, such as during the invasion of Kuwait, the defence of the nation then became a powerful recruitment tool: 200,000 volunteers followed the call for enlistment, when a maximum of 20,000 were expected. Given Saudi Arabia's consistent lack of military manpower—estimated to be short of 25–50 per cent of its staff since at least the 1980s–conscription would be a suitable answer.[58] Although regularly supported, by then former

Defence Minister Sultan ibn Abd al-Aziz and more recently the grand mufti of Saudi Arabia, it is also regularly rebuffed by particularly the National Guard, chiefly in charge of internal security.[59] More importantly, it is the military's involvement in campaigns in Yemen that might provide, at last, the necessary attachment to its own population.

## *The political force which will: Egypt, Algeria*

A military force which is capable, willing and unchecked by either civilians or itself will ultimately use its power to influence politics to its own advantage. Forces can do so in multiple ways: they can remove governments but preserve the system (guardian coup); they can change the system as a whole (breakthrough coup); or they can bar a larger group from political participation (veto coup).

The most far-reaching, the breakthrough coups, are of revolutionary nature and change the system and its structures in its entirety.[60] Consequently, putschists have the largest degree of latitude following a coup of this type, which in turn implies that a large degree of organisational frustration prevailed beforehand. The cases of Egypt in 1952, Libya in 1969 or Iraq in 1958 are examples of breakthrough coups, as they abolished the monarchy and removed all the elites connected to the previous system. These coups led many observers to the conclusion that Arab military forces are essentially agents of change. Although this type of coup is most certainly the most invasive, it is not the most prevalent in the Arab world.

In pure numerical terms, this would be the guardian coup, which changes the leadership without altering the system as such. More often than not, guardian coups occur as a result of a factional power struggle within the armed forces, and therefore do not question the political system so much as those who hold the reins of power. Guardian coups are driven by factional interests and change personalities rather than profound structures or indeed policies, although their stated interests do not differ much from breakthrough coups.

Veto coups are the rarest form of Arab coups, as they are decidedly directed against the "actual or prospective victory at the polls of a party or movement which the military oppose or which represents groups which the military wish to exclude from political power" or a "government in power (which) begins to promote radical policies or to develop an appeal to groups whom the military wishes to exclude from power".[61] In other words, a veto coup bars a larger group from political participation and therefore usually encounters the highest degree of opposition. The motivations for this kind of coup must therefore be strong. In this context, the armed forces are agents of revision rather than change. Veto coups do not change the system in its entirety when they are successful, and they are possible only if the armed forces already play a political role.

Of course, different coups bring different regimes to power; the armed forces do not necessarily seek direct governance as in military dictatorships, but often prefer civilian oligarchs in power if they are assured the protection of their interests. The difference between the three coup types is the target of the intervention as such; whereas breakthrough coups aim at a certain system, guardian coups target a military faction, and veto coups aim at the exclusion of a certain group from power.

## The Egyptian military: from political to economic power

Military influence on politics cannot be solely measured in coup occurrence—after all, Egypt does not lead Arab coup statistics but its armed forces certainly influence politics decisively. In fact, the role the Egyptian armed forces play and have played in the country's politics goes way beyond the simple removal from power of a leader. In addition to ousting King Farouk in 1952 and President Morsi in 2013, Egypt's armed forces collectively disobeyed President Mubarak in 2011, were the springboard for a violent mutiny which led to the death of President Sadat in 1981, launched an aborted coup in 1971, were directly involved in governance in the 1950s, have fielded numerous governors and other, nominally civilian, personnel, and have expanded, since the 1970s, their role in the Egyptian economy. Although the extent of the military's influence on politics has fluctuated, it has never subsided entirely and may now very well be at an all-time high.

In several ways, the Egyptian armed forces were, and are, the ideal case of an Arab force intervening in politics: not only capable and cohesive, but also pushed by military-intrinsic motives, unopposed by effective civilians and capitalising on a positive image in society. They have consequently been able, more so than most of their regional counterparts, to establish and enlarge their political say over time.

The first precondition for this is of course its military capability, which ironically is the result of two crucial battlefield failures. The defeats of 1948 and 1967 drove home the point that an armed force neglected or politicised by the civilian leadership will fail in its mission. President Sadat, who succeeded Nasser in power in 1970, embarked not only on a mission of professionalisation, but also of streamlining the civil–military decision-making. In 1974, Sadat published his "October Working Paper", in which he laid out the idea of a "state of institutions". Educational levels of officers were dramatically increased—the number of officers with university education rose from not even 1 per cent of officers in 1967 to 70 per cent in 1994[62]—while military conscription became more selective; the switch from Soviet to American aid facilitated the modernisation of the institution further. In addition, he removed military officers from politics—twenty-two out of twenty-six governorships were held by military personnel in 1964, which was reduced to five in 1980; the number of cabinet members with a military background was decreased from a third to a tenth. The military was no longer a battleground for competing powers, but was placed under firm civilian supervision while left to its business of war.[63] In 1973, this led to a much-improved performance against Israel.[64] In 1991, Egypt participated in Operation Desert Storm against Iraq as part of a multinational coalition, fielding one of the largest contingents with over 40,000 troops and 400 tanks. In spite of several issues with flexibility and leadership at the junior officer level, the Egyptian military showed:

> areas of consistently competent performance. The bravery of the individual soldier is beyond question. Similarly, unit cohesion has been inconsistent, though tending more toward the positive side of the spectrum. In general, one is struck by the fact that Egyptian forces regularly have fought tenaciously in impossible situations. (…) Egyptian logistics and combat engineering were also real areas of strength. (…) Overall, Egyptian forces fought well.[65]

More recently, the armed forces have been involved in an extended campaign in the Sinai against Jihadi networks. Its performance there has been questionable; however, not only is it the first time the Egyptian military has fought a counter-insurgency operation in a mountainous and desert area, but political turmoil also made its task more difficult.[66] Its capacity to act as a collective whole, however, is undisputed.

While the Egyptian military had motives to remove King Farouk in 1952, it was scarcely noticed that it was also building up resentment towards President Mubarak and later President Morsi. In 2008, leaked cables from the United States Embassy in Cairo noted disgruntled mid-level officers referring to military chief Field Marshal Tantawi as "Mubarak's poodle"—incompetent, valuing loyalty over skills in subordinates and submissive to the president. In part, this was because military salaries had fallen compared to those in the private sector; but it also had to do with the fact that Mubarak's son Gamal was being groomed to be his successor—not only a man without any military experience, but also with dangerously liberal attitudes towards the economy. Since the 1970s, the armed forces had been involved in ever-growing economic activities going far beyond mere military production—an endeavour now under threat, should Gamal's neoliberalism come into full force.[67] Lastly, long-term political and military stability under Mubarak—the longest-serving Egyptian president with nearly 30 years in power—meant that the officer corps was static and consequently promotions slow; defence minister Field Marshal Tantawi, for instance, had been in his post for 21 years. In contrast to Nasser, Mubarak did not purge the officer corps; and in contrast to Sadat, he did not reshuffle the commanders of the armed forces regularly.[68]

Ironically, coups and combat operations can be to the benefit of those officers who remain in the corps after purges and dismissals, eligible for decorations and promotion. While these motivations fed into the collective disobedience—indeed, ordered disobedience by the highest military echelons—in 2011, somewhat different motives contributed to the ousting of President Morsi in 2013. Mid-level officers' interests had been met somewhat by the dismissal of Defence Minister Field Marshal Tantawi, Chief of Staff Sami Annan, Navy Commander Mohab Memish and Air Force Commander Reda Hafez; the removal of the upper echelons meant that promotions were now in store for junior and mid-level officers.[69] Then, a different set of motives emerged particularly with the jihadi insurgency in the Sinai and protracted instability hurting Egypt's economy.

While on the surface Morsi's overturning of the constitutional dec-laration the military had issued in 2012 seemed to compromise civilian control over the armed forces, in practice the constitution of the same year gave the military almost the same amount of autonomy and inde-pendence. In December 2012, he even gave army officers the right to arrest civilians, even if only for a week; and promoted several senior officers shortly before the coup, so that superficially, the military did not seem disgruntled.[70] Clearly, Morsi was looking for an accommoda-tion with the military, not a confrontation. In his first national address after the elections, he began by thanking the army and added, "Only God knows how much love I have in my heart (for it)."[71]

However, a closer look revealed increasing discontent with Morsi's policies: violent protests erupted when the draft constitution seemed entirely written by Islamist forces, escalating further with Morsi's con-stitutional declaration. Although the armed forces ensured security and cooperated with the presidency initially, it issued a somewhat disobedi-ent declaration a few days into the protests:

> The armed forces (…) realise their responsibility to preserve the higher interests of the country and to secure and protect vital targets, public institutions and the interests of innocent citizens. (…) The armed forces affirm that dialogue is the best and only way to reach consensus. (…) The opposite of that will bring us to a dark tunnel that will result in catastro-phe and that is something we will not allow.[72]

Constant unrest had hurt Egypt's economy: revenues from foreign investment and tourism had dropped, foreign exchange reserves shrunk by around 60 per cent, 1,500 factories had closed since 2011 and the Egyptian pound had lost 12 per cent of its value, increasing the prices of fuel and food staples imports.[73] All this impacted on the Egyptian military's economic activities. Without clearing his decision with the armed forces, Morsi announced that the "Egyptian people and army" would help free Syria.[74] Meanwhile, the insurgency in the Sinai kept growing; when seven soldiers were kidnapped, Morsi aborted an operation against the kidnappers—and rumours emerged of a military cutback intended by Morsi.[75]

Arguably, the Egyptian military was already influencing politics heavily before it ousted Morsi in summer 2013; but as its moves proved not to achieve the desired results, a coup became ever more likely—

particularly because Morsi's backtracking policy on issues such as constitutional control over the armed forces only confirmed that he was not a serious antagonist. In contrast to other leaders discussed in the previous chapter, neither Morsi nor his aides had a power base in the military, the necessary intelligence or network, nor indeed an understanding of how the armed forces think as a collective. Whereas Morsi was seeking to buy himself support through the granting of promotions and independence, he instead proved to the armed forces that he was not a political match.

Lastly, the Egyptian military was confident of its popular support. After all—and in contrast to Tunisia, for instance—the decision to stop backing Mubarak was triggered by fraternisation of demonstrators with soldiers rather than the other way around. Although bruised by its governing experience during the interregnum, the armed forces knew that they could capitalise on a positive image in society. The open calls for the military to intervene—perhaps innocuously funded by the UAE and channelled through the defence ministry[76]–ultimately provided the force with the necessary popular mandate to do so. In a statement designed to portray the armed forces as subordinate not to the government but to the population, then Defence Minister Sisi declared that "this army receives orders only from Egyptians".[77] A song lauding the soldiers which had saved the nation, commissioned by the military's public relations department, became so popular that it was frequently played at weddings.[78]

Taken together, these four dynamics have given the armed forces the possibility to influence politics not only by removing the government, but by expanding its political clout even further than before. Although present on Egypt's political scene since 1952, the extent to which the military played a role fluctuated over time: while at its peak in the very early days of the Free Officers' reign, it was pushed back somewhat under Sadat. And although it transformed itself from the institution leading the revolution to one subordinate to the civilian side of the state (visible in its withdrawal into the many military cities created for their accommodation), this subordination came with conditions and was never total. The military enjoyed autonomy in terms of budget and management, and handled American aid directly, without civilian mediation.[79] It was also allowed to engage in far-reaching economic activities well beyond its military scope.

All of these trends have evolved further since 2011 and particularly 2013, in spite of the military's public declaration that it would not be allotted the right to vote or indeed "be part of the political scene or rule".[80] For while it is true that the government itself has a very civilian face, the armed forces play an increasingly political role.

The military's most important gain was the enshrining of its institutional independence in the constitution of 2012—most of which was preserved in the 2014 constitution. Its 2012 constitutional declaration, issued only days before President Morsi's election and later abrogated by him, was comparatively timid. Now, the armed forces (as well as parliament) need to be consulted before the president, as the supreme commander, declares war; the defence minister is now the commander in chief (somewhat in competition with the position of supreme commander) and, although common practice before, the defence minister now by law has to hail from the military's ranks. Before parliament was elected in 2015, Sisi ruled by decree, occasionally expanding the military's prerogatives—for instance having the military protect vital infrastructure alongside the police.[81]

More generally, the armed forces' influence is creeping further and further into the civilian political realm; the military did not just secure the constitutional referendum of 2014, but also monitored the national and international media coverage of the event.[82] Former military staff have also arrived in Egypt's legislative for the first time, representing more than 50 out of 596 MPs, and the parliament's secretary general (in charge of running its daily business) is now a former army general.[83] Retired officers are in charge of the sea and Nile ports, government entities in charge of industrial development, agricultural development and subways, as well as of state-owned companies for grain silos, chemicals, land and sea transportation.[84] Several of the 27 governors also have a military background—though Sisi's cabinet itself contains only two officers out of 33 portfolios, that of defence and military production.[85]

Perhaps more worryingly, the armed forces have become a topic that can no longer be discussed publicly, displaying more and more authoritarian tendencies. A TV show was suspended for "demotivating the army", although the guest had simply mentioned how the Egyptian people had stood by the military after the defeat of 1967. Facebook-users have been arrested for making derogatory comments about the military, and the religious ministry has announced dismissal of preachers criticising army, police or Sisi. University presidents, who are appointed by Sisi, have been given the right to dismiss students who "disturb the educational process"—which some have interpreted to mean "insulting the army". Differing from official military accounts on events such as the attack on a military outpost in the Sinai is now punishable by an exorbitant fine. Former military staff have been publicly warned against publishing their memoirs.[86]

Already very present in Egypt's economy before 2013, the armed forces have since managed to expand their role even further.[87] They do so through a variety of outlets such as the National Service Projects Organisation (created in 1979), the Arab Organisation for Industralisation (created in 1975), and the National Organisation for Military Production—all of which run multiple outlets running themselves, which makes it impossible to establish a clear picture. Economic activities are also run from the Armed Forces Lands Projects, a government agency attached to the ministry of defence. The extent of the military's economic activities is difficult to assess, due to the opacity of the system: estimates range from 5 to 60 per cent of Egypt's GDP, but the trend goes clearly towards expansion. More importantly, it goes way beyond the production of military equipment.

Since 2013, the Egyptian military has been involved, through its subsidiary companies, in a series of major as well as minor infrastructure projects including roads, bridges, tunnels and apartment blocks worth several billion dollars. Most of the projects resulting from the Emirati economic stimulus package of $4.9 billion have been channelled through the military as well, such as the building of a million housing units alongside the UAE-based Arabtec Company. Similarly, digging the second Suez Canal was executed by the Army Corps of Engineers and Suez Canal Authority, itself headed by a former SCAF (Supreme Council of the Armed Forces) member. Over the course of one year, the military also accomplished 473 projects including roads, bridges, ports, airports renovation of hospitals, schools, youth centres, extension of water pipes and construction of desalination plants. Private companies now need a security clearance in order to rent billboards on Cairo's ring road, which are operated by the military-owned National Service Project Organisation; and the defence ministry now owns 60 per cent of the newly created national entity for telecommunications. Telecoms companies will now have no role in extending or installing communication cables; instead, they will only be able to rent cables from the company of which the army holds the majority stake.[88]

The armed forces defend their prominent role by pointing to their low defence budget, which is admittedly 3.5 per cent lower than most in the region; and to their provision of services and products below market price, at 60 per cent less for construction services as well as 10–25 per cent lower food staple prices in the military-run supermarkets (claimed to be bulwarks against monopolies). When public transport prices rose because the government cut subsidies, the military operated buses to assuage public anger.[89]

The main reason for this operation is that the armed forces not only manage these projects and services with low-paid conscripts (who receive 250 Egyptian pounds or $35 a month), but they pay no taxes on their revenues. Even profit-oriented military installations such as cinemas, hotels, supermarkets and theatres are exempt from real estate tax: in 2015, 574 of such installations were exempted alone. Military imports are tariff-free, and according to a 1997 decree, the armed forces allow the military to manage all undeveloped non-agricultural land, which happens to constitute 87 per cent of Egypt. While this latter decree has caused some recent controversy in parliament, it is unlikely to change the fact that none of the military's economic endeavours are subject to civilian supervision.[90]

Things are certainly facilitated by a 2013 law which allows ministers to sign off contracts without competitive bidding. Moreover, a May 2011 amendment to the law on the military judiciary stipulated that only military prosecutors and judges can investigate illicit gains by officers.[91] Although it is arguable that Egypt's economy requires such massive projects to relaunch an ailing economy, the risk of deterring civilian business long-term is real.[92]

Lastly, a new trend has emerged which was unseen under Sadat or Mubarak, that of a personality cult revolving especially, but not only, around Sisi. A lawsuit was filed in 2013 in order to "force Sisi to run for President to protect the nation"; when Sisi's candidacy to the presidency in 2014 was finally announced by the SCAF, it was in the "approval of the Egyptian people's willingness" for Sisi to run. The "Yes to Field

Marshal" campaign supporting Sisi issued a collection of biographies modestly called *Best Soldiers on Earth* in which he was described as the "saviour" who had protected Egypt from civil war.[93] Famously, Sisi publicly orders projects to speed up their completion, including the Suez Canal project, the repair of a runway at Cairo International Airport, roads and medical installations, earning him a certain amount of ridicule. In one joke he is said to order a pregnant woman to give birth earlier than expected.[94] In contrast to other Egyptian presidents of military origin, Sisi invokes his army origins regularly; although rarely donning the uniform—once to visit troops in the Sinai—he is pictured on billboards and posters across the country in uniform, sometimes along with Sadat and Nasser (Mubarak is famously missing).[95] More importantly, the military features prominently in his speeches, as do military values. Sisi has famously said that he expects his ministers in the office by 7 a.m., urging Cairo commuters to "take the bicycle to work" and has called on Egyptians to "listen only to him".[96]

But the personality cult extends to other military personnel: Field Marshal Tantawi, who was defence minister at the time of the 2011 demonstrations, has been honoured with not only a road ("in recognition of his distinctive history in times of war and peace and for his leading role in the adoption and protection of the 25 January Revolution", as a military statement said) but also a large mosque in his name—built with public funds by a military-owned company.[97] All over Cairo, schools have been named after military martyrs.[98]

Meanwhile, the Egyptian military is under pressure: it faces not only an ongoing insurgency in the Sinai, but has deployed also to Yemen in support of Saudi Arabia's operation, and remains vigilant on the border with Libya where the air force has flown sorties against IS.[99] Since 2011, over 200 soldiers have died in the conflict with jihadi networks.[100] Perhaps in recognition of these efforts, Sisi passed a law which allowed him to increase the pensions of "some" soldiers, and has gone on a defence spending spree. He has signed several arms deals with France, including 24 Rafale fighter jets, vessels, a satellite communication system, missiles and helicopter carriers, worth over 2 billion euros; and with Russia, worth €3.5 billion.[101]

As all military men who have come to power, Sisi knows all too well that the armed forces continue to be a potential threat, and in spite of its cohesion the Egyptian military is not immune to strife. This concerns not only the presence of Islamist soldiers in the ranks—the assassin of prosecutor general Hisham Barakat was allegedly a former army officer—but, more worryingly, the officer corps.[102] Regular reports about rivalries between Sisi and former chief of staff Sami Anan—supposedly favoured by the United Arab Emirates—or indeed his defence minister Sedki Sobhi are perhaps only tools to destabilise the regime.[103]

## From revolutionary to conservative: the Algerian armed forces

Of all Arab forces, the Algerian military is the only one which truly emerged from a protracted battle against a colonial power; more so than any other, it can claim therefore the title of midwife of the state. Its influence on Algerian politics has consequently been interlinked not only with the struggle for independence, but with Algeria as a political concept writ large. While it gradually transformed from a guerrilla force into a modern military organisation over the decades, its influence and presence on Algeria's political scene evolved and indeed diminished in spite of a somewhat positive image. Nevertheless, the military is still an important power player and continues to influence Algerian politics decisively: because it has the capacity, the interest as well as the clout over the civilian leadership to do so.

The capacity of the Algerian military to act as a collective was determined by two instances: the first occurred in the early days of independence, the second in the 1980s. The first had to do with its origins: while it is true that the Algerian military is the descendant of the armed wing of the independence movement of the Front de Libération Nationale (FLN), the Armée de Libération Nationale (ALN), it is indeed the descendant of only a part of the ALN. An important split had occurred during the last war years between those forces fighting within Algeria (known as the armée de l'intérieur or maquisards, so called after the *maquis* or shrubland, the natural hideout of guerrilla forces) and those which emerged, a little later, on the borders with Tunisia and Morocco (known as the armée des frontières). The two forces, originally even under two separate command structures, were in theory united under one chief of general staff in 1960; in practice, however, they were at odds, not only over the question of which of the two did more of the fighting. The border force under Houari Boumediene (later also the chief of general staff) was more organised, more structured and resembled more a conventional force, whereas the armée de l'intérieur was a revolutionary, guerrilla, asymmetric force, although it had been given some structure in 1956 with ranks, codified codes of conduct and leadership structures.

As the war against France came to an end in 1962, three warring power centres emerged in the Algerian resistance on the eve of independence: the civilian leadership or Provisional Government based in Tunisia, which negotiated independence with France; the armée de l'intérieur; and the more regular forces under Boumediene. The latter were supported by a network of influential Algerians based in Morocco, the so-called Oujda clan. When Boumediene threw his military weight behind one of the founders of the liberation movement in 1962, Ahmed Ben Bella, the latter managed to oust Algeria's first Prime Minister Benyoucef Benkhedda. Both the provisional government and the armée de l'intérieur were outmanoeuvred.

These events largely shaped Algerian civil–military relations for the coming years. Had the less organised and more guerrilla-oriented forces from the *maquis* prevailed, the military might not have developed the necessary cohesion and capacity for collective and coordinated action as fast as it did. But because the regular forces or armée des frontières prevailed, the nucleus of the newly created Armée Nationale Populaire was a body capable not just of exerting pressure on the civilian government, but of deploying troops and tanks on the streets of Algiers—which it did as early as 1965.

Although Ben Bella had come to power with the help of Boumediene, the Oujda clan and the military, he was soon at odds with all three. He had misgivings about Boumediene's highly personalised grip on the armed forces as defence minister, as well as his push for military professionalisation at the expense of revolutionary fighters of the *maquis*. Already a partisan for military modernisation, Boumediene was convinced of the necessity of a professional force after the army's rather poor performance against Moroccan forces in 1963 in the border areas around Tindouf and Figuig.

Ben Bella however pushed for the integration of former *maquisards* into the armed forces, to promote the somewhat romantic notion of "popular defence"; indeed, the Party Congress of 1964 drafted a document, the Charter of Algiers, which called not only for full party control over the armed forces, but also for the establishment of popular militias—both of which Boumediene saw as hostile acts against the military he was trying to build. He nevertheless proceeded with his professionalisation programme, demobilised 70,000 troops and built the new armed force on the remaining 60,000. These, while vetted politically, were retained more for their actual skills than for their contribution to the revolutionary cause.

But while Boumediene sought to create a regular and capable force, he encountered significant opposition against this not only from Ben Bella, but also from influential former guerrilla leaders. A classical armed force was seen as unproductive and a drain on resources; and, of course, as a dangerous tool in the hands of an opponent. More importantly, it would rely at least in part on Algerian officers who had previously served in, and deserted, the French military, since they were better educated—which was controversial as they were accused of collaborating with the enemy. In an overt show of force, one vocal opponent of their integration, former guerrilla fighter and Boumediene-ally Mohammed Chaabani, was executed in 1964.[104] A 1967 coup attempt by chief of staff Tahar Zbiri was a further expression of this power struggle within the officer corps.

Ben Bella was equally in disagreement with Boumediene over the ubiquitous presence of Oujda clan members throughout the government and the officer corps. He gradually began to assert his power by dismissing clan members from their posts, in the ministries of the interior, education and tourism. When he moved against Abdelaziz Bouteflika, equally a member of the clan and foreign minister, he was ousted by the armed forces under the leadership of Boumediene. A newly created Revolutionary Council assumed all power, with Boumediene as its president and defence minister. The council, composed of twenty-six members, all officers, combined civilian and military power in Algeria.

Boumediene and his professionalisation programme laid the decisive groundwork for the political role the armed forces were playing not only under his regime but also in the decade after his passing. Without the emphasis on modernisation and technical skill, the military would not have had the capacity to act the way it did first in 1965 and later in 1991.

This trend continued in the 1980s: the Algerian military was allowed to develop further into a professional force; it received largely Soviet equipment and quickly became the third strongest military on the African continent. It had also learned, from the Chaabani incident, to close ranks in the officer corps in spite of ongoing power struggles between the remnants of the French-educated officers, those from the armée des frontières and the usually Arabic-educated officers from the armée de l'intérieur. When Boumediene passed away, the military leadership consequently managed to agree to nominate one of the French-educated officers, Chadly Bendjedid, as the consensus candidate to the presidency. Although the revolutionary council no longer existed, the military leadership presented their candidate to the FLN congress as a *fait accompli* in an expression of its de facto power.

Lacking the network Boumediene had, Bendjedid never controlled the armed forces though—rather, he had assumed power because the military leadership had given it to him.[105] In the years until 1989, when an economic crisis and ongoing protests forced the leadership to open up Algeria's political space for parties and ultimately elections, the armed forces were an unchallenged power. Supervised de facto by defence ministers hailing from the force (most presidents kept the portfolio) since independence, the Algerian military experienced very little civilian control. It was not engaged in combat (largely because it is constitutionally banned from deployment outside the national territory, and therefore has by default an internal role) and therefore had the luxury to grow further and further into a settled institution.

When the parliamentary elections of 1991 projected a victory of the Islamist Party *Front Islamique du Salut* (FIS), the military therefore had enough collective interest, as well as capacity to act against it, and returned the state to military rule under General Liamine Zéroual. It also paid an unexpectedly high price for the abortion of the election, as it triggered a decade of violence between the armed forces and several different Islamist insurgent groups, causing 200,000 civilian casualties.

However, it proved flexible and responded with the swift creation of a special force command dedicated to the "execution and coordination of anti-subversive actions", which would unite units from both the army and the intelligence services in the most comprehensive way. Its founder, General Mohammad Lamari, would later become the armed forces' chief of staff for most of the decade, and act forcefully against the terrorist structures; in the absence of counter-insurgency experience, its violent reprisal would lead to more violence in the immediate term, however.

The military efficiency which allowed for such rather unusual power clusters is proof of the fact that the Algerian armed forces were internally not restricted by political concerns, and therefore able to structure, plan and act according to military considerations. In an almost extra-constitutional way, the top commanders of the forces would meet regularly in conclave fashion, circumventing civilian decision-makers to thrash out their tactics against the Islamists. It was the military leaders who eventually negotiated a truce, finally bringing an extremely violent conflict to an end.[106] Since then, the Algerian military has embarked on a modernisation programme in equipment terms, while maintaining its strong emphasis on cohesion and professional criteria for its personnel.

While it has managed to reduce terrorist activity, it is still challenged in the Sahel zone by al-Qaeda in the Islamic Maghreb (AQIM). To combat AQIM, Algeria joined forces with Niger, Mauritania and Mali to create a joint military headquarters in 2010, located in Algeria's south. But the problem is far from being contained; the Algerian military's operation against a terrorist group which had taken a gas facility hostage in January 2013 led to the deaths of twenty-nine kidnappers and thirty-nine hostages. Subsequently, this led to the restructuring of the Algerian defence intelligence system, largely held accountable for the hostage crisis and its outcome, and the dismissal of several high-ranking officers. The incident has drawn international attention to the Algerian armed forces' capacity, and raised doubts about its counter-insurgency operations techniques. That notwithstanding, the Algerian military is solidly intertwined with the regime; it is militarily capable and enjoys the regime's trust, meanwhile being subordinate to President Bouteflika who has fired high-ranking officers on a number of occasions, imposing his rule when necessary. Although the military is influential and an important part of the regime, it is not the regime itself.

Somewhat ironically, the armed forces have progressively left Algeria's political stage since they have become ever more embroiled in its actual mission of war-fighting. After nearly a decade of violence,

Oujd clan member Abdelaziz Bouteflika arrived in power in 1999. He is the first civilian in power since Ben Bella (with the exception of the very short-lived stint of Mohamed Boudiaf, who was assassinated on camera after only months of being in power), and has asserted his hold over the armed forces progressively.

The interests which have driven the Algerian military into politics were, and are, very much institutional, although to different extents. In an overlap of civilian and military interests, of French-educated officers and the Oujda clan, the armed forces have never single-handedly ruled, but always been part of a larger conglomerate of Algerian interest groups. Its interests were therefore always less clearly distinguished as military ones and more broadly a mixture of political and military concerns. In the early days of independence, this concerned firstly the nature of the military and, by extension, of the Algerian state. Distribution of power amongst the different components which had fought for independence was at the centre stage of this period. The military, as an organisation aspiring to be a professional force, was at odds with the popular guerrilla forces; but it was in step with the interests of other political forces.

The interests to maintain power in the 1980s then turned more personal than institutional. Benefits in the shape of subsidised food staples, cars, housing and other allowances ensured for the Algerian officer class, especially the war veterans, preferential treatment in a society struggling economically.[107] Yet the motivations to abort the elections of 1990 were never stated outright. After all, the armed forces were largely supportive of the democratic process as long as, as defence minister General Khaled Nezzar stated, a "just mean" was established, with no party dominating the National People's Assembly.[108] Arguably, the FIS was highly critical of several state institutions, including the military, but its onslaught was modest when it came to the armed forces. FIS leader Abassi stated that the coup of 1965 was an error as it had disrupted Algeria's proper political development; it called on the release of prisoners convicted in state security courts and a security police free from abuse and oppression—referring probably to the brutal crushing of demonstrators by the armed forces in 1988—and severely criticised Algeria's siding with the international coalition against Iraq.

Perhaps its most salient attacks on the armed forces were, however, the insinuations that the military was in fact not Algerian but French-dominated—a reference to the French-educated officers who continued to dominate the officer corps. In response, the military's magazine *el-Djeich* attempted to discredit the FIS as a foreign agent: "in its manifestation a small group, a social movement, or political party, the religious extremist sphere of influence serves Western strategy aimed at maintaining a balance between monarchies and nationalist regimes in order to prevent the birth of Arab unity".

Yet, at the same time, the FIS espoused typical Algerian post-independence rhetoric. In its political programme, the FIS stated that "after the colonial invasion our army was subjugated, but the people's army never capitulated and the popular resistance and organisation testifies to the tenacity and courage of our faithful people. (...) The successive revolutions in our land and particularly liberation have demonstrated that the army is the people and the people are the army."[109] With this statement, the FIS was moving towards the military's most important monopoly: the one on Algerian nationalism, itself centred on the war of independence. So intertwined are the conflict, the armed forces and nationalism that "the officer corps maintains almost exclusive control over the struggle's official narrative".[110] Additionally, the FIS and its liberal and anti-corruption economic programme clearly began to threaten those business links which had expanded under Bendjedid (although never reaching Egyptian proportions).

It was at this point that the officers began to warn the FIS on several occasions not to go too far. General Mustapha Chelloufi, secretary general of the defence ministry, warned that "I will not be tolerant of those who use democracy in order to return dictatorship once they have achieved power." Major General Khaled Nezzar, the defence minister, stated that the military was resolved to "respond to any organised excesses that might jeopardise the national unity of the country (...) and would not hesitate to intervene to re-establish order and unity so that force remains in the hands of the law".[111] Unsurprisingly, soldiers and officers suspected to be sympathisers of Islamism were purged after the coup.[112]

What allowed the Algerian military to abort the elections of 1991 was not just its capacity, its interests and its monopoly on Algerian nationalism. The FIS had clearly overstated its power base, and underestimated the readiness of the armed forces to go to war over power in the country—indeed, the military had overstated the same for itself as the ensuing conflict showed. Both parties eventually lost support in the population due to the violence both inflicted.

Since the conflict came to an end in the early 2000s, the Algerian military no longer plays the same role in politics as before. Algeria eventually returned to a multi-party system (albeit somewhat constrained) and put a Charter of Peace and National Reconciliation to referendum in 2005. An amnesty was extended to those members of the armed groups who had not committed collective crimes, families of persons gone missing during the violence received pensions, religious parties remained banned and, most importantly, immunity was granted to members of the security and defence forces for their actions during the conflict. Since then, more distance has been created between the military and the civilian leadership; several high-ranking officers involved in the conflict have been retired (such as Mohamed Lamari and Larbi Belkheir). In 2013, Bouteflika began successively dismantling the last bastion of military power: military intelligence concentrated in the Department for Information and Research (DRS); first it was dismembered and its units allotted to other military departments, and later it was disbanded altogether. Several officers in charge of DRS departments were dismissed (such as the infamous General Toufik and Generals Bachir Tartag and Mehenna Djebbar) or very publicly put on trial (such as Generals Hassan and Benhadid).[113] In total, nearly seventy generals attached to the DRS were retired. Several midranking officers in charge of regional military expenditure control were similarly dismissed in 2014.[114]

While much debate ensued over the objectives of this reshuffle, the civilians prevailed. Prime Minister Abdelmallek Sellal stated that "we are aware that the changes would be met with resistance and attempts to oppose them, motivated by customs and interests, but despite all that we cannot escape our destiny".[115] In parallel—and perhaps entirely unrelatedly—the army chief of staff reiterated repeatedly the military's neutrality with regard to the ongoing election process, as political parties similarly and repeatedly questioned the said neutrality.[116] Neither the reshuffle nor such statements should, however, be read as the

Algerian military being a fully neutral and controlled force. Perhaps more accurately, power within the Algerian officer corps has moved to a different network from before: a network which approves of the departure of the war generation.

# CONCLUSION

## THE FOUR PRECONDITIONS OF COUPS, AND THEIR AFTERMATH

Staging a coup with the help of the armed forces seems comparatively easy because of their organisational nature; it requires the identification not of masses but just the right individuals, the right units in terms of coercive equipment, and the right nodes in the command structure to move these units while paralysing the opponents'; with these, the clusters of power will be either besieged or taken over in order to enforce a political change, and potential opponents will be neutralised. Technically, this involves remarkably few people and relatively small units, and can happen within a few hours if the chosen time (very often at night and, in the Arab case, very often in July or August) facilitates movement in the streets, which is crucial if tanks are involved. Since coups are technically ground operations, they fall into the realm of the army more than the navy or air force. At their forefront are armoured and mechanised brigades, mainly due to the tanks they have at their disposal, as well as communications units which can prevent not only potential opposition from forming, but also serve as the connector between the conspirators. The successful execution of a coup therefore depends on the co-option of few critical military units necessary at the planned time and place, as well as the penetration of the relevant command and technical structure of those units—and on the acceptance or neutralisation of potential opponents.

With the units in question, critical infrastructure is taken over in order to create a situation in which the government in power has no alternative but to step down (if it has not already been neutralised by force, as happened in Iraq in 1958). Frequently, putschists strike while the head of state is out of the country, as in Libya in 1969, in Mauritania in 1984 or in Sudan in 1985. These strikes target first and foremost the centres of effective power, such as the offices of head of state, the main administrative buildings such as the Ministry of Defence, of Interior, police headquarters, but also symbolic buildings more generally. In Iraq, both coups of 1963 and 1968 were considered a success once the radio station as well as ministry of defence had been taken. By default, coups therefore usually take place in the capital of the country.

In the case of Egypt in 2013, for example, tanks began to surround the presidential palace hours before the ousting of President Morsi, as well as around rallies of Muslim Brotherhood supporters in Cairo. In 1952, the Egyptian putschists arrested first officers they suspected of posing a threat and then took control of the military headquarters with an artillery battalion. In Libya in 1969, troops and tanks took the royal palace as well as the military and internal security headquarters of the capital within two hours in the early morning. The Syrian coup of 1949 struck at 2.30 a.m., when army units surrounded the presidency, parliament and various ministries and arrested the president and prime minister.[1]

In addition, the military usually attempts to close off the main roads leading in and out of the capital in order to prevent movement of potential opposition forces, control focal traffic points to filter movement as well as airports and other transport facilities to prevent the escape of former government officials (in Egypt, a travel ban on Morsi and other top aides was imposed).

In the twentieth century, the putschists placed additional emphasis on the control of the mass media, mainly radio stations and the existing TV stations, and usually announced the coup in a Communiqué No. 1. During the Iraqi coup of 1958, the broadcasting station was seized even before the royal palace. In the twenty-first century, this has changed somewhat due to a less controllable media landscape. Rather than pre-empting a media leak, the armed forces now build dramatic momentum. The Egyptian military announced its intentions 48 hours before it struck in 2013, broadcasting its ultimatum on TV as well as posting it on Facebook: "The armed forces reiterate their call that the demands of the people be met, as a last chance to bear the historical burden that the nation is currently facing."[2] When President Morsi refused to step down, the armed forces arrested him and other members of the leadership and declared a road map for political transition on TV, including the suspension of the constitution.[3] They then shut down the Brotherhood's satellite television network, along with two other popular Islamist channels, arrested journalists sympathetic to the Morsi regime and shut down a website which featured Morsi's last video statement denouncing the military.[4] While the role of the media during a coup has evolved, it has remained an important ingredient of its execution and success.

Although coups are neither time- nor manpower-intensive affairs, they crucially require a capable military force, which is highly trained and equipped; indeed, the more developed its military features, the better. And not just with coups: all kinds of political activities in which the armed forces engage as a collective require first and foremost unity and military capacity, a desire to act, the absence of an opponent and sufficient acquiescence from the population.

The question of this book was simple: why do Arab armies become political actors when they are, in theory, only a state institution with a specific and technical task? It is not only a simple but an old question, puzzling military sociologists and political scientists since the last century. In essence, the phenomenon (and the four dynamics which lead to it) can be traced back to two key paradoxes of defence, which are as unchangeable as they are universal: military superiority over civilians in terms of collective violence, and the need to cooperate on defence matters. Just as war is a continuation of politics, so the military is a continuation of civilian governance. The two can never be fully separated, even though it might seem a desirable goal. Whoever wants to understand why the Arab world seems so much more prone to military meddling (followed closely by Africa; Latin America and Asia)[5] therefore also needs to look closely at the surrounding civilian context; after all, military organisations are created by civilians. Wherever armed forces become political actors, this constitutes a crisis going well beyond the institution alone: be it a highly polarised society, a delegitimised government incapable of delivering, civil–military relations out of joint or an economic crisis. In that sense, the solution is not simply returning the armed forces to the barracks, and it explains why the removal of the military from politics takes almost two decades on average.[6]

Previous studies seeking to explain the interference of the military in politics have looked at variables such as military size, object of the coup, aftermath of the coup and many more. But as is often the case in social sciences, simple questions require a complex answer: there is no single cause for why Arab (or other) military forces become political (although some theories will say otherwise), but indeed there are four—which are placed in a certain sequence. Only where a force is militarily capable to act as a collective will the question of its desire to do so emerge; only where this will is present will a strong civilian opponent be necessary; and only where the civilian population is likely to acquiesce to military intervention will such a move occur. The desire of a force without the capability to act is consequently irrelevant, as it does not lead to military intervention; a force which is checked by a strong civilian counterpart might have the capacity and the will to act, but it will not be able to. Students of coups will find that elements of all four preconditions are usually present when an armed force (Arab or other) begins to meddle with politics.

So what does this fourfold insight imply for the future of Arab military forces? The current strategic context has propelled the forces back to the forefront of not just politics but security, too. Counter-insurgency operations are being fought on the ground in Egypt, Iraq, Lebanon, Tunisia and Algeria; the forces of Syria, Libya and Yemen had suffered large-scale desertion amidst a heavy internal conflict; the air forces of the Gulf were flying strike sorties over Iraq, Syria, Libya and Yemen. Perhaps not coincidentally, the prospect of a joint Arab force, tabled since the 1950s, has resurfaced at the same time. Now more than before, Arab leaders need their forces to be operationally capable; coup-proofing activities which led to the demise of the Iraqi or Libyan military are therefore not an option. At the same time, Arab forces empowered by the wave of public approval in 2011 have slammed the door on reform they perceive as intrusive; discarded political pluralism as divisive; and rejected cooperation with civilians as unnecessary. Security sector reform, as promised in 2011, never occurred. Instead, armed militias are appearing across the region, as Arab military forces are incapable of managing alone.

# CONCLUSION

Now, more than before, Arab leaders need to rethink how they relate to their armed forces, how they can control them without weakening them, how they can team up with rather than tame an organisation that is vital for the survival not just of regimes but of populations more generally. This requires a reassessment of civilian leadership, civilian legitimacy and civilian threat perceptions—because while Arab military forces are by and large still capable of producing change, when they have an interest to do so, when they have social backing and a weak civilian adversary, they continue to be unable to manage the aftermath of political change. At the end of the day, politics is a civilian business for which the military is ill-equipped. Whoever wants the armed forces to stay out of politics needs to reform the civilians, too.

# NOTES

## 1. INTRODUCTION: OF KINGMAKERS AND GAME-CHANGERS

1. For a detailed account of the military role in 2011, see William C. Taylor, *Military Responses to the Arab Uprisings and the Future of Civil–Military Relations in the Middle East* (New York: Palgrave Macmillan, 2014).

2. Coups are defined as "actions of conspiratory groups of Arab army officers, carried out by surprise and utilization, or threat of utilization, of military force, calculated to overthrow the existing government and to seize power". Eliezer Be'eri, "The Waning of the Military Coup in Arab Politics", *Middle Eastern Studies*, Vol. 18, No. 1 (Jan. 1982), p. 81.

3. These numbers do not include coups which were aborted before any action took place (as in Saudi Arabia in 1969), military mutinies, revolutions, palace coups without military support, or the appointment/election of retired military officers in office. See also Naunihal Singh, *Seizing Power: The Strategic Logic of Military Coups* (Baltimore: Johns Hopkins University Press, 2014) p. 2.

4. Mark N. Cooper, "The Demilitarisation of the Egyptian Cabinet", *International Journal of Middle East Studies* Vol.14, No. 2 (1982); Kees Koonings and Dirk Kruijt, *Political Armies* (London: Zed Books, 2002), p. 18.

5. BBC Monitoring, "Syrian military, security forces to cast their votes 'for the first time'", 28 March 2016, Syrian State TV.

6. William C. Taylor, *Military Responses to the Arab Uprisings and the Future of Civil–Military Relations in the Middle East: Analysis from Egypt, Tunisia, Libya, and Syria* (New York: Palgrave Macmillan, 2014).

7. Samuel P. Huntington, *Political Order in Changing Societies* (New Haven: Yale University Press, 1968), p. 203. For more on modernisation theory's take on the armed forces, see Lucian W. Pye, "Armies in the Process of Political Modernization", in John J. Johnson, ed., *The Role*

*of the Military in Underdeveloped Countries* (Princeton: Princeton University Press 1967); Edward Shils, "The Military in the Political Development of the New States", in John J. Johnson, ibid.; William Gutteridge, *Military Institutions and Power in the New States* (London: Pall Mall Press, 1964); Morris Janowitz, *Military institutions and Coercion in the Developing Nations* (Chicago: University of Chicago Press, 1977).

8. Donald Horowitz, *Ethnic Groups in Conflict* (Los Angeles: University of California Press, 1985), ch. 11; Cynthia Enloe, *Ethnic Soldiers* (Athens: University of Georgia Press, 1980).

9. John B. Londregan and Keith T. Poole, "Poverty, The Coup Trap, and the Seizure of Executive Power", *World Politics*, Vol. 42, No. 2 (Jan. 1990), pp. 151–83. Rosemary O'Kane, "Coups d'Etat in Africa: A Political Economy Approach", *Journal of Peace Research*, Vol. 30, No. 3 (1993), pp. 251–70; Paul Collier and Anke Hoeffler, "On economic causes of civil war", Oxford Economic Papers, Vol. 50, No. 4 (1998), pp. 563–73.

10. Juan J. Linz, "The Perils of Presidentialism", *Journal of Democracy*, Vol. 1, No. 1 (Winter 1990), pp. 51–69; James D. Fearon and David Laitin, "Ethnicity, Insurgency, and Civil War", *American Political Science Review*, Vol. 97, No. 1 (2003), pp. 75–90; Alexander Galetovic and Ricardo Sanhueza, "Citizens, Autocrats, and Plotters: A Model and New Evidence on Coups D'État", *Economics & Politics*, Vol. 12, No. 2 (July 2000), pp. 183–204; Aaron Belkin and Evan Schofer, "Toward a Structural Understanding of Coup Risk", *Journal of Conflict Resolution*, Vol. 47, No. 5 (Oct. 2003), pp. 594–620; Barbara Geddes, "How Autocrats Defend Themselves Against Armed Rivals", SSRN eLibrary, 2009; Clayton L. Thyne and Jonathan Powell, "Coup d'état or Coup d'Autocracy? How Coups Impact Democratisation, 1950–2008", *Foreign Policy Analysis* (2014), pp. 1–22.

11. Naunihal Singh, *Seizing Power: The Strategic Logic of Military Coups* (Baltimore: Johns Hopkins University Press, 2014); Paul Collier and Anke Hoeffler, "Military Spending and the Risks of Coups d'Etat", Centre for the Study of African Economies, Department of Economics, Oxford University (Oct. 2007), available at http://users.ox.ac.uk/~econpco/research/pdfs/MilitarySpendingandRisksCoups.pdf; Gabriel Leon, "Loyalty for Sale? Military Spending and Coups d'Etat", *Public Choice*, Vol. 159, Nos. 3–4 (June 2014), pp. 363–83; Vincenzo Bove and Roberto Nisticò, "Coups d'état and Defence Spending: a Counterfactual Analysis", Centre for Studies in Economics and Finance, Department of Economics, University of Naples (July 2014), p. 2, available at http://www.csef.it/WP/wp366.pdf; Vincenzo Bove and Jennifer Brauner, "The Demand for Military Expenditure in Authori-

tarian Regimes", Birkbeck Working Papers in Economics and Finance No. 1106 (Oct. 2011); Gary Zuk and William R. Thompson, "The Post-Coup Military Spending Question: A Pooled Cross-Sectional Time Series Analysis", *American Political Science Review*, Vol. 76, No. 1 (Mar. 1982), p. 66; Edward Luttwak, *Coup d'État: A Practical Handbook* (Harmondsworth: Penguin Books, 1968); Bruce W. Farcau, *The Coup: Tactics in the Seizure of Power* (London: Praeger, 1994).

12. James T. Quinlivan, "Coup-Proofing: Its Practice and Consequences in the Middle East", *International Security*, Vol. 24, No. 2 (Autumn 1999); Jonathan Powell, "Coups and Conflict: The Paradox of Coup-Proofing", diss., University of Kentucky, 2012; Holger Albrecht, "Does Coup-Proofing Work? Political–Military Relations in Authoritarian Regimes amid the Arab Uprisings", *Mediterranean Politics*, Vol. 20, No. 1 (2015).

2. THE VIEW FROM WITHIN: MILITARY REASONS

1. *Le Matin Algérie*, "Saïd Bouteflika est un 'malade mental', affirme le général à la retraite Benhadid", 23 September 2015.

2. William R. Thompson, "Toward Explaining Arab Military Coups", *Journal of Political and Military Sociology*, Vol. 2, No. 2 (Fall 1974), p. 238.

3. Khaled Fahmy, *All the Pasha's Men: Mehmed Ali, his army and the making of modern Egypt* (Cairo: American University in Cairo Press, 2003).

4. Ministry of National Defence, Tunisia, *The Tunisian Armed Forces* (Tunis: Alif, Les Editions de la Méditerranée, 1996), pp. 69–77.

5. George L. Mosse, *Fallen Soldiers: Reshaping the Memory of the World Wars* (Oxford: Oxford University Press, 1990).

6. International Institute for Strategic Studies, *The Military Balance 2014* (London: Routledge, 2014), pp. 311–17. For civil aviation, see http://www.airfleets.net/home/

7. Morris Janowitz, *The Professional Soldier: A Social and Political Portrait* (New York: Collier-Macmillan 1960), p. 40.

8. For example, the current US force contains 15% officers, which constitutes a historical high; during the Vietnam war it stood at 12%. The Israeli military's officer corps had 6% officers during the war of 1967. US Department of Defence, *2011 Demographics: Profile of the Military Community* (Nov. 2010), available at http://www.militaryonesource. mil/12038/MOS/Reports/2011_Demographics_Report.pdf; Donald E. Vandergriff, *Officer Manning: Armies of the Past*, available at www.john-smilitaryhistory.com%2FVandergriff_Officers_Briefing.ppt&ei=9vK_U9DZE-2W0QWY04HABQ&usg=AFQjCNE2Jfp2k4dyKeaYbojHKldN mvGo0Q&sig2=sI3pRt8vl5q11jybm2lYJQ

9. Edward Luttwak, *Coup d'État: A Practical Handbook* (Harmondsworth: Penguin Books, 1968), p. 72.

10. Ibid., pp. 74, 88, 120–29.

11. Gordon H. Torrey, *Syrian Politics and the Military, 1945–1958* (Columbus: Ohio State University Press, 1964), p. 162; Tarek Osman, *Egypt on the Brink: From the Rise of Nasser to Mubarak* (New Haven: Yale University Press, 2010), p. 48.

12. Risa A. Brooks, "Abandoned at the Palace: Why the Tunisian Military Defected from the Ben Ali Regime in January 2011", *Journal of Strategic Studies*, Vol. 36, No. 2 (2013), p. 206; *Jeune Afrique*, "Le général Ammar, l'homme qui a dit non", 7 February 2011, http://www.jeuneafrique.com/192799/politique/le-g-n-ral-ammar-l-homme-qui-a-dit-non/

13. Reuters, "UPDATE 1-Egypt army: will not use violence against citizens", 31 January 2011, available at http://www.reuters.com/article/2011/01/31/egypt-army-idAFLDE70U2JC20110131

14. Luttwak, *Coup d'État*, pp. 74, 88, 120–29.

15. Adel Beshara, *Lebanon: The Politics of Frustration–The Failed Coup of 1961* (London: Routledge, 2005).

16. Joel Gordon, *Nasser's Blessed Movement: Egypt's Free Officers and the July Revolution* (Oxford: Oxford University Press, 1992), pp. 47–8.

17. Frederick Manning, "Morale, unit cohesion, and esprit de corps", in Reuven Gal and D. Mangelsdorff (eds), *Handbook of Military Psychology* (New York: Wiley, 1991).

18. Darryl Henderson, *Cohesion: The Human Element in Combat* (Washington, DC: National Defense University Press, 1985), p. 4; Edward A. Shils and Morris Janowitz, "Cohesion and Disintegration in the Wehrmacht in World War II", *Public Opinion Quarterly*, Vol. 2 (Summer 1948).

19. Risa A. Brooks, "An Autocracy at War: Explaining Egypt's Military Effectiveness, 1967 and 1973", *Security Studies*, No. 3 (July–Sept. 2006), p. 420.

20. Guy Siebold, "Military Group Cohesion", in Thomas W. Britt, Amy B. Adler, Carl Andrew Castro (eds), *Military Life: The Psychology of Serving in Peace and Combat*, Vol. 1 (Westport: Praeger Security International, 2006), p. 193.

21. Robert MacCoun, Elizabeth Kier, Aaron Belkin, "Does Social Cohesion Determine Motivation in Combat? An Old Question with an Old Answer", *Armed Forces and Society*, Vol. 32, No. 4 (July 2006); Leonard Wong, Thomas A. Kolditz, Raymond A. Millen, Terrence M. Potter, *Why They Fight: Combat Motivation in the Iraq War* (Carlisle Barracks, PA: Strategic Studies Institute, 2003).

22. Quoted in Robert MacCoun, "What is Known about Unit Cohesion and Military Performance", in *Sexual Orientation and US Military*

*Personnel Policy: Options and Assessment* (Santa Monica: RAND, 1993), p. 300.

23. David Marlowe, *Cohesion, Anticipated Breakdown, and Endurance in Battle: Considerations for Severe and High Intensity Combat*, unpublished draft (Washington, DC: Walter Reed Army Institute of Research, 1979), p. 50, quoted in MacCoun, "What is Known about Unit Cohesion and Military Performance".

24. Anthony King, "The Word of Command: Communication and Cohesion in the Military", *Armed Forces and Society*, Vol. 32, No. 4 (July 2006), p. 508.

25. Yehoshofat Harkabi, "Basic Factors in the Arab Collapse during the Six-Day War", *Orbis* (Fall 1967).

26. Kenneth M. Pollack, *Arabs at War: Military Effectiveness, 1948–1991* (Lincoln: University of Nebraska Press, 2002), pp. 553–5.

27. Timothy D. Hoyt, "Social Structure, Ethnicity, and Military Effectiveness: Iraq, 1980—2004", in Risa A. Brooks and Elizabeth A. Stanley (eds), *Creating Military Power: the sources of military effectiveness* (Stanford, CA: Stanford University Press, 2007), p. 65.

28. Morris Janowitz, *Sociology and the Military Establishment* (Beverly Hills: Sage Publications, 1974), pp. 103–4.

29. US Department of Defence, *Dictionary of Military Terms and Acronyms* (Seattle: Praetorian Press, 2011).

30. Neville Stanton, Christopher Baber, Don Harris, *Modelling Command and Control: Event Analysis of Systemic Teamwork* (Aldershot: Ashgate, 2008), p. 11.

31. Risa A. Brooks, "An Autocracy at War: Explaining Egypt's Military Effectiveness, 1967 and 1973", *Security Studies*, No. 3 (July–Sept. 2006), pp. 414–15.

32. Mehran Kamrava, "Military professionalization and civil–military relations in the Middle East", *Political Science Quarterly*, Vol. 115, No. 1 (2000), p. 69.

33. James T. Quinlivan, "Coup-Proofing: Its Practice and Consequences in the Middle East", *International Security*, Vol. 24, No. 2 (Autumn 1999), p. 133.

34. Nikolaos van Dam, "Middle Eastern Political Clichés: 'Tikriti' and 'Sunni Rule' in Iraq; 'Alawi Rule' in Syria: A Critical Appraisal", *Orient* (Jan. 1980), pp. 42–57; Florence Gaub, "The Libyan Armed Forces between Coup-Proofing and Repression", *Journal of Strategic Studies*, Vol. 36, No. 2 (April 2013), p. 12.

35. Quinlivan, "Coup-Proofing", p. 137.

36. Cynthia Enloe, *Ethnic Soldiers* (Athens: University of Georgia Press, 1980), p. 52.

37. Ibid., p. 16.

38. N. E. Bou-Nacklie, "*Les troupes spéciales*: religious and ethnic recruitment, 1916–1946", *International Journal for Middle East Studies*, Vol. 25, No.4 (1993), pp. 645–60.

39. Florence Gaub, *Military Integration after Civil Wars: Multiethnic Armies, Identity and Post-Conflict Reconstruction* (London: Routledge, 2010), p. 55.

40. Pollack, *Arabs at War*, p. 404.

41. Michael Knights, "The Military Role in Yemen's Protests: Civil–Military Relations in the Tribal Republic", *Journal of Strategic Studies*, Vol. 36, No. 2 (2013).

42. Stephen Hosmer, *Why the Iraqi Resistance to the Coalition Invasion was so Weak* (Santa Monica: RAND, 2007), p. 56.

43. *CNN*, "Shadowy Iraq office accused of sectarian agenda", 1 May 2007, available at http://edition.cnn.com/2007/WORLD/meast/05/01/iraq.office/

44. Toby Dodge, *Iraq: From War to Authoritarianism* (London: Routledge for the IISS, 2012), p. 124.

45. "More Than 1,000 in Iraq's Forces Quit Basra Fight", *New York Times*, 4 April 2008; "Battle to retake Basra was 'Complete Disaster'", *Daily Telegraph*, 20 April 2008.

46. Report of the Independent Commission on the Security Forces of Iraq, 6 September 2007, pp. 56, 66, http://media.csis.org/isf.pdf

47. Patrick Seale, *Asad of Syria: The Struggle for the Middle East* (Los Angeles: University of California Press, 1988), pp. 72–85, 102.

48. Ronald Bruce St John, *Historical Dictionary of Libya* (Lanham, MD: Scarecrow Press, 1998), p. 55; John Cooley, *Libyan Sandstorm: The Complete Account of Gaddafi's Revolution* (New York: Holt, Rinehart and Winston, 1982), p. 167; *Independent*, "Libyan commander 'attempted a coup'", 24 October 1993, available at http://www.independent.co.uk/news/world/libyan-commander-attempted-a-coup-1512701.html

49. *LA Times*, "Coup Attempt, Military Purge Reported in Iraq: As Many as 200 Executed After Move Against President Hussein in January, Dissidents Assert", 8 February 1989, available at http://articles.latimes.com/1989_02_08/news/mn-2132_1_coup-attempt; *New York Times*, "U.S. and Iraqis tell of a coup attempt against Baghdad", 3 July 1992, available at http://www.nytimes.com/1992/07/03/world/us-and-iraqis-tell-of-a-coup-attempt-against-baghdad.html; *Independent*, "Iraqi officers pay dear for West's coup fiasco", 17 February 1998, available at http://www.independent.co.uk/news/iraqi-officers-pay-dear-for-wests-coup-fiasco-1145298.html

50. Kevin M. Woods, Williamson Murray, Elizabeth A. Nathan, Laila

Sabara, Ana M. Venegas, *Saddam's Generals: Perspectives of the Iran–Iraq War* (Alexandria, VA: Institute for Defense Analyses, 2011), p. 36.

51. Hicham Bou Nassif, "Wedded to Mubarak: The Second Careers and Financial Rewards of Egypt's Military Elite, 1981–2011", *Middle East Journal*, Vol. 67, No. 4 (Autumn 2013), p. 512.

52. Pollack, *Arabs at War*, p. 28.

53. *Sarasota Herald Tribune*, "Egyptian Army Officers said arrested in Purge", 16 January 1954; *Christian Science Monitor*, "Nasser purges air force", 27 June 1969; Stephen H. Gotowicki, "The Role of the Egyptian Military in Domestic Society", US Army, Foreign Military Studies Office, 1997, available at http://fmso.leavenworth.army.mil/documents/egypt/egypt.htm

54. William Bache, "Transferring American Military Values to Iraq", *Middle East Review of International Affairs*, Vol. 11, No. 3 (Sept. 2007), p. 2.

55. Risa A. Brooks, *Political–Military Relations and the Stability of Arab Regimes*, Adelphi Paper 324 (Oxford: International Institute for Strategic Studies, 1998), p. 46.

56. George W. Gawrych, "The Egyptian High Command in the 1973 War", *Armed Forces and Society*, Vol. 13, No. 4 (Summer 1987), pp. 535–59.

57. Khaled Fattah, "A political history of civil–military relations in Yemen", *Alternative Politics*, Special Issue 1 (Nov. 2010).

58. Florence Gaub, ""Multi-ethnic Armies in the Aftermath of Civil War: Lessons Learned from Lebanon", *Defence Studies*, Vol. 7, No. 1 (2007), pp. 5–20.

59. Ulrich Bröckling and Michael Sikora (eds), *Armeen und ihre Deserteure: Vernachlässigte Kapitel einer Militärgeschichte der Neuzeit* (Goettingen: Vandenhoeck & Ruprecht, 1998).

60. Florence Gaub, "Syria's Military: Last Man Standing?", *Carnegie Europe*, 29 July 2014, available at http://carnegieeurope.eu/strategiceurope/?fa=56274

61. Ulrich Pilster and Tobias Boehmelt, "Coup-Proofing and Military Effectiveness in Interstate Wars, 1967–1999", *Conflict Management and Peace Science*, Vol. 28, No. 4 (Sept. 2011), p. 333.

62. Israel Program for Scientific Translations, *Middle East Record*, Vol. 2, 1961 (Tel Aviv: Tel Aviv University, 1962), p. 608; Itamar Rabinovich and Haim Shaked, *Middle East Contemporary Survey, 1984–1985* (Boulder, CO: Westview Press, 1987), p. 627; Alison Pargeter, *Libya: The Rise and Fall of Qaddafi* (New Haven: Yale University Press, 2012), p. 60.

63. Steven A. Cook, *The Struggle for Egypt: From Nasser to Tahrir Square* (Oxford: Oxford University Press, 2012), p. 11.

64. William Thompson, "Explanations of Military Coup", PhD diss. (Seattle: University of Washington, 1972), pp. 161–7; Paul Collier, *Wars,*

*Guns and Votes: Democracy in Dangerous Places* (New York: HarperCollins, 2009), pp. 141–54.

65. Eric A. Nordlinger, *Soldiers in Politics: Military Coups and Governments* (Upper Saddleback River, NJ: Prentice Hall, 1977), p. 78.

66. Friedrich V. Kratochwil, *Rules, Norms and Decisions: On the conditions of practical and legal reasoning in international relations and domestic affairs* (Cambridge: Cambridge University Press, 1990), p. 75.

67. Robert D. Miewald, "Weberian Bureaucracy and the Military Model", *Public Administration Review*, Vol. 30, No. 2 (March/April 1970), pp. 129–33.

68. Cyril Northcote Parkinson, "Parkinson's Law: The Pursuit of Progress", *The Economist*, 19 November 1955; Leif Lewin, *Self-Interest and Public Interest in Western Politics* (Oxford: Oxford University Press, 1991).

69. Charles C. Moskos, "From Institution to Occupation: Trends in Military Organisation", *Armed Forces and Society*, Vol. 4, No. 1 (Nov. 1977), p. 42.

70. Charles C. Moskos, "The All-Volunteer Military: Calling, Profession, or Occupation?", *Parameters*, Vol. 7, No. 1, p. 4.

71. Paul Collier and Anke Hoeffler, "Military Spending and the Risks of Coups d'Etat", Centre for the Study of African Economies, Department of Economics, Oxford University (Oct. 2007), available at http://users.ox.ac.uk/~econpco/research/pdfs/MilitarySpendingandRisks Coups.pdf

72. Gabriel Leon, "Loyalty for Sale? Military Spending and Coups d'Etat", *Public Choice*, Vol. 159, Nos. 3–4 (June 2014), pp. 363–83.

73. Vincenzo Bove and Roberto Nisticò, "Coups d'état and Defence Spending: a Counterfactual Analysis", Centre for Studies in Economics and Finance, Department of Economics, University of Naples (July 2014), p. 2, available at http://www.csef.it/WP/wp366.pdf; Vincenzo Bove and Jennifer Brauner, "The Demand for Military Expenditure in Authoritarian Regimes", Birkbeck Working Papers in Economics and Finance No. 1106 (Oct. 2011).

74. See International Institute for Strategic Studies, *The Military Balance 2014* (London: Routledge, 2014), p. 494.

75. Richard B. Parker, *The Politics of Miscalculation in the Middle East* (Bloomington: Indiana University Press, 1993), p. 84.

76. Joseph Sassoon, *Saddam Hussein's Ba'th Party: Inside an Authoritarian Regime* (New York: Cambridge University Press, 2012) pp. 140–41, 214–15.

77. Torrey, *Syrian Politics and the Military*, p. 129; Eliezer Be'eri, *Army Officers in Arab Politics and Society* (New York: Praeger, 1970), p. 55.

78. Malcolm Knight, Norman Loayza, Delano Villanueva, "The Peace Dividend: Military Spending Cuts and Economic Growth", Policy

Research Working Paper 1577 (Washington, DC: World Bank and International Monetary Fund, 1996), p. 7.

79. David Whynes, *The Economics of Third World Military Expenditure* (London: Macmillan Press, 1979), p. 11.

80. Gary Zuk and William R. Thompson, "The Post-Coup Military Spending Question: A Pooled Cross-Sectional Time Series Analysis", *American Political Science Review*, Vol. 76, No. 1 (Mar. 1982), p. 66.

81. Ronald Bruce St John, *Historical Dictionary of Libya* (Lanham, MD: Scarecrow Press 1998), p. 40; *The National*, "Libya to spend billions on defence", 24 March 2013, available at http://www.thenational.ae/business/industry-insights/aviation/libya-to-spend-billions-on-defence

82. *LA Times*, "Weapons imports to Syria surged sevenfold in 10 years, report says", 20 March 2012, available at http://latimesblogs.latimes.com/world_now/2012/03/syria-weapons-increase-imports-russia.html

83. Staffan Wiking, *Military Coups in Sub-Saharan Africa: How to justify illegal assumptions of power* (Uppsala: Scandinavian Institute of African Studies, 1983), available at http://www.diva-portal.org/smash/get/diva2:278002/FULLTEXT01.pdf

84. Ibrahim Marashi and Sammy Salama, *Iraq's Armed Forces: An Analytical History* (New York: Routledge, 2008), p. 142.

85. *Al-Ahram Online*, "Egypt military budget allocations to reach LE31 bn in 2013/14: Source", 29 May 2013, available at http://english.ahram.org.eg/NewsContent/3/0/72493/Business/0/-Egypt-military-budget-allocations-to-reach-LE-bn-.aspx

86. *New York Times*, "Succession Gives Army a Stiff Test in Egypt", 11 September 2010, available at http://www.nytimes.com/2010/09/12/world/middleeast/12egypt.html?_r=0; Aljazeera, "Army 'could block' Egypt succession", 15 December 2010, available at http://www.aljazeera.com/news/middleeast/2010/12/201012158103985404.html

87. *Al-Monitor*, "Egyptian Army Considered Economic Stakes in Coup", 10 July 2013, available at http://www.al-monitor.com/pulse/politics/2013/07/egypt-army-economic-interests-coup-morsi.html

88. Stephan Roll, "The Military and the Muslim Brotherhood: Will a Power-sharing Agreement be Reached in Egypt?" SWP Comments 2012/C 04, February 2012, available at http://www.swp-berlin.org/en/publications/swp-comments-en/swp-aktuelle-details/article/egypt_military_and_muslim_brotherhood.html

89. Amr Adly, "The Military Economy and the Future of the Private Sector in Egypt", Carnegie Middle East Center, 6 September 2014, available at http://carnegie-mec.org/2014/09/06/military-economy-and-future-of-private-sector-in-egypt/ho7x

90. Philippe Droz-Vincent, "From Political to Economic Actors: The

Changing Role of Middle Eastern Armies", in Oliver Schlumberger (ed.), *Debating Arab Authoritarianism: Dynamics and Durability in Non-democratic Regimes* (Stanford, CA: Stanford University Press, 2007), p. 202.

91. International Institute for Strategic Studies, *The Military Balance 2014* (London: Routledge, 2014), p. 311.

92. *Al-Akhbar*, "Lebanese Budget Skimps on Overloaded Army", 10 July 2013, available at http://english.al-akhbar.com/node/16385

93. *Foreign Policy*, "The Egyptian Republic of Retired Generals", 8 May 2012, available at http://mideastafrica.foreignpolicy.com/posts/2012/05/08/the_egyptian_republic_of_retired_generals

94. International Institute for Strategic Studies, *The Military Balance 2014*, (London: Routledge, 2014) p. 307.

95. *The National*, "Army and police officers' Dh100,000 pension gap", available at http://www.thenational.ae/news/uae-news/army-and-police-officers-dh100-000-pension-gap

96. *Arabian Business*, "UAE monthly household income revealed", 3 February 2009, available at http://www.arabianbusiness.com/uae-monthly-household-income-revealed-80418.html

97. *Al-Shorfa*, "Qatari government workers and military personnel receive salary increases", 15 September 2011, available at http://al-shorfa.com/en_GB/articles/meii/features/main/2011/09/15/feature-02; *Arabian Business*, "Saudi Arabia to raise wages for most military", 31 August 2010, available at http://www.arabianbusiness.com/saudi-arabia-raise-wages-for-most-military-345848.html; *Reuters*, "Saudi king orders one-month salary bonus for security personnel", 29 April 2015, available at http://www.reuters.com/article/saudi-military-bonuses-idUSL5N0XQ1S020150429

98. *Middle East Eye*, "Syria to raise army salaries to fight 'economic migration'", 7 October 2015, available at http://www.middleeast-eye.net/news/syria-raise-army-salaries-fight-economic-migration-65331448

99. Risa A. Brooks, "An Autocracy at War: Explaining Egypt's Military Effectiveness, 1967 and 1973", *Security Studies*, Vol. 15, No. 3 (July–Sept. 2006), p. 407.

100. *Associated Press*, "Mauritania army stages coup; junta takes charge", 6 August 2008, available at http://web.archive.org/web/20080812110822/http://ap.google.com/article/ALeqM5hmqqO8XJixmimcunkNvDYctnppTgD92CQJ180

101. Brooks, "An Autocracy at War", pp. 419–20.

102. Florence Gaub, "Whatever happened to Yemen's army?", EUISS brief 9, 2015, available at http://www.iss.europa.eu/uploads/media/Brief_9_Yemen.pdf

103. Stephen C. Pelletiere and Douglas V. Johnson, *Lessons Learned: The Iraq–Iran War*, Vol. I (Carlisle Barracks, PA: Strategic Studies Institute, US Army War College, 1991), pp. 65–6.

104. Michael Eistenstadt, *Like a Phoenix from the Ashes? The Future of Iraqi Military Power*, Policy Papers, No. 36 (Washington, DC: Washington Institute for Near East Policy, 1993), available at http://www.washingtoninstitute.org/uploads/Documents/pubs/PP_36_FutureofIraqiMilitaryPower.pdf

105. Ehud Ya'ari, "Sadat's Pyramid of Power", *Jerusalem Quarterly*, No. 14 (Winter 1980), p. 115.

106. Hicham Bou Nassif, "Wedded to Mubarak: The Second Careers and Financial Rewards of Egypt's Military Elite, 1981–2011", *Middle East Journal*, Vol. 67, No. 4 (Autumn 2013).

107. Robert Springborg, "The President and the Field Marshal: Civil–Military Relations in Egypt Today", *Middle East Report* (July–Aug. 1987), p. 8.

108. *New York Times*, "Fateful Choice on Iraq Army Bypassed Debate", 17 March 2008, available at http://www.nytimes.com/2008/03/17/world/middleeast/17bremer.html?pagewanted=all&_r=0

109. *New York Times*, "Their Jobs in Jeopardy, Iraqi Troops Demand Pay", 25 May 2003, available at http://www.nytimes.com/2003/05/25/international/worldspecial/25IRAQ.html

110. James P. Pfiffner, "US Blunders in Iraq: De-Baathification and Disbanding the Army", *Intelligence and National Security*, Vol. 25, No. 1 (Feb. 2010), pp. 76–85; Robert S. Weiler, "Eliminating Success During Eclipse II: An Examination of the Decision to Disband the Iraqi Military", United States Marine Corps, Command and Staff College, March 2009, pp. 17–19, available at http://www.dtic.mil/dtic/tr/fulltext/u2/a511061.pdf

111. *Time*, "How Disbanding the Iraqi Army Fueled ISIS", 28 May 2015, available at http://time.com/3900753/isis-iraq-syria-army-united-states-military/; David H. Ucko, "Militias, tribes and insurgents: The challenge of political integration in Iraq", in Mats Berdal and David H. Ucko (eds), *Reintegrating Armed Groups after Conflict: Politics, Violence and Transition* (New York: Routledge, 2009) pp. 89–118; *Haaretz*, "ISIS Top Brass Is Iraqi Army's Former Best and Brightest", 8 August 2015, available at http://www.haaretz.com/israel-news/1.670177

112. J. C. Hurewitz, *Middle East Politics: The Military Dimension* (Boulder, CO: Westview Press, 1969), p. 237.

113. Florence Gaub, "Multi-Ethnic Armies in the Aftermath of Civil War: Lessons Learned from Lebanon", *Defence Studies*, Vol. 7, No. 1 (March 2007), p. 7.

114. Torrey, *Syrian Politics and the Military*, p. 129.

115. Be'eri, *Army Officers in Arab Politics and Society*, p. 139.

116. Quoted in Be'eri, *Army Officers in Arab Politics and Society*, p. 139.

117. Ibid., p. 323.

118. Risa A. Brooks, *Shaping Strategy: the civil–military politics of strategic assessment* (Princeton: Princeton University Press, 2008), p. 74.

119. *New York Times*, "Egypt Lifts a Junior Corps Impatient Over Military Failure", 13 August 2012, available at http://www.nytimes.com/2012/08/14/world/middleeast/purge-by-morsi-shows-impatience-within-egypts-military.html?pagewanted=all

120. Quoted in Fawaz A. Gerges, "Egypt and the 1948 War: internal conflict and regional ambition", in Eugene L. Rogan and Avi Shlaim (eds), *The War for Palestine: Rewriting the History of 1948*, Cambridge Middle East Studies 15, 2nd edn (Cambridge: Cambridge University Press, 2007), p. 155.

121. Ibid., p. 155.

122. Pollack, *Arabs at War*, pp. 24–5.

123. Gamal Abdel Nasser, *Egypt's Liberation: The Philosophy of the Revolution* (Washington, DC: Public Affairs Press, 1955), p. 23.

124. Torrey, *Syrian Politics and the Military*, p. 122.

125. Quoted in Joshua Landis, "Syria and the Palestine War: fighting King 'Abdullah's "Greater Syria Plan"", in Rogan and Shlaim (eds), *The War for Palestine*, p. 179.

126. Elizabeth Whitman, "The Awakening of the Syrian Army: General Husni al-Za'im's Coup and Reign, 1949", Senior Thesis, Columbia University (April 2011), p. 13.

127. Pollack, *Arabs at War*, p. 184.

128. Pelletiere and Johnson, *Lessons Learned*, Vol.I, p. 65.

129. Ibrahim Marashi and Sammy Salama, *Iraq's Armed Forces: An Analytical History* (New York: Routledge, 2008), p. 148.

130. Pollack, *Arabs at War*, p. 208.

131. Kevin M. Woods, Williamson Murray, Elizabeth A. Nathan, Laila Sabara, Ana M. Venegas, *Saddam's Generals: Perspectives of the Iran–Iraq War* (Alexandria, VA: Institute for Defense Analyses, 2011), p. 36.

132. *LA Times*, "Coup Attempt, Military Purge Reported in Iraq: As Many as 200 Executed After Move Against President Hussein in January, Dissidents Assert", 8 February 1989, available at http://articles.lat-imes.com/1989–02–08/news/mn-2132_1_coup-attempt; *New York Times*, "U.S. and Iraqis tell of a coup attempt against Baghdad", 3 July 1992, available at http://www.nytimes.com/1992/07/03/world/us-and-iraqis-tell-of-a-coup-attempt-against-baghdad.html; *Independent*, "Iraqi officers pay dear for West's coup fiasco", 17 February 1998,

available at http://www.independent.co.uk/news/iraqi-officers-pay-dear-for-wests-coup-fiasco-1145298.html

133. Brooks, *Shaping Strategy*, p. 121.
134. Robert Springborg, "The President and the Field Marshal: Civil–Military Relations in Egypt Today", *Middle East Report* (July–Aug. 1987), p. 6.
135. Florence Gaub, *Military Integration after Civil Wars: Multiethnic Armies, Identity and Post-Conflict Reconstruction* (New York: Taylor and Francis, 2010), p. 50.
136. *Haaretz*, "The root of Egypt's coup: Morsi giving free hand to Sinai Islamists", 18 July 2013, available at http://www.haaretz.com/news/middle-east/1.536623
137. Dirk Vandewalle, *Libya Since Independence: Oil and State-Building* (Ithaca, NY: Cornell University Press, 1998), p. 56.
138. Manfred Halpern, "Egypt and the New Middle Class: Reaffirmations and New Explorations", *Comparative Studies in Society and History*, Vol. 11, No. 1 (Jan. 1969).
139. Manfred Halpern, *The Politics of Social Change in the Middle East and North Africa* (Santa Monica: RAND, 1963), p. 260. Be'eri, *Army Officers in Arab Politics and Society*, pp. 351–9.
140. Miles D. Wolpin, "The military as a conservative socio-political force: Marxian and non-Marxian Perspectives", in Miles D. Wolpin, *Militarism and Social Revolution in the Third World* (Allanheld, Osmun, 1981).
141. Hurewitz, *Middle East Politics*, p. 124; see also Ahmed Abdalla, "The Armed Forces and the Democratic Process in Egypt", *Third World Quarterly*, Vol. 10, No. 4 (Oct. 1988), p. 1452.
142. Amos Perlmutter, "From Obscurity to Rule: The Syrian Army and the Ba'th Party", *Western Political Quarterly*, Vol. 22 (1969), p. 829.
143. Amos Perlmutter, "Egypt and the Myth of the New Middle Class: A Comparative Analysis", *Comparative Studies in Society and History*, Vol. 10, No. 1 (Oct. 1967), pp. 46–65.
144. Joel Gordon, *Nasser's Blessed Movement: Egypt's Free Officers and the July Revolution* (Oxford: Oxford University Press, 1992), p. 19; Stella Margold, "Agrarian Land Reform in Egypt", *American Journal of Economics and Sociology*, Vol. 17, No. 1 (Oct. 1957), pp. 9–19.
145. Uriel Dann, *King Hussein and the Challenge of Arab Radicalism, Jordan 1955–1967* (Oxford: Oxford University Press, 1989), p. 35.
146. Juan Romero, *The Iraqi Revolution of 1958: A Revolutionary Quest for Unity and Security* (New York: University Press of America, 2011), pp. 98–9.
147. Oren Barak, *The Lebanese Army: A National Institution in a Divided Society* (Albany, NY: State University of New York Press, 2009), p. 30.

## 3. THE COMPANY THEY KEEP: SOCIO-POLITICAL REASONS

1. Rebecca L. Schiff, *The Military and Domestic Politics: A concordance theory of civil–military relations* (Routledge: New York, 2009), pp. 32–48.
2. Claude Welch, "Civilian Control of the Military: Myth and Reality", in Claude Welch (ed.), *Civilian Control of the Military: Theory and Cases from Developing Countries* (Albany, NY: State University of New York Press, 1976), p. 3.
3. A. R. Luckham, "A Comparative Typology of Civil–Military Relations", *Government and Opposition*, Vol. 6, No. 1 (Jan. 1971), pp. 26–34; Amos Perlmutter, "The Praetorian State and the Praetorian Army: Toward a Taxonomy of Civil-Military Relations in Developing Polities", *Comparative Politics* (April 1969), p. 384.
4. Peter D. Feaver, *Armed Servants: Agency, Oversight and Civil–Military Relations* (Cambridge, MA: Harvard University Press, 2003), p. 61.
5. Claude E. Welch and Arthur K. Smith, *Military Role and Rule: Perspectives on Civil–Military Relations* (Belmont: Duxbury Press, 1974), p. 40.
6. David Hirst, "The Terror from Tikrit", *Guardian*, 26 November 1971.
7. Farid El-Khazen, *The Breakdown of the State in Lebanon, 1967–1976* (London: I. B. Tauris, 2000), p. 296.
8. Abdo I. Baaklini, "Civilian Control of the Military in Lebanon: A Legislative Perspective", in Claude Welch (ed.), *Civilian Control of the Military: Theory and Cases from Developing Countries* (Albany, NY: State University of New York Press, 1976), pp. 255–80.
9. Peter D. Feaver, 'The Civil–Military Problematique: Huntington, Janowitz, and the Question of Civilian Control", *Armed Forces and Society*, Vol. 23, No. 2 (Winter 1996), p. 169.
10. Samuel E. Finer, *The Man on Horseback: The role of the military in politics* (Boulder, CO: Westview, 1988), pp. 64–76.
11. Risa A. Brooks, "An Autocracy at War: Explaining Egypt's Military Effectiveness, 1967 and 1973", *Security Studies*, Vol. 15, No. 3 (2006), pp. 396–430.
12. David M. Witty, "A Regular Army in Counterinsurgency Operations: Egypt in North Yemen, 1962–1967", *Journal of Military History*, Vol. 65, No. 2 (April 2001), p. 417.
13. Amos Perlmutter, "From Obscurity to Rule: the Syrian Army and the Ba'th Party", *Western Political Quarterly*, Vol. 22, No. 4 (Dec. 1969), pp. 827–45.
14. Samuel Huntington, "Civilian Control of the Military: A Theoretical Statement", in Heinz Elau et al. (eds), *Political Behavior: A Reader in Theory and Research* (Glencoe, IL: Free Press, 1956), p. 380.
15. Oren Barak, *The Lebanese Army: A National Institution in a Divided Society*

(Albany, NY: State University of New York Press, 2009), p. 31. Adel Beshara, *Lebanon: The politics of frustration—the failed coup of 1961* (London: Routledge, 2005).

16. Cynthia Enloe, *Ethnic Soldiers* (Athens: University of Georgia Press, 1980).

17. Max Weber, *On Charisma and Institution Building* (Chicago: University of Chicago Press, 1968), p. 12.

18. Gabriel Ben-Dor, "Civilianization of Military Regimes in the Arab World", *Armed Forces and Society*, Vol. 1, No. 3 (May 1975).

19. Ibid., p. 168.

20. *Reuters*, "Egypt army: will not use violence against citizens", 31 January 2011, available at http://www.reuters.com/article/2011/01/31/egypt-army-idAFLDE70U2JC20110131

21. *New York Times*, "Chief of Tunisian Army Pledges His Support for 'the Revolution'", 24 January 2011, available at http://www.nytimes.com/2011/01/25/world/africa/25tunis.html?_r=0

22. *Jeune Afrique*, "Le général Ammar, l'homme qui a dit non", 7 February 2011, available at http://www.jeuneafrique.com/Article/ARTJAJA2612p044–049.xml1/mohamed-ghannouchi-tunis-armee-zine-el-abidine-ben-ali-tunisie-le-general-ammar-l-homme-qui-a-dit-non.html

23. *Daily Star Lebanon*, "Lebanese break through army cordon with roses", 5 March 2005, available at http://www.dailystar.com.lb/News/Lebanon-News/2005/Mar-01/4994-lebanese-break-through-army-cordon-with-roses.ashx#axzz3HdBPJGlB

24. Arab Center for Research and Policy Studies, "The Arab Opinion Project: The Arab Opinion Index", Doha (March 2012), pp. 47–8.

25. Gallup, "Egypt from Tahrir to Transition", April 2011, available at http://www.gallup.com/poll/157046/egypt-tahrir-transition.aspx; Zogby Research Services, "Egyptian Attitudes: September 2013", available at http://static.squarespace.com/static/52750dd3e4b08c252c723404/t/5294bf5de4b013dda087d0e5/1385480029191/Egypt%20October%202013%20FINAL.pdf%20%20t

26. Pew Research Center, "Egyptians embrace revolt leaders, religious parties and military, as well", 25 April 2011, available at http://www.pewglobal.org/2011/04/25/egyptians-embrace-revolt-leaders-religious-parties-and-military-as-well/; "Egyptian military gets higher ratings than most political parties", 1 July 2013, available at http://www.pewresearch.org/fact-tank/2013/07/01/egyptian-military-gets-higher-ratings-than-most-political-parties/

27. *Daily Star Lebanon*, "Army scores highest on Lebanese trust index poll", 14 August 2014, available at http://www.dailystar.com.lb/News/Lebanon-News/2014/Aug-14/267244-army-scores-highest-on-lebanese-trust-index-poll.ashx#ixzz3Hdq5AyVl

28. Florence Gaub, "Multi-Ethnic Armies in the Aftermath of Civil War: Lessons Learned from Lebanon", *Defence Studies*, Vol. 7, No. 1 (2007); Oren Barak, "Commemorating Malikiyya: Political Myth, Multiethnic Identity and the Making of the Lebanese Army", *History & Memory*, Vol. 13, No. 1, pp. 60–84.

29. Najah Abdallah, "L'image de l'armée libanaise à travers de la presse quotidienne au Liban en 1984", PhD diss. (University Michel de Montaigne, Bordeaux III, 1992) pp. 188–91, 207, 252, 284.

30. Department of Defense, "Measuring Stability and Security in Iraq", Report to Congress In accordance with the Department of Defense Supplemental Act 2008 Section 9204, Public Law 110–252 (Washington, DC, December 2009), pp. 34–5.

31. Zogby Research Services, "Tunisia: Divided and Dissatisfied with Ennahda", 2013, available at http://b.3cdn.net/aai/b8cc8e61b78158d8 47_8pm6b1oog.pdf

32. Magharebia, "Les Tunisiens manifestent leur soutien à l'armée", 2 August 2013, available at http://magharebia.com/fr/articles/awi/features/2013/08/02/feature-01

33. *Jordan Times*, "Overwhelming majority trusts army, security agencies", 30 September 2014, available at http://jordantimes.com/overwhelming-majority-trusts-army-security-agencies

34. Florence Gaub, *Military Integration after Civil Wars: Multiethnic Armies, Identity and Post-Conflict Reconstruction* (London: Routledge, 2010) pp. 72–7.

35. Elizabeth Picard, "Arab Military in Politics: from Revolutionary Plot to Authoritarian Regime", in Giacomo Luciani (ed.), *The Arab State* (London: Routledge, 1990), pp. 202–8.

36. BBC Monitoring, "Saudi mufti urges compulsory military service of youths—pan-Arab daily report", Al-Quds al-Arabi, 11 April 2015; BBC Monitoring, "Saudi paper highlights benefits of military conscription, urges state to recruit", 11 February 2016, Al-Watan.

37. Lucian Pye, "Armies in the Process of Political Modernization", in John J. Johnson (ed.), *The Role of the Military in Underdeveloped Countries* (Princeton: Princeton University Press, 1962), p. 78; Samuel Huntington, *Political Order in Changing Societies* (New Haven: Yale University Press, 1968), p. 203.

38. Joel Gordon, *Nasser's Blessed Movement: Egypt's Free Officers and the July Revolution* (Oxford: Oxford University Press, 1992), p. 19.

39. Fuad I. Khuri and Gerald Obermeyer, "The Social Bases for Military Intervention in the Middle East", in Catherine McArdle Kelleher (ed.), *Political Military Systems: Comparative Perspectives* (London: Sage Publications: 1974), pp. 64–5.

40. Ronald Bruce St John, *Historical Dictionary of Libya* (Lanham, MD: Scarecrow Press 1998), p. 40.

41. Arab Center for Research and Policy Studies, "The Arab Opinion Project: The Arab Opinion Index", Doha (March 2012), p. 46; Zogby Research Services, "Egyptian Attitudes in the post-Tamarrud, post-Morsi Era", July 2013, available at http://b.3cdn.net/aai/6eaeff56 ba538229a3_gom6bhktx.pdf

42. Pew Research Center, "Egyptians embrace revolt leaders".

43. Eliezer Be'eri, *Army Officers in Arab Politics and Society* (Praeger: London, 1970) p. 102; Joel Beinin, *Workers and Peasants in the Modern Middle East* (New York: Cambridge University Press, 2001), pp. 126–8.

44. Joel Gordon, *Nasser's Blessed Movement: Egypt's Free Officers and the July Revolution* (Oxford University Press: Oxford, 1992) p. 51

45. Ibid., p. 33.

46. Ibid., p. 50.

47. Ibid., p. 14.

48. Gordon H. Torrey, *Syrian Politics and the Military, 1945–1958* (Columbus: Ohio State University Press, 1964), p. 74.

49. Quoted in Be'eri, *Army Officers in Arab Politics and Society*, p. 55.

50. Phebe Marr, *The Modern History of Iraq* (Boulder, CO: Westview Press, 2012), pp. 61–79; Majid Khadduri, "The Role of the Military in Iraqi Society", in Sydney Nettleton Fisher (ed.), *The Military in the Middle East* (Columbus: Ohio State University Press, 1963), p. 44.

51. Dirk Vandewalle, *A History of Modern Libya* (New York: Cambridge University Press, 2012), p. 76.

52. Middle Eastern Values Study, "The Birthplace of the Arab Spring: Values and Perceptions of Tunisians and a Comparative Assessment of Egyptian, Iraqi, Lebanese, Pakistani, Saudi, Tunisian, and Turkish Publics", 2014, p. 66, available at http://mevs.org/files/tmp/Tunisia_FinalReport.pdf, p. 67.

53. Zogby Research Services, "Tunisia: Divided and Dissatisfied with Ennahda", 2013, available at http://b.3cdn.net/aai/b8cc8e61b78158d8 47_8pm6b1oog.pdf

54. Zogby Research Services, "Egyptian Attitudes: September 2013", available at http://static.squarespace.com/static/52750dd3e4b08c252c7234 04/t/5294bf5de4b013dda087d0e5/1385480029191/Egypt%20 October%202013%20FINAL.pdf%20%20t; Pew Research Center, "One Year after Morsi's Ouster, Divides Persist on El-Sisi, Muslim Brotherhood", 22 May 2014, available at http://www.pewglobal. org/2014/05/22/one-year-after-morsis-ouster-divides-persist-on-el-sisi-muslim-brotherhood/

55. Shibley Telhami, "2012: Public Opinion Survey", Anwar Sadat Chair

for Peace and Development, University of Maryland, available at http://www.brookings.edu/~/media/research/files/reports/2012/5/21%20egyptian%20elections%20poll%20telhami/egypt_poll_results

56. Zogby Research Services, "Tunisia: Divided and Dissatisfied with Ennahda", 2013, available at http://b.3cdn.net/aai/b8cc8e61b78158d847_8pm6b1oog.pdf

57. *NOW Lebanon*, "Nine Unforgettable Years: A Tribute to President Emile Lahoud", 25 November 2007, available at https://now.mmedia.me/lb/en/archive/Nine-Unforgettable-Years-A-Tribute-to-President-Emile-Lahoud21320

58. *NOW Lebanon*, "A State of Minds: Lebanon in Numbers—Views on President Suleiman's term", 22 July 2014, available at https://now.mmedia.me/lb/en/a-state-of-minds/556942-views-on-president-suleimans-term

59. National News Agency of the Lebanese Republic, "Jumblatt: History shall do Sleiman justice", 5 May 2014, available at http://www.nna-leb.gov.lb/en/show-news/26254/Jumblatt-History-shall-do-Sleiman-justice

60. *Mada Masr*, "Polls show high approval ratings for Sisi after first 100 days in office", 22 September 2014, available at http://www.madamasr.com/news/polls-show-high-approval-ratings-sisi-after-first-100-days-office

61. Zeinab Abul-Magd, "Understanding SCAF", Cairo Review of Global Affairs, 30 June 2012, available at http://www.aucegypt.edu/gapp/cairoreview/pages/articleDetails.aspx?aid=216

62. *Aljazeera*, "Background: SCAF's last-minute power grab", 18 June 2012, available at http://www.aljazeera.com/indepth/spotlight/egypt/2012/06/201261812449990250.html; International Crisis Group, "Lost in Transition: The World According to Egypt's SCAF", Middle East/North Africa Report No. 121, available at http://www.crisisgroup.org/~/media/files/middle%20east%20north%20africa/north%20africa/egypt/121-lost-in-transition-the-world-according-to-egypts-scaf.pdf

63. Pew Research Center, "Egyptians embrace revolt leaders; "Egyptian military gets higher ratings".

64. Shibley Telhami, "2012: Public Opinion Survey".

65. *Aljazeera*, "Transcript: Egypt's army statement", 3 July 2013, available at http://www.aljazeera.com/news/middleeast/2013/07/201373203740167797.html; *The Arabist*, "Sisi's speech to the army, and Morsi", 15 July 2013, available at http://arabist.net/blog/2013/7/15/sisis-speech-to-the-army-and-morsi

66. Eric A. Nordlinger, "Soldiers in Mufti: The Impact of Military Rule upon Economic and Social Change in the Non-Western States", *American Political Science Review*, Vol. 64, No. 4 (Dec. 1970), p. 1140; Robert W. Jackman, "Politicians in Uniform: Military Governments and Social Change in the Third World", *American Political Science Review*, Vol. 70, No. 4 (Dec. 1976), pp. 1078–97.

67. Uriel Dann, *Iraq under Qassem: A Political History, 1958–1963* (New York: Praeger, 1969), p. 376.

68. Eric A. Nordlinger, *Soldiers in Politics: Military Coups and Governments* (Upper Saddleback River, NJ: Prentice Hall, 1977), p. 109.

69. Ibid., p. 117.

70. Kirk J. Beattie, "Egypt: Thirty-Five Years of Praetorian Politics", in Constantine Danopoulos (ed.), *Military Disengagement from Politics* (London: Routledge, 1988), pp. 210–30.

71. Mark N. Cooper, "The Demilitarisation of the Egyptian Cabinet", *International Journal of Middle East Studies*, Vol. 14, No. 2 (1982).

72. Mada Masr, "Calls for Sisi's nomination a public sentiment, says military spokesperson", 22 September 2013, available at http://www.madamasr.com/news/calls-sisi%E2%80%99s-nomination-public-sentiment-says-military-spokesperson

73. *Financial Times*, "Egyptians become victims of soaring crime rate", 1 May 2013, available at http://www.ft.com/intl/cms/s/0/7ffac226-adab-11e2-a2c700144feabdc0.html#axzz2xWywGjZl

74. *Guardian*, "Egyptian police go on strike", 10 March 2013, available at http://www.theguardian.com/world/2013/mar/10/egypt-police-strike

75. Steven A. Cook, *Ruling but not Governing: The Military and Political Development in Egypt, Algeria and Turkey* (Baltimore, MD: Johns Hopkins University Press, 2007), pp. 32–62.

76. Gamal Abdel Nasser, *Egypt's Liberation: The Philosophy of the Revolution* (Washington, DC: Public Affairs Press, 1955), p. 19.

77. Quoted in Eliezer Be'eri, *Army Officers in Arab Politics and Society* (New York: Praeger, 1970), p. 101.

78. Nasser, *Egypt's Liberation*, pp. 33–4.

79. *Daily Beast*, "Egyptians: Stop Calling Our Revolution a Coup", 7 October 2013, available at http://www.thedailybeast.com/articles/2013/07/10/egyptians-stop-calling-our-revolution-a-coup.html; *Foreign Policy*, "The Wikipedia war over Egypt's 'Coup'", 7 July 2013, available at http://blog.foreignpolicy.com/posts/2013/07/07/the_wikipedia_war_over_egypts_coup; *Al-Monitor*, "Was Morsi's Ouster a Coup Or New Egyptian Revolution?", 4 July 2013, available at http://www.al-monitor.com/pulse/originals/2013/07/was-morsi-ouster-a-coup-or-new-egyptian-revolution.html#ixzz3I0STko00

80. Ibrahim Al-Marashi and Sammy Salama, *Iraq's Armed Forces: An Analytical History* (London: Routledge, 2008), p. 82.

81. Joel Gordon, *Nasser's Blessed Movement: Egypt's Free Officers and the July Revolution* (Oxford: Oxford University Press, 1992), p. 74.

82. *Ahram Online*, "Egypt's armed forces advised Morsi to be inclusive: Defence Minister El-Sisi", 7 October 2013, available at http://english.ahram.org.eg/NewsContent/1/64/83454/Egypt/Politics-/Egypts-armed-forces-advised-Morsi-to-be-inclusive-.aspx

83. George L. Mosse, *Fallen Soldiers: Reshaping the Memory of the World Wars* (Oxford: Oxford University Press, 1990).

## 4. MODELS OF NON-POLITICAL ARMIES

1. A. Abbas, "The Iraqi Armed Forces, Past and Present", in Committee Against Repression and for Democratic Rights in Iraq (CARDRI) (ed.), *Saddam's Iraq: Revolution or Reaction?* (London: Zed Books, 1989), p. 203.

2. *Stars and Stripes*, "Iraqi army remains on defensive as extent of June debacle becomes clearer", 14 July 2014, available at http://www.stripes.com/news/middle-east/iraqi-army-remains-on-defensive-as-extent-of-june-debacle-becomes-clearer-1.293417

3. *New York Times*, "More Than 1,000 in Iraq's Forces Quit Basra Fight", 4 April 2008; *Daily Telegraph*, "Battle to retake Basra was 'Complete Disaster'", 20 April 2008.

4. *New York Times*, "Iraq Army Woos Deserters Back to War on ISIS", 28 September 2014, available at http://www.nytimes.com/2014/09/29/world/middleeast/iraq-army-woos-deserters-back-to-war-on-isis.html?_r=0

5. *Washington Post*, "The US military is back training troops in Iraq, but it's a little different this time", 8 January 2015, available at http://www.washingtonpost.com/world/the-us-military-is-back-training-troops-in-iraq-but-its-a-little-different-this-time/2015/01/08/11b9aa58-95f2-11e4-8385-866293322c2f_story.html

6. *New York Times*, "Facing Militants With Supplies Dwindling, Iraqi Soldiers Took to Phones", 26 September 2014, available at http://www.nytimes.com/2014/09/27/world/middleeast/facing-isis-with-few-supplies-iraqi-soldiers-took-to-phones.html; Reuters, "How Mosul fell: An Iraqi general disputes Baghdad's story", 14 October 2014, available at http://uk.reuters.com/article/2014/10/14/uk-mideast-crisis-gharawi-special-report-idUKKCN0I30ZA20141014

7. Ulrich Bröckling and Michael Sikora (eds), *Armeen und ihre Deserteure. Vernachlässigte Kapitel einer Militärgeschichte der Neuzeit* (Göttingen: Vandenhoeck and Ruprecht, 1998), p. 9.

8. Arnold M. Rose, "The social psychology of Desertion from combat", *American Sociological Review*, 16 (1951), p. 614.

9. Christoph Jahr, "'Der Krieg zwingt die Justiz, ihr Innerstes zu revidieren': Desertion und Militärgerichtsbarkeit im Ersten Weltkrieg", in Ulrich Bröckling, Ulrich and Michael Sikora (eds), *Armeen und ihre Deserteure. Vernachlässigte Kapitel einer Militärgeschichte der Neuzeit* (Göttingen: Vandenhoeck and Ruprecht, 1998), pp. 190–94.

10. Bruce Allen Watson, *When Soldiers Quit. Studies in Military Disintegration* (London: Praeger, 1997), p. 2.

11. Edward A. Shils and Morris Janowitz, "Cohesion and Disintegration in the Wehrmacht in World War II", *Public Opinion Quarterly*, Vol. 2 (1948), pp. 280–315. Omer Bartov rejects this hypothesis in his book *Hitler's Army: Soldiers, Nazis and War in the Third Reich* (New York: Oxford University Press, 1991).

12. Leonard Wong et al., "Why They Fight: Combat Motivation in the Iraq War", Strategic Studies Institute, July 2003, p. 7, available at http://www.strategicstudiesinstitute.army.mil/pdffiles/PUB179.pdf

13. Watson, *When Soldiers Quit*, pp. 156–63.

14. *New York Times*, "Iraq Army Woos Deserters Back to War on ISIS", 28 September 2014, available at http://www.nytimes.com/2014/09/29/world/middleeast/iraq-army-woos-deserters-back-to-war-on-isis.html?_r=0

15. James Pfiffner, "US Blunders in Iraq: De-Baathification and Disbanding the Army", *Intelligence and National Security*, Vol. 25, No. 1 (February 2010), pp. 76–85.

16. Douglas Feith, *War and Decision* (New York: Harper, 2008), p. 432.

17. Anthony Cordesman, "The US Transition in Iraq: Iraqi Forces and US Military Aid", Center for Strategic and International Studies, 21 October 2010, p. 22; Special Inspector General for Iraq Reconstruction, Quarterly Report to the United States Congress, 30 July 2010, p. 61; Ibid., 30 April 2008, p. 98; Anthony Cordesman, "Inexcusable Failure: Progress in Training the Iraqi Army and Security Forces as of Mid-July 2004", Center for Strategic and International Studies, 20 July 2004, p. 8.

18. Lieutenant Colonel Carl D. Grunow, US Army, "Advising Iraqis: Building the Iraqi Army", *Military Review* (July–Aug. 2006), p. 15.

19. US Congress, House, Armed Services Committee, Subcommittee on Oversight and Investigations Hearing, *Development of Operational Capability of the Iraqi Security Forces* (110th Congress, 1st sess., 12 June 2007), Lieutenant General Martin F. Dempsey, former Commanding General, Multi-National Security Transition Command–Iraq, the coalition command responsible for recruiting, training and equipping the Iraqi Security Forces.

20. *Aljazeera America*, "Veterans not surprised Iraq's Army collapsed", 28 June 2014, available at http://america.aljazeera.com/watch/shows/america-tonight/articles/2014/6/28/how-did-iraq-s-armycollapseso-quickly.html

21. *New York Times*, "Minister Sees Need for US help in Iraq Until 2018", 15 January 2008, available at http://www.nytimes.com/2008/01/15/world/middleeast/15military.html?_r=0; *The Hill*, "US to help Iraq security for another 10 years, says general", 17 January 2008, available at http://thehill.com/homenews/administration/4510-us-to-help-iraq-security-for-another-10-years-says-general; *Guardian*, "Iraqi army not ready to take over until 2020, says country's top general", 12 August 2010, available at http://www.theguardian.com/world/2010/aug/12/iraqi-army-not-ready-general; *New York Times*, "Ready or Not, Iraq's Military Prepares to Stand on its Own", 28 June 2009.

22. *Wall Street Journal*, "Iraqis Face Uncertain Future as US Ends Combat Mission", 27 August 2010, available at http://www.wsj.com/articles/SB10001424052748704913704575453303215595156

23. Toby Dodge, *Iraq: From War to Authoritarianism* (London: International Institute for Strategic Studies/Routledge, 2012), p. 127.

24. Department of Defense, "Measuring Stability and Security in Iraq", Quarterly report to Congress, May 2006, p. 52, available at http://www.defense.gov/pubs/pdfs/May%2006%20Security%20and%20Stabilty%20Report%20Final%20with%20errata.pdf

25. International Institute for Strategic Studies, *The Military Balance 2008* (London: Routledge, 2008), p. 229.

26. Michael Eisenstadt, "Like a Phoenix from the Ashes? The Future of Iraqi Military Power", Policy Papers No. 36 (Washington, DC: Washington Institute for Near East Policy, 1993), p. 8.

27. *Foreign Policy*, "How Maliki Ruined Iraq", 19 June 2014, available at http://foreignpolicy.com/2014/06/19/how-maliki-ruined-iraq/?wp_login_redirect=0

28. Author interviews with Iraqi officers, Baghdad, 2010 and 2012.

29. International Crisis Group, "Loose Ends: Iraq's Security Forces between US Drawdown and Withdrawal", *Middle East Report*, No. 99 (26 October 2010), p. 19.

30. International Institute for Strategic Studies, *The Military Balance 2010* (London: Routledge, 2010), p. 294; Department of Defense, *Measuring Stability and Security in Iraq*, Quarterly report to Congress, March 2008, p. 45; Interview conducted by the author with NATO Training Mission Iraq Personnel, Baghdad, 7 June 2010.

31. Ahmed Hashim, "Saddam Husayn and Civil–Military Relations in Iraq: The Quest for Legitimacy and Power", *Middle East Journal*, Vol. 57,

No. 1 (Winter 2003), p. 38; US Congress, House, Armed Services Committee, Subcommittee on Oversight and Investigations Hearing, *Hearing on Iraqi Security Forces, Non-Government Perspectives* (110ᵗʰ Congress, 1ˢᵗ sess., 28 March 2007), Dr Anthony Cordesman testimony.

32. *New York Times*, "Text of Colonel Reese's Memo", 30 July 2009, available at http://www.nytimes.com/2009/07/31/world/middleeast/31 advtext.html?pagewanted=all&_r=0

33. Ronald Bruce St John, *Historical Dictionary of Libya* (Lanham, MD: Scarecrow Press, 1998), p. 40.

34. John Cooley, *Libyan Sandstorm: The Complete Account of Qaddafi's Revolution* (New York: Holt, Rinehart and Winston, 1982), p. 167.

35. St John, *Historical Dictionary of Libya*, p. 55.

36. Kenneth Pollack, *Arabs at War: Military Effectiveness 1948–1991* (Lincoln: University of Nebraska, 2002), pp. 358–424.

37. *Alarabiya News*, "Warfalla, Libya's largest tribe", 1 September 2011, available at http://www.alarabiya.net/articles/2011/09/01/164993. html; Luiz Martínez, *The Libyan Paradox* (New York: Columbia University Press, 2007), p. 71.

38. *The Australian*, "Gaddafi's Libyan Army collapsing, say defectors", 5 June 2011, available at http://www.theaustralian.com.au/news/world/gad-dafis-libyan-army-collapsing-say-defectors/story-e6frg6so-12260 69500257; International Institute for Strategic Studies, *The Military Balance 2011* (London: Routledge, 2011), p. 320; Florence Gaub, 'Libya in Limbo: How to Fill the Security Vacuum', NATO Defense College Research Report, 31 August 2011, p. 3; *New York Times*, "Rebels in Libya Gain Power and Defectors", 27 February 2011, http://www. nytimes.com/2011/02/28/world/africa/28unrest.html?pagewanted= all

39. Civil–Military Fusion Centre, "The Libyan rebels: evolution of a fighting force", July 2011, p. 2.

40. *Tripoli Post*, "Nations' Feedback on Libyan Uprising", 23 February 2011, available at http://tripolipost.com/articledetail.asp?c=1&i=5463

41. *Reuters*, "Son's unit may be one of Gaddafi's last lines of defense", 25 February 2011, available at http://www.reuters.com/article/2011/ 02/25/us-libya-commandos-idUSTRE71N8GT20110225

42. *BBC News*, "Profile: Khamis Ghaddafi", 4 September 2011, available at http://www.bbc.co.uk/news/world-africa-14723041

43. Amnesty International, "The Battle for Libya: Killings, Disappearances and Torture", London, 2011, available at http://www.amnesty.org/ en/library/info/MDE19/025/2011/en; United Nations Human Rights Council, *Report of the International Commission of Inquiry on Libya* (New York, 2 March 2012), available at www.ohchr.org%2FDocuments%2

FHRBodies%2FHRCouncil%2FRegularSession%2FSession19%2FA_
HRC_19_68_en.doc&ei=6VxrT_3RFMXOsgaU2pGtAg&usg=AFQj
CNFQAOsidSQiRewVmC5_8gxQtSOGdA

44. *Reuters*, "Some 5,000 militia men join new Libyan army", 15 February
    2012, available at http://www.reuters.com/article/2012/02/15/us-
    libya-militias-idUSTRE81E23H20120215

45. *Agence France Presse*, "Libya to integrate 50,000 anti-Kadhafi fighters",
    1 December 2011, available at http://www.google.com/hostednews/
    afp/article/ALeqM5hIWIuNlAOLc-Sh8JQJt1MnkCJzBQ?docId=CNG
    .104a1c9e9c71e179b33042a465c95d6c.831

46. International Crisis Group, "Holding Libya Together", p. 24.

47. *Libya Herald*, "Security is under control—Interior Minister Sheikh",
    26 July 2013, available at http://www.libyaherald.com/2013/07/26/
    security-is-under-control-interior-minister-sheikh/

48. Katherine Glassmyer and Nicholas Sambanis, "Rebel–Military Integra-
    tion and Civil War Termination", *Journal of Peace Research*, Vol. 45, No. 3
    (May 2008), pp. 365–84.

49. *Al-Defaiya*, "Two Libyan Rebel Groups Reject Chief-of-Staff Nomina-
    tion", 6 January 2012, available at http://www.defaiya.com/defaiya-
    online/index.php?option=com_content&view=article&id=2672%3A
    two-libyan-rebel-groups-reject-chief-of-staff-nomination&catid=78%3
    Alibya&Itemid=27&lang=en

50. *Middle East Eye*, "Head of Libya's army: 'no control' over government-
    funded rebels",11 August 2014, available at http://www.middleeast-
    eye.net/news/head-libyas-army-no-control-over-government-funded-
    rebels-221789896

51. Andrew Engel, "Libya's Divided Security Establishment: Who
    Commands?", *War on the Rocks*, 20 February 2014, available at http://
    warontherocks.com/2014/02/libyas-divided-security-establishment-who-
    commands/

52. *New York Times*, "Libya: Minister of Defence to be Dismissed", 27 June
    2013, available at http://www.nytimes.com/2013/06/28/world/
    africa/libya-minister-of-defense-to-be-dismissed.html?_r=0; Al Jazeera
    TV, "Libya's new army chief says building of military obstructed by
    squabbling", 24 June 2013, BBC Monitoring.

53. *Agence France Presse*, "New Chief for Libya's revamped national army",
    17 November 2011, available at http://www.google.com/hosted-
    news/afp/article/ALeqM5i2GtUw73moWubwhdFPXQ-ZouMDzg?
    docId=CNG.a3f2fe1bf5ddf5725a77594ecefbea23.211

54. *The National*, "Libya Army Officers want Chief dismissed", 24 April
    2013, available at http://www.thenational.ae/news/world/africa/
    libya-army-officers-want-chief-dismissed; *Libya al-Ahrar TV*, "Libyan offi-

cers at Mu'aytiqah airbase oppose appointment of new chief of staff", 29 August 2014, BBC Monitoring; *National Libyan TV*, "Libyan General Chief of Staff Office urges forces to obey ousted chief", 24 August 2014, BBC Monitoring.

55. WAL, "Libyan officers, soldiers in Al-Jufrah express support for combating 'terrorism'", 21 May 2014, BBC Monitoring; *Al-Arabiya TV*, "Libyan air defence, Interior Ministry declare support for Haftar", 20 May 2014, BBC Monitoring; *Middle East Eye*, "Libya army command 'loyal' to constitutional legitimacy", 20 May 2014, available at http://www.middleeasteye.net/news/libya-army-command-loyal-constitutional-legitimacy-230572364; *Libya Herald*, "Libyan Air Force commander sacked for publicly supporting Maj-Gen Haftar", 21 March 2014, BBC Monitoring; *Libya al-Ahrar TV*, "Libyan army commands reject House of Representatives' decisions", 24 August 2014, BBC Monitoring.

56. *Libya Herald*, "Haftar appointed army commander, promoted Colonel-General—Libyan official", 5 February 2015, BBC Monitoring.

57. *Libya Herald*, "Libyan HoR creates position of army commander-in-chief—paper", 19 February 2015, BBC Monitoring; *Al-Sharq al-Awsat*, "Former Libyan defence minister says 'army must be under civilian authority'", 7 October 2015, BBC Monitoring.

58. *Libya Herald*, "Libya army chief says removed senior official due to incompetence, betrayal", 25 June 2015, BBC Monitoring; *Al Jazeera*, "Libyan parliament 'split' over government, military spending, Al Jazeera says", 24 August 2015, BBC Monitoring.

59. International Crisis Group, "Yemen's Military-Security Reform: Seeds of a New Conflict?", 4 April 2013, pp. 7–10.

60. *BBC News*, "Top Yemeni general, Ali Mohsen, backs opposition", 21 March 2011, available at http://www.bbc.com/news/world-middle-east-12804552

61. Michael Knights, "The Military Role in Yemen's Protests: Civil–Military Relations in the Tribal Republic", *Journal of Strategic Studies*, Vol. 36, No. 2 (2013).

62. Khaled Fattah, "Ensuring the Success of Yemen's Military Reforms", Carnegie Europe, 13 December 2012, available at http://carnegieeurope.eu/publications/?fa=50349; International Crisis Group, "Yemen's Military-Security Reform: Seeds of a New Conflict?", 4 April 2013.

63. *Yemen Observer*, "Marib Tribal Men Demand Recruiting 85 Thousand People", 27 November 2014; *Yemen Post*, "Hadi Reinstates, Promotes 8009 Officers, Soldiers from South", 24 November 2014; *Yemen Post*, "Yemen officially including Huthi militants within forces", 23 November 2014; *Yemen Fox*, "President urges Partnership with Huthi Group", 18 November 2014.

64. *Yemen Times*, "Rebels in Disguise", 16 October 2014.

65. *Asharq Al-Awsat*, "Hadi, Salih and the Huthis Share Army Capabilities", 20 March 2015, Mideastwire.com; *Yemen Fox*, "Mutiny inside Yemen's special forces", 22 November 2014.

66. *Yemen Post*, "Al-Subaihi slams army chiefs, Huthi militias", 28 November 2014.

67. *Al-Wasat*, "Yemeni military official allegedly starts establishment of new army", 21 May 2015, BBC Monitoring; *Wall Street Journal*, "Yemen Leader Moves to Unify Fractured Fighting Force", 29 July 2015, available at http://www.wsj.com/articles/yemen-leader-moves-to-unify-fractured-fighting-force-1438225287; *Asharq Al-Awsat*, "Yemeni army leaders to reform military after takeover of Aden from pro-Huthis", 4 August 2015, BBC Monitoring; Aden al-Ghad, "Yemeni colonel calls for forming of new southern army", 4 August 2015, BBC Monitoring.

68. Oren Barak, *The Lebanese Army: a National Institution in a Divided Society* (Albany, NY: SUNY Press, 2009), pp. 100–104.

69. Stéphane Malsagne, "L'armée libanaise dans la guerre de Palestine (1948–1949): vers un renouveau historiographique", *Confluences Méditerranée*, No. 65 (Spring 2008).

70. *Daily Star*, "Lebanese break through army cordon with roses", 1 March 2005, available at http://www.dailystar.com.lb/News/Lebanon-News/2005/Mar-01/4994-lebanese-break-through-army-cordon-with-roses.ashx

71. Amnesty International, "Lebanon: Security forces using excessive force against protestors must be held to account", 29 August 2015, available at https://www.amnesty.org/en/latest/news/2015/08/lebanon-security-forces-using-excessive-force-against-protestors-must-be-held-to-account/; *Arab News*, "Lebanese Army seals Parliament after Syria-linked demonstrations", 22 June 2013, available at http://www.arabnews.com/news/455765

72. Aram Nerguizian, "Between Sectarianism and military development: The Paradox of the Lebanese Armed Forces", in Bassel F. Salloukh et al. (ed.), *The Politics of Sectarianism in Postwar Lebanon* (London: Pluto Press, 2015), pp. 118–22.

73. Oren Barak, "Towards a Representative Military? The Transformation of the Lebanese Officer Corps", *Middle East Journal*, Vol. 60, No. 1 (Winter 2006).

74. Nayla Moussa, "Loyalties and Group Formation in the Lebanese Officer Corps", Carnegie Middle East Center, 3 February 2016, available at http://carnegie-mec.org/2016/02/03/loyalties-and-group-formation-in-lebanese-officer-corps/itga

75. Donald Horowitz, *Ethnic Groups in Conflict* (Los Angeles: University of California Press, 1985), ch.12.

76. Stéphane Malsagne, *Fouad Chéhab, 1902–1973: Une figure oubliée de l'histoire libanaise* (Paris: Editions Karthala, 2011), p. 109.

77. *La Croix*, "Émile Lahoud: Un Marin en Eaux Troubles", 1 December 1989; André Rondé, "L'Armée libanaise et la restauration de l'Etat de droit", *Revue Droit et Défense*, No. 2 (1998), p. 30; Sean Boyne, "Lebanon rebuilds its army", *Jane's Intelligence Review*, Vol. 7, No. 3 (1995), pp. 122–5.

78. Author interview with Lebanese general, Beirut, January 2015.

79. Samuel P. Huntington, *The Soldier and the State: The Theory and Politics of Civil–military Relations* (Cambridge, MA: Belknap Press, 1957), p. 8.

80. Oren Barak, *The Lebanese Army: a National Institution in a Divided Society* (Albany, NY: SUNY Press, 2009), p. 95.

81. Quoted in Adel Beshara, *Lebanon: The Politics of Frustration—The Failed Coup of 1961* (London: Routledge, 2005), p. 142.

82. Author interview with Lebanese general, Beirut, December 2015.

83. R. D. McLaurin, "From professional to political: the redecline of the Lebanese Army", *Armed Forces and Society*, Vol. 17, No. 4 (Summer 1991).

84. Elizabeth Picard, "The Demobilization of the Lebanese Militias", Centre for Lebanese Studies, 1999.

85. Lebanese Army Operate, available at https://www.youtube.com/watch?v=4OGUg72rE5Y

86. Fabiola Azar and Etienne Mullet, 'Muslims and Christians in Lebanon: Common Views on Political Issues', *Journal of Peace Research*, Vol. 39, No. 6 (2002); Arab Center for Research and Policy Studies, 'The Arab Opinion Index 2011', available at http://english.dohainstitute.org/release/5083cf8e-38f8-4e4a-8bc5-fc91660608b0

87. *L'Orient–Le Jour*, "Chamel Roukoz, l'homme qui commande les commandos", 7 September 2015, available at http://www.lorientlejour.com/article/942891/chamel-roukoz-lhomme-qui-commande-les-commandos.html

88. *Tunisie Numerique*, "Tunisie—Le centre Carter pour le droit au vote des militaires et agents de l'ordre", 22 April 2014, available at http://www.tunisienumerique.com/tunisie-le-centre-carter-pour-le-droit-au-vote-des-militaires-et-agents-de-lordre/219304; *Direct Info*, "Tunisie: Accorder ou non le droit de voter et de se porter candidats aux militaires", 4 November 2015, available at http://directinfo.webmanagercenter.com/2015/11/04/tunisie-accorder-le-droit-de-vote-aux-militaires-et-aux-securitaires-implique-loctroi-du-droit-de-se-porter-candidat/; *Leaders*, "Pourquoi les agents des Corps Armés ne doivent pas bénéficier du droit de vote", 17 April 2014, available at http://www.leaders.com.tn/article/13849-pourquoi-les-agents-des-corps-armes-ne-

doivent-pas-beneficier-du-droit-de-vote; *Mosaique FM*, "Chawki Gaddes: Les agents de sécurité et les militaires ont le droit de voter", 22 April 2014, available at http://archivev2.mosaiquefm.net/fr/index/a/ActuDetail/Element/36209

89. Ministry of National Defence, Tunisia, *The Tunisian Armed Forces* (Tunis: Alif, Les Editions de la Méditerranée, 1996), pp. 69–77.

90. *Tunisie Numerique*, "Tunisie: Identification des corps de 5 personnes ayant pris part au putsch de décembre 1962", 5 September 2012, available at http://www.tunisienumerique.com/tunisie-identification-des-corps-de-5-personnes-ayant-pris-part-au-putsch-de-decembre-1962/142217

91. Kapitalis, "Tunisie. Les putschistes de 1962 sont-ils des 'martyrs'?", 8 September 2012, available at http://www.kapitalis.com/politique/11650-tunisie-les-putschistes-de-1962-sont-ils-des-lmartyrsr.html

92. L. B. Ware, "The Role of the Tunisian Military in the Post-Bourguiba Era", *Middle East Journal*, Vol. 39, No. 1 (Winter 1985).

93. *Jeune Afrique*, "Tunisie: la torture de l'ère Ben Ali en procès", 2 December 2011, available at http://www.jeuneafrique.com/189037/societe/tunisie-la-torture-de-l-re-ben-ali-en-proc-s/

94. *Direct Info*, "Tunisie—ANC: Les militaires victimes de l'affaire de Barraket Essahel réhabilités par la loi", 13 June 2014, available at http://directinfo.webmanagercenter.com/2014/06/13/tunisie-anc-les-militaires-victimes-de-laffaire-de-barraket-essahel-rehabilites-par-la-loi/

95. Sharan Grewal, "A quiet revolution: The Tunisian Military after Ben Ali", Carnegie Middle East Center, 24 February 2016.

96. L. B. Ware, "The Role of the Tunisian Military in the Post-Bourguiba Era", p. 38.

97. Quoted in Sharan Grewal, "A quiet revolution", p. 9.

98. *Babnet Tunisie*, "Tunisie: L'association d'anciens militaires dénonce l'exploitation médiatique de la souffrance des familles des victimes du terrorisme", 7 June 2013, available at http://www.babnet.net/cadredetail-66419.asp

99. *Magharebia*, "Les Tunisiens manifestent leur soutien à l'armée", 2 August 2013.

100. *Al Jazeera TV*, "Tunisian Defence Ministry says army to recruit thousands of jobless youths", 4 March 2016, BBC Monitoring; Hamza Meddeb, "Conscription Reform Will Shape Tunisia's Future Civil–Military Relations", 21 October 2015, Carnegie Endowment for International Peace, available at http://carnegieendowment.org/syriaincrisis/?fa=61704

## 5. MODELS OF POTENTIALLY POLITICAL ARMIES

1. The Emirate of Transjordan was renamed the Hashemite Kingdom of Jordan in 1946.
2. Dana Adams Schmidt, *Armageddon in the Middle East* (New York: John Day Company, 1974), p. 59.
3. P. J. Vatikiotis, *Politics and the Military in Jordan: a study of the Arab Legion 1921–1957* (London: Frank Cass, 1967), p. 137.
4. Kenneth M. Pollack, *Arabs at War: Military Effectiveness, 1948–1991* (Lincoln: University of Nebraska Press, 2002), pp. 267–357.
5. Uriel Dann, *King Hussein and the Challenge of Arab Radicalism, Jordan 1955–1967* (Oxford: Oxford University Press, 1989), p. 10.
6. Peter Snow, *Hussein: A Biography* (London: Barrie & Jenkins, 1972), p. 95.
7. Lawrence Tal, *Politics, the Military and National Security in Jordan, 1955–1967* (Basingstoke: Palgrave, 2002), p. 27.
8. Uriel Dann, *King Hussein*, p. 35.
9. Eliezer Be'eri, *Army Officers in Arab Politics and Society* (New York: Praeger, 1970), pp. 233–4.
10. Peter Snow, *Hussein: A Biography* (London: Barrie & Jenkins, 1972), p. 110.
11. Tal, *Politics, the Military and National Security in Jordan*, p. 49.
12. Ghazi bin Muhammad, *The Tribes of Jordan at the Beginning of the Twenty-first Century* (Amman: Rutab, 1999), p. 17; Ann Furr and Muwafaq Al-Serhan, "Tribal Customary Law in Jordan", *South Carolina Journal of International Law and Business*, Vol. 4, No. 2 (Spring 2008), p. 19; Kamal Salibi, *The Modern History of Jordan* (London: I. B. Tauris, 1993), p. 99.
13. Syed Ali El-Edroos, *The Hashemite Arab Army 1908–1979* (Amman: The Publishing Committee, 1980), p. 321.
14. *Jordan Times*, "Jordan marks Arabisation of army today", 29 February 2016, available at http://www.jordantimes.com/news/local/jordan-marks-arabisation-army-today
15. Salibi, *The Modern History of Jordan*, pp. 188–9; Snow, *Hussein*, p. 32.
16. Quoted in Tal, *Politics, the Military and National Security in Jordan*, p. 81.
17. Alexander Bligh, "The Jordanian Army: Between Domestic and External Challenges", in Barry Rubin and Thomas A. Keaney, *Armed Forces in the Middle East: politics and strategy* (Portland, OR: Frank Cass, 2002), p. 151.
18. Quoted in Tal, *Politics, the Military, and National Security in Jordan*, p. 90.
19. Federal Research Division of the Library of Congress, Country Studies Series, "Jordan Personnel: Composition, Recruitment, and Training", 1989; Hillel Frisch, *The Palestinian Military: Between Militias and Armies* (New York: Routledge, 2008), p. 50.

20. *Business Insider*, "11 photos showing King Abdullah II of Jordan being a total badass", 5 February 2015, available at http://uk.businessinsider.com/king-abduallh-of-jordan-is-a-total-badass-2015–2?r=US&IR=T

21. *Al-Monitor*, "Jordan's king pushes to expand military, intelligence authority", 25 August 2014, available at http://www.al-monitor.com/pulse/originals/2014/08/jordan-king-constitution-amendments.html#ixzz48LltS0Zq; Dana El Kurd, "The Jordanian Military: A Key Regional Ally", *Parameters*, Vol. 44, No. 3 (Autumn 2014).

22. Tamer Khorma, "The Myth of the Jordanian Monarchy's Resilience to the Arab Spring", Stiftung Wissenschaft und Politik Comments 33, July 2014; *Al-Ra'y*, "Military retirees: Suspicious Relations and Sudden Riches", 20 March 2014, BBC Monitoring; Tariq Tell, "Early Spring in Jordan: The Revolt of the Military Veterans", Carnegie Middle East Center, 4 November 2015.

23. Bligh, "The Jordanian Army", p. 151; *Jordan Times*, "Jordan military committed to defending all Arab causes—King", 2 November 2014, available at http://www.jordantimes.com/news/local/jordan-military-committed-defending-all-arab-causes-%E2%80%94-king#sthash.RczSoPVg.dpuf

24. Gordon H. Torrey, *Syrian Politics and the Military, 1945–1958* (Lincoln: Ohio State University Press, 1964), p. 121.

25. Patrick Seale, *Asad of Syria: The Struggle for the Middle East* (Los Angeles: University of California Press, 1988), pp. 58–68.

26. Kenneth M. Pollack, *Arabs at War: Military Effectiveness, 1948–1991* (Lincoln: University of Nebraska Press, 2002), p. 457.

27. Torrey, *Syrian Politics and the Military*, p. 247.

28. Hanna Batatu, "Some Observations on the Social Roots of Syria's Ruling, Military Group and the Causes for Its Dominance", *Middle East Journal*, Vol. 35, No. 3 (Summer 1981), p. 343.

29. Alasdair Drysdale, "Ethnicity in the Syrian Officer Corps: A Conceptualisation", *Civilisations*, Vol. 29, Nos. 3/4 (1979).

30. Hicham Bou Nassif, "'Second-Class': The Grievances of Sunni Officers in the Syrian Armed Forces", *Journal of Strategic Studies*, Vol. 38, No. 5, pp. 626–49.

31. Dorothy Ohl et al., "For Money or Liberty? The political economy of military desertion and rebel recruitment in the Syrian civil war", Carnegie Middle East Center, 24 November 2015.

32. Amos Perlmutter, "From Obscurity to Rule: The Syrian Army and the Ba'th Party", *Western Political Quarterly*, Vol. 22, No. 4 (December 1969), pp. 827–45.

33. Pollack, *Arabs at War*, pp. 479–80.

34. Kheder Khaddour, "Strength in Weakness: The Syrian Army's Accidental Resilience", Carnegie Middle East Center, 14 March 2016; Kheder Khaddour, "Assad's Officer Ghetto: Why the Syrian Army Remains Loyal", Carnegie Middle East Center, 4 November 2015.

35. Eyal Zisser, "The Syrian Army: Between the Domestic and the External Fronts", *Middle East Review of International Affairs Journal*, Vol. 5, No. 1 (March 2001).

36. *The Economist*, "Cracks in the army: Defections from Bashar Assad's armed forces are growing", 29 October 2011.

37. *Al-Hayat*, "Syrian opposition ponders appealing to army officers to remove al-Asad", 4 September 2013, BBC Monitoring; *Elaph*, "Syrian dissident urges army to overthrow al-Asad", 5 September 2013, BBC Monitoring.

38. *Daily Star*, "Assad: Syrian army fatigued but will prevail", 27 July 2015; Institute for the Study of War, "The Regime's Military Capabilities: Part 1", 26 May 2015, available at http://iswresearch.blogspot.fr/2015/05/the-regime-military-capabilities-part-1.html

39. *Middle East Eye*, "Syria to raise army salaries to fight 'economic migration'", 7 October 2015, available at http://www.middleeasteye.net/news/syria-raise-army-salaries-fight-economic-migration-65331448

40. BBC Monitoring, "Syrian President condemns West, vows to survive protests", 11 January 2012; BBC Monitoring, "We will engage in dialogue—Syria's al-Asad", 6 January 2013; BBC Monitoring, "Syria's Al-Asad salutes army for 'heroism, sacrifice', says confident of victory", 1 August 2013; BBC Monitoring, "Syrian leader gives speech on war, terrorism, role of West and media—full text", 27 July 2015.

41. *The New Arab*, "Syria Army conscription and poor conditions stir anger", 11 November 2015, available at https://www.alaraby.co.uk/english/news/2015/11/13/syria-army-conscription-and-poor-conditions-stir-anger

42. Institute for the Study of War, "The Regime's Military Capabilities: Part 1", 26 May 2015, available at http://iswresearch.blogspot.fr/2015/05/the-regime-military-capabilities-part-1.html

43. *Al-Monitor*, "CIA Director Brennan says Syria army remains resilient", 11 March 2014, available at http://www.al-monitor.com/pulse/originals/2014/03/cia-director-john-brennan-assesses-saudi-arabia-syria-iran.html

44. Stephanie Cronin, "Tribes, Coups and Princes: Building a Modern Army in Saudi Arabia", *Middle Eastern Studies*, Vol. 49, No. 1 (Jan. 2013), pp. 2–28.

45. Nadav Safran, *Saudi Arabia: The Ceaseless Quest for Security* (Cambridge, MA: Belknap Press, 1985), pp. 59–71, 70, 108.

46. Ibid., p. 105.
47. Ibid., p. 94.
48. Ibid., p. 195.
49. Joseph A. Kechichian, *Succession in Saudi Arabia* (New York: Palgrave, 2001), pp. 102–6.
50. Pollack, *Arabs at War*, p. 427.
51. Ibid., p. 434.
52. *Alarabiya*, "Saudi pilot who made history by downing two fighters in 30 secs", 30 March 2015, available at http://english.alarabiya.net/en/perspective/features/2015/03/30/Saudi-pilot-who-made-history-by-downing-two-fighters-in-30-secs-.html
53. Quoted in Joseph A. Kechichian, *Succession in Saudi Arabia* (New York: Palgrave, 2001), p. 105.
54. Bernard Haykel, Thomas Hegghammer, Stéphane Lacroix (eds), *Saudi Arabia in Transition: Insights on Social, Political, Economic and Religious Change* (New York: Cambridge University Press, 2015), p. 107.
55. *Guardian*, "Saudi pilots receive online death threats after air strikes on Isis", 24 September 2014, available at http://www.theguardian.com/world/2014/sep/24/saudi-pilots-online-death-threats-twitter-air-strikes-isis
56. Safran, *Saudi Arabia*, p. 130.
57. *Alarabiya*, "Saudi's decision to send troops in Syria 'final'", 11 January 2016, available at http://english.alarabiya.net/en/News/middle-east/2016/02/11/Spokesman-Saudi-decision-to-send-troops-in-Syria-is-final.html
58. Pollack, *Arabs at War*, p. 431.
59. *Arab News*, "Conscription call by grand mufti finds strong support from intellectuals", 17 April 2015, available at http://www.arabnews.com/featured/news/733766; *Arabian Business*, "Saudi rules out imminent military conscription", 14 August 2014, available at http://www.arabianbusiness.com/saudi-rules-out-imminent-military-conscription-561278.html#.VzsOG0akxJg; Safran, *Saudi Arabia*, p. 439.
60. Samuel Huntington, *Political Order in Changing Societies* (New Haven: Yale University Press, 1968), p. 232.
61. Ibid., pp. 223–4.
62. Mark N. Cooper, "The Demilitarisation of the Egyptian Cabinet", *International Journal of Middle East Studies*, Vol. 14 (1982).
63. Risa A. Brooks, "Explaining Egypt's Military Effectiveness, 1967 and 1973", *Security Studies*, No. 3 (July–Sept. 2006), p. 421.
64. Risa A. Brooks, *Shaping Strategy: the civil–military politics of strategic assessment* (Princeton University Press, 2008), pp. 101–42; George W. Gawrych, "The Egyptian High Command in the 1973 War", *Armed Forces and Society*, Vol. 13, No. 4 (Summer 1987), pp. 535–59.

65. Pollack, *Arabs at War*, p. 147.

66. *Defense News*, "Egypt Military Winds Down Sinai Campaign Against IS", 23 September 2015, available at http://www.defensenews.com/story/defense/international/mideast-africa/2015/09/23/egypt-military-winds-sinai-campaign/72689540/

67. *New York Times*, "Egypt Stability Hinges on a Divided Military", 5 February 2011; *New York Times*, "Succession Gives Army a Stiff Test in Egypt", 11 September, 2010, available at http://www.nytimes.com/2010/09/12/world/middleeast/12egypt.html?_r=0; *Aljazeera*, "Army 'could block' Egypt succession", 15 December 2010, available at http://www.aljazeera.com/news/middleeast/2010/12/201012158103985404.html; Stephan Roll, "The Military and the Muslim Brotherhood: Will a Power-sharing Agreement Be Reached in Egypt?" SWP Comments 2012/C 04, February 2012, available at http://www.swp-berlin.org/en/publications/swp-comments-en/swp-aktuelle-details/article/egypt_military_and_muslim_brotherhood.html

68. Hicham Bou Nassif, "Wedded to Mubarak: The Second Careers and Financial Rewards of Egypt's Military Elite, 1981–2011", *Middle East Journal*, Vol. 67, No. 4 (Autumn 2013), p. 516.

69. *Hürriyet Daily News*, "Egypt promotes junior corps impatient over military failure", 15 August 2012, available at http://www.hurriyetdailynews.com/egypt-promotes-junior-corps-impatient-over-military-failure.aspx?pageID=238&nID=27820&NewsCatID=352

70. Ahram Online, "Egypt army officers granted arrest powers until 15 December", 9 December 2012, available at http://english.ahram.org.eg/NewsContent/1/64/60159/Egypt/Politics-/Egypt-army-officers-granted-arrest-powers-until-D.aspx

71. Zeinab Abul-Magd, "The Military", in Emile Hokayem (ed.), *Egypt After the Spring: Revolt and Reaction* (London: International Institute for Strategic Studies, 2016), p. 61.

72. *BBC News*, "Egypt: Army warns it will not allow 'dark tunnel'", 8 December 2012, available at http://www.bbc.com/news/world-middle-east-20651896

73. *Guardian*, "Egypt 'suffering worst economic crisis since 1930s'", 16 May 2013, available at http://www.theguardian.com/world/2013/may/16/egypt-worst-economic-crisis-1930s; *Al-Monitor*, "Egyptian Army Considered Economic Stakes in Coup", 10 July 2013, available at http://www.al-monitor.com/pulse/politics/2013/07/egypt-army-economic-interests-coup-morsi.html

74. Zeinab Abul-Magd, "The Military", p. 63.

75. *Al-Rai al-Aam*, "Morsi promised Washington to decrease army forces, establish military base", 24 October 2013.

76. *New York Times*, "Recordings Suggest Emirates and Egyptian Military Pushed Ousting of Morsi", 1 March 2015, available at http://www.nytimes.com/2015/03/02/world/middleeast/recordings-suggest-emirates-and-egyptian-military-pushed-ousting-of-morsi.html?_r=0

77. *Channel 1 TV*, "Egyptian defence minister says army is united", 24 July 2013, BBC Monitoring.

78. Zeinab Abul-Magd, "The Military", p. 64.

79. Philippe Droz-Vincent, "Le militaire et le politique en Egypte", *Monde arabe, Maghreb Machrek*, No. 165 (July/Sept. 1999), p. 18.

80. *Nile News TV*, "Egyptian Armed Force will not be part of political scene, ruling", 1 July 2013, BBC Monitoring; *Ahram Online*, "Egypt's military vote to be postponed to 2020", 9 June 2013, available at http://english.ahram.org.eg/NewsContent/1/64/73581/Egypt/Politics-/Egypts-military-vote-to-be-postponed-to-.aspx

81. *MENA News Agency*, "Egypt's Sisi decides that army help police in protecting facilities", 27 October 2014, BBC Monitoring.

82. *MENA News Agency*, "Egyptian Armed Forces open centre for monitoring media coverage of referendum", 14 January 2014, BBC Monitoring.

83. *Ahram Online*, "Military officer takes charge as first secretary-general of Egypt's parliament", 18 October 2014, available at http://english.ahram.org.eg/NewsContent/1/64/113379/Egypt/Politics-/Military-officer-takes-charge-as-first-secretaryge.aspx; *Gulf News*, "Ex-military raises profile in new Egypt parliament", 6 December 2015, available at http://gulfnews.com/news/mena/egypt/ex-military-raises-profile-in-new-egypt-parliament-1.1632584

84. Zeinab Abdul-Magd, "Egypt's adaptable officers: power, business, and discontent", ISPI Analysis No. 265, July 2014.

85. *Ahram Online*, "Who's Who in Egypt's New Cabinet", 19 September 2015, available at http://english.ahram.org.eg/NewsContent/1/64/141883/Egypt/Politics-/Whos-Who-in-Egypts-New-Cabinet.aspx

86. *Middle East Eye*, "Egypt to dismiss preachers who criticise army or police during Eid sermons", 16 July 2015, available at http://www.middleeasteye.net/news/egypt-dismiss-preachers-who-criticise-police-or-army-during-eid-sermons-21761084; *MENA News Agency*, "Egyptian university to 'sack' students over 'insulting' army", 27 October 2014, BBC Monitoring; *MENA News Agency*, "Egypt's police pursue Brotherhood member for creating anti-army Facebook page", 5 February 2015, BBC Monitoring; *MENA News Agency*, "Egyptian police arrest Facebook admin for instigating against army", 7 April 2014, BBC Monitoring; *Ahram Online*, "Egyptian TV host suspended as network slams content 'demotivating the army'", 26 October 2014, available at http://english.ahram.org.eg/News/114009.aspx; *Guardian*, "Egypt

imposes anti-terror law that punishes 'false' reporting of attacks", 17 August 2015, available at http://www.theguardian.com/world/2015/aug/17/egyptian-president-ratifies-law-to-punish-false-reporting-of-terror-attacks; *MENA News Agency*, "Egypt Armed Forces warns against publishing 'memoirs' of ex-military officials", 28 September 2013, BBC Monitoring.

87. Shana Marshall, "The Egyptian Armed Forces and the remaking of an economic empire", 15 April 2015, Carnegie Middle East Center, available at http://carnegie-mec.org/2015/04/15/egyptian-armed-forces-and-remaking-of-economic-empire

88. *MENA News Agency*, "Egyptian President opens upgraded Armed Forces factories", 14 May 2015, BBC Monitoring; *MENA News Agency*, "Egypt's Sisi assigns army with evacuating lands of new capital", 19 March 2015, BBC Monitoring; *MENA News Agency*, "Egypt's Sisi says Armed Forces projects provide job opportunities for civilians", 4 December 2014, BBC Monitoring; *Middle East Monitor*, "Egyptian military expands control over economy", 26 January 2015, available at https://www.middleeastmonitor.com/20150126-egyptian-military-expands-control-over-economy/

89. *MENA News Agency*, "Egyptian army operates buses to cope with uncontrolled rise in transport fare", 7 July 2014, BBC Monitoring.

90. *Mada Masr*, "The Armed Forces and Egypt's Land", 27 April 2016, available at http://www.madamasr.com/sections/economy/armed-forces-and-egypts-land; *Al-Monitor*, "Will Egyptian parliament cut into the military's profit margin?", 1 April 2016, available at http://www.al-monitor.com/pulse/originals/2016/03/egypt-military-economic-empire-sisi-parliament-limit.html

91. *Al-Ahram Weekly*, "Military Inc.?", 31 December 2014, available at http://weekly.ahram.org.eg/News/10053/18/Military-Inc-.aspx; MENA News Agency, "Egypt's news agency lists national projects implemented by army", 10 June 2015, BBC Monitoring; *Mada Masr*, "Companies clash with military over ad rights", 19 October 2015, available at http://www.madamasr.com/sections/politics/companies-clash-military-over-ad-rights; Amr Adly, "The Military Economy and the Future of the Private Sector in Egypt", Carnegie Middle East Center, 6 September, 2014, available at http://carnegie-mec.org/2014/09/06/military-economy-and-future-of-private-sector-in-egypt/ho7x; *Egypt Independent*, "Army will control 60% of Egypt's national entity for telecommunications", 11 May 2015, available at http://www.egyptindependent.com/news/newspaper-army-will-control-60-egypt-s-national-entity-telecommunications; *Al-Masry al-Youm*, "Defense Minister exempts 574 military installations from real estate

tax", 3 June 2015, available at http://www.marsad.eg/2015/06/03/defense-minister-exempts-574-military-installations-from-real-estate-tax/; *MENA News Agency*, "Army combats monopoly in Egyptian markets", 29 August 2014, BBC Monitoring; *MENA News Agency*, "Egyptian army takes part in reducing food prices", 6 December 2015, BBC Monitoring.

92. Ahmed Morsy, "The Military Crowds Out Civilian Business in Egypt", 24 June 2014, Carnegie Endowment for International Peace, available at http://carnegieendowment.org/2014/06/24/military-crowds-out-civilian-business-in-egypt

93. *MENA News Agency*, "Egyptian court refuses to force Sisi to run for president", 29 December 2013, BBC Monitoring; *MENA News Agency*, "Army commanders approve Egyptians' will to name Al-Sisi for president", 11 January 2014, BBC Monitoring; *MENA News Agency*, "Egypt's Sisi supports print book named *Best soldiers on earth*", 10 February 2014, BBC Monitoring.

94. *MENA News Agency*, "Egypt's Sisi orders army to end road construction by 6 Aug", 7 June 2015, BBC Monitoring; *MENA News Agency*, "Egypt's Sisi oders army to revamp Heart Institute in month", 7 June 2015, BBC Monitoring; *Daily News Egypt*, "Al-Sisi inaugurates housing, infrastructure projects across Egypt", 6 February 2016, available at http://www.dailynewsegypt.com/2016/02/06/al-sisi-inaugurates-housing-infrastructure-projects-across-egypt/

95. *Al-Monitor*, "Sisi dusts off uniform for Sinai visit", 5 August 2015, available at http://www.al-monitor.com/pulse/originals/2015/08/egypt-sisi-military-uniform-visit-north-sinai.html

96. *Daily News Egypt*, "Cabinet ministers must start work at 7am: Mehleb", 17 June, 2014, available at http://www.dailynewsegypt.com/2014/06/17/cabinet-ministers-must-start-work-7am-mehleb/. *Aljazeera*, "Sisi tells Egyptians: Don't listen to anyone but me", 24 February 2016, available at http://www.aljazeera.com/news/2016/02/sisi-tells-egyptians-don-listen-160224181547015.html; *Daily News Egypt*, "Al-Sisi urges Egyptians to cycle", 13 June 2014, available at http://www.dailynewsegypt.com/2014/06/13/al-sisi-urges-egyptians-cycle/

97. *Arab Contractors*, "President Sisi Inaugurated Marshal Hussein Tantawi Mosque in the Fifth Settlement", 9 March 2015, available at http://www.arabcont.com/English/News/Release-2015–971%20.aspx; *Daily News Egypt*, "Name change angers activists", 10 November 2012, available at http://www.dailynewsegypt.com/2012/11/10/name-change-angers-activists/

98. *MENA News Agency*, "Egypt's Cairo governor names schools after army, police 'martyrs'", 19 January 2014, BBC Monitoring.

99. *New York Times*, "Egypt Launches Airstrike in Libya Against ISIS Branch", 26 February 2015, available at http://www.nytimes.com/2015/02/17/world/middleeast/isis-egypt-libya-airstrikes.html?_r=0

100. *Foreign Policy*, "How to get Egypt's Generals Back on Our Side", 5 January 2015, available at http://foreignpolicy.com/2015/01/05/how-to-get-egypts-generals-back-on-our-side-sisi-military-us-foreign-policy/

101. *Defense News*, "Egypt, France To Sign Arms Deal Mid-April", 6 April 2016, available at http://www.defensenews.com/story/defense/policy-budget/industry/2016/04/06/egypt-france-fighter-jet-frigate-satellite/82695674/; *Defense Industry Daily*, "All Over Again: Egypt Looks Beyond the USA for New Arms", 7 April 2016, http://www.defenseindustrydaily.com/all-over-again-egypt-looks-beyond-the-usa-for-new-arms-019091/; *MENA News Agency*, "Egyptian leader issues decree to give exceptional pension to former soldiers", 16 October 2014, BBC Monitoring.

102. *Middle East Eye*, "Egypt hunts former army officer over assassination of prosecutor general", 3 July 2015, available at http://www.middleeasteye.net/news/egypt-hunts-former-army-officer-over-assassination-prosecutor-general-513631553

103. *Middle East Eye*, "Sami Anan: Former chief of staff with ambition to replace Egypt's Sisi", 1 December 2015, available at http://www.middleeasteye.net/news/profile-egypts-former-army-chief-staff-sami-anan-publishing-tbc-431751869; *Middle East Eye*, "Observers point toward discord in Sisi's visit to Sinai barracks", 8 July 2015, available at http://www.middleeasteye.net/news/observers-point-toward-disaccord-sisis-visit-sinais-military-barracks-1464347557

104. William B. Quandt, "Algerian Military Development: The Professionalization of a Guerrilla Army", March 1972, RAND Corporation, available at http://www.rand.org/pubs/papers/P4792.html; François Gèze, "Armée et nation en Algérie: l'irrémédiable divorce?", *Hérodote*, No. 1 (2005), pp. 175–203.

105. José Garçon and Pierre Affuzi, "L'armée algérienne: le pouvoir de l'ombre », *Pouvoirs*, No. 86 (1998), pp. 45–56.

106. Habib Souaidia, *La Sale Guerre: Le témoignage d'un ancien officier des forces spéciales de l'armée algérienne, 1992—2000* (Paris: La Découverte, 2001).

107. Luis Martinez, *The Algerian Civil War, 1990–1998* (London: Hurst & Co., 2000), pp. 84–5.

108. Steven A. Cook, *Ruling but not Governing: The Military and Political Development in Egypt, Algeria, and Turkey* (Baltimore, MD: Johns Hopkins University Press, 2007), pp. 42–62.

109. Quoted in Cook, *Ruling but not Governing*, p. 52.

110. Ibid., p. 53.
111. Ibid., p. 53.
112. Souaïdia, *La Sale Guerre*, pp. 54–6.
113. *Al-Quds al-Arabi*, "Algeria: New dismissals of officers and judges", 23 September 2015; *Echourouk El Youmi*, "Algerian former counter-terrorism chief charged with breaching military rules", 1 October 2015, BBC Monitoring; *Aljazeera TV Arabic*, "Algerian army chief of staff is reportedly set to force 74 generals to retire", 8 June 2014, BBC Monitoring.
114. *Eshourouk El Youmi*, "Algerian president dismisses senior officers in military expenditure control", 21 September 2014, BBC Monitoring.
115. *El-Khabar*, "…changes in the army will be met with resistance, attempts to oppose…", 14 October 2015.
116. *L'Expression*, "Algeria's chief of staff reiterates army's refusal to engage in politics", 25 June 2014, BBC Monitoring; *El-Khabar*, "Algerian opposition parties form alliance, urge army to be neutral", 18 April 2013, BBC Monitoring; *El-Khabar*, "Algerian opposition not convinced of army neutrality regarding elections", 18 February 2014, BBC Monitoring.

## CONCLUSION: THE FOUR PRECONDITIONS OF COUPS, AND THEIR AFTERMATH

1. *BBC News*, "Bloodless coup in Libya", 1 September 1969, available at http://news.bbc.co.uk/onthisday/hi/dates/stories/september/1/newsid_3911000/3911587.stm; Gordon H. Torrey, *Syrian Politics and the Military, 1945–1958* (Lincoln: Ohio State University Press, 1964), p. 121.
2. *Ahram Online*, "Egypt military gives political forces 48 hours to resolve crisis", 1 July 2013, available at http://english.ahram.org.eg/NewsContent/1/64/75415/Egypt/Politics-/Egypt-military-gives-political-forces-hours-to-re.aspx
3. *Ahram Online*, "Egypt military unveils transitional roadmap", 3 July 2013, available at http://english.ahram.org.eg/News/75631.aspx
4. *International New York Times*, "Army Ousts Egypt's President; Morsi is Taken into Military Custody", 3 July 2013, available at http://www.nytimes.com/2013/07/04/world/middleeast/egypt.html?pagewanted=all&_r=0
5. Jonathan M. Powell and Clayton L. Thyne, "Global instances of coups from 1950 to 2010: A new dataset", *Journal of Peace Research*, Vol. 48, No. 2, (2011) p. 257.
6. Lant Pritchett and Frauke de Weijer, "Fragile States: Stuck in a Capability Trap?", World Development Report 2011, Background Paper, October 2011, p. 11.

# BIBLIOGRAPHY

Abbas, A., "The Iraqi Armed Forces, Past and Present", in Committee Against Repression and for Democratic Rights in Iraq (CARDRI) (ed.), *Saddam's Iraq: Revolution or Reaction?* (London: Zed Books, 1989).

Abdallah, Najah, "L'image de l'armée libanaise à travers de la presse quotidienne au Liban en 1984", PhD dissertation, University Michel de Montaigne, Bordeaux III, 1992.

Abul-Magd, Zeinab, "Egypt's adaptable officers: power, business, and discontent", *ISPI Analysis*, No. 265, July 2014.

———, "The Military", in Emile Hokayem (ed.), *Egypt After the Spring: Revolt and Reaction* (London: International Institute for Strategic Studies, 2016).

———, "Understanding SCAF", *Cairo Review of Global Affairs*, 30 June 2012, http://www.aucegypt.edu/gapp/cairoreview/pages/articleDetails. aspx?aid=216, last accessed 21 July 2016.

Adams Schmidt, Dana, *Armageddon in the Middle East* (New York: John Day Company, 1974).

Adel Beshara, *Lebanon: The Politics of Frustration—The Failed Coup of 1961* (London: Routledge, 2005).

*Aden al-Ghad*, "Yemeni colonel calls for forming of new southern army", 4 August 2015, BBC Monitoring.

Adly, Amr, "The Military Economy and the Future of the Private Sector in Egypt", Carnegie Middle East Center, 6 September 2014, http://carnegie-mec.org/2014/09/06/military-economy-and-future-of-private-sector-in-egypt/ho7x, last accessed 21 July 2016.

*Agence France Presse*, "Libya to integrate 50,000 anti-Kadhafi fighters", 1 December 2011, http://www.google.com/hostednews/afp/article/ ALeqM5hIWIuNlAOLc-Sh8JQJt1MnkCJzBQ?docId=CNG.104a1c9e9c7 1e179b33042a465c95d6c.831, last accessed 21 July 2016.

———, "New Chief for Libya's revamped national army", 17 November

2011, http://www.google.com/hostednews/afp/article/ALeqM5i2GtU w73moWubwhdFPXQ-ZouMDzg?docId=CNG.a3f2fe1bf5dd-f5725a77594ecefbea23.211, last accessed 21 July 2016.

Ahmed Abdalla, "The Armed Forces and the Democratic Process in Egypt", *ThirdWorld Quarterly*, Vol. 10, No. 4, 1988.

Ahmed Hashim, "Saddam Husayn and Civil-Military Relations in Iraq: The Quest for Legitimacy and Power", *Middle East Journal*, Vol. 57, No. 1, 2003.

Ahmed Morsy, "The Military Crowds Out Civilian Business in Egypt", 24 June 2014, Carnegie Endowment for International Peace, http://carnegieendowment.org/2014/06/24/military-crowds-out-civilian-business-in-egypt, last accessed 21 July 2016.

*Ahram Online*, "Egypt's armed forces advised Morsi to be inclusive: Defence Minister El-Sisi", 7 October 2013, http://english.ahram.org.eg/News Content/1/64/83454/Egypt/Politics-/Egypts-armed-forces-advised-Morsi-to-be-inclusive-.aspx, last accessed 21 July 2016.

———, "Egypt army officers granted arrest powers until 15 December", 9 December 2012, http://english.ahram.org.eg/NewsContent/1/64/60159/Egypt/Politics-/Egypt-army-officers-granted-arrest-powers-until-D.aspx, last accessed 21 July 2016.

———, "Egypt military budget allocations to reach LE31 bn in 2013/14: Source", 29 May 2013, http://english.ahram.org.eg/NewsContent/3/0/72493/Business/0/-Egypt-military-budget-allocations-to-reach-LE-bn-.aspx, last accessed 21 July 2016.

———, "Egypt military gives political forces 48 hours to resolve crisis", 1 July 2013, http://english.ahram.org.eg/NewsContent/1/64/75415/Egypt/Politics-/Egypt-military-gives-political-forces-hours-to-re.aspx, last accessed 21 July 2016.

———, "Egypt military unveils transitional roadmap", 3 July 2013, http://english.ahram.org.eg/News/75631.aspx, last accessed 21 July 2016.

———, "Egypt's military vote to be postponed to 2020", 9 June 2013, http://english.ahram.org.eg/NewsContent/1/64/73581/Egypt/Politics-/Egypts-military-vote-to-be-postponed-to-.aspx, last accessed 21 July 2016.

———, "EgyptianTV host suspended as network slams content 'demotivating the army'", 26 October 2014, http://english.ahram.org.eg/News/114009.aspx, last accessed 21 July 2016.

———, "Military Officer takes charge as first secretary-general of Egypt's parliament", 18 October 2014, http://english.ahram.org.eg/News Content/1/64/113379/Egypt/Politics-/Military-officer-takes-charge-as-first-secretaryge.aspx, last accessed 21 July 2016.

———, "Who's Who in Egypt's New Cabinet", 19 September 2015, http://english.ahram.org.eg/NewsContent/1/64/141883/Egypt/Politics-/Whos-Who-in-Egypts-New-Cabinet.aspx last accessed, 21 July 2016.

*Al-Ahram Weekly*, "Military Inc.?", 31 December 2014, http://weekly.ahram. org.eg/News/10053/18/Military-Inc-.aspx, last accessed 21 July 2016.

*Al-Akhbar*, "Lebanese Budget Skimps on Overloaded Army", 10 July 2013, http://english.al-akhbar.com/node/16385, last accessed 21 July 2016.

*Alarabiya*, "Saudi pilot who made history by downing two fighters in 30 secs", 30 March 2015, http://english.alarabiya.net/en/perspective/features/ 2015/03/30/Saudi-pilot-who-made-history-by-downing-two-fighters-in-30-secs-.html, last accessed 21 July 2016.

————, "Saudi's decision to send troops in Syria 'final'", 11 January 2016, http://english.alarabiya.net/en/News/middle-east/2016/02/ 11/Spokesman-Saudi-decision-to-send-troops-in-Syria-is-final.html, last accessed 21 July 2016.

*Alarabiya News*, "Warfalla, Libya's largest tribe", 1 September 2011, http:// www.alarabiya.net/articles/2011/09/01/164993.html, last accessed 21 July 2016.

*Al-Arabiya TV*, "Libyan air defence, Interior Ministry declare support for Haftar", 20 May 2014, BBC Monitoring.

Albrecht, Holger, "Does Coup-Proofing Work? Political–Military Relations in Authoritarian Regimes amid the Arab Uprisings", *Mediterranean Politics*, Vol. 20, No. 1, 2015.

*Al-Defaiya*, "Two Libyan Rebel Groups Reject Chief-of-Staff Nomination", 6 January 2012, http://www.defaiya.com/defaiyaonline/index.php? option=com_contentandview=articleandid=2672%3Atwo-libyan-rebel-groups-reject-chief-of-staff-nominationandcatid=78%3AlibyaandItemid= 27andlang=en, last accessed 21 July 2016.

*Al-Hayat*, "Syrian opposition ponders appealing to army officers to remove al-Asad", 4 September 2013, BBC Monitoring.

*Aljazeera America*, "Veterans not surprised Iraq's Army collapsed", 28 June 2014, http://america.aljazeera.com/watch/shows/america-tonight/ articles/2014/6/28/how-did-iraq-s-armycollapsesoquickly.html, last accessed 21 July 2016.

*Al Jazeera TV*, "Libya's new army chief says building of military obstructed by squabbling", 24 June 2013, BBC Monitoring.

————, "Tunisian Defence Ministry says army to recruit thousands of jobless youths", 4 March 2016, BBC Monitoring.

*Al Jazeera TV Arabic*, "Algerian army chief of staff is reportedly set to force 74 generals to retire", 8 June 2014, BBC Monitoring.

*Aljazeera*, "Army 'could block' Egypt succession", 15 December 2010, http:// www.aljazeera.com/news/middleeast/2010/12/2010121581 03985404.html, last accessed 21 July 2016.

————, "Background: SCAF's last-minute power grab", 18 June 2012, http://www.aljazeera.com/indepth/spotlight/egypt/2012/06/2012618 12449990250.html, last accessed 21 July 2016.

————, "Libyan parliament 'split' over government, military spending, Al Jazeera says", 24 August 2015, BBC Monitoring.

————, "Sisi tells Egyptians: Don't listen to anyone but me", 24 February 2016, http://www.aljazeera.com/news/2016/02/sisi-tells-egyptians-don-listen-160224181547015.html.

————, "Transcript: Egypt's army statement", 3 July 2013, http://www.aljazeera.com/news/middleeast/2013/07/201373203740167797.html, last accessed 21 July 2016.

Al-Marashi, Ibrahim and Sammy Salama, *Iraq's Armed Forces: An Analytical History* (London: Routledge, 2008).

*Al-Masry al-Youm*, "Defense Minister exempts 574 military installations from real estate tax", 3 June 2015, http://www.marsad.eg/2015/06/03/defense-minister-exempts-574-military-installations-from-real-estate-tax/, last accessed 21 July 2016.

*Al-Monitor*, "CIA Director Brennan says Syria army remains resilient", 11 March 2014, http://www.al-monitor.com/pulse/originals/2014/03/cia-director-john-brennan-assesses-saudi-arabia-syria-iran.html, last accessed 21 July 2016.

————, "Egyptian Army Considered Economic Stakes in Coup", 10 July 2013, http://www.al-monitor.com/pulse/politics/2013/07/egypt-army-economic-interests-coup-morsi.html, last accessed 21 July 2016.

————, "Jordan's king pushes to expand military, intelligence authority", 25 August 2014, http://www.al-monitor.com/pulse/originals/2014/08/jordan-king-constitution-amendments.html#ixzz48LltS0Zq, last accessed 21 July 2016.

————, "Sisi dusts off uniform for Sinai visit", 5 August 2015, http://www.al-monitor.com/pulse/originals/2015/08/egypt-sisi-military-uniform-visit-north-sinai.html, last accessed 21 July 2016.

————, "Was Morsi's Ouster a Coup or New Egyptian Revolution?", 4 July 2013, http://www.al-monitor.com/pulse/originals/2013/07/was-morsi-ouster-a-coup-or-new-egyptian-revolution.html#ixzz3I0STko00, last accessed 21 July 2016.

————, "Will Egyptian parliament cut into the military's profit margin?", 1 April 2016, http://www.al-monitor.com/pulse/originals/2016/03/egypt-military-economic-empire-sisi-parliament-limit.html, last accessed 21 July 2016.

*Al-Quds al-Arabi*, "Algeria: New dismissals of officers and judges", 23 September 2015.

*Al-Ra'y*, "Military retirees: Suspicious Relations and Sudden Riches", 20 March 2014, BBC Monitoring.

*Al-Rai al-Aam*, "Morsi promised Washington to decrease army forces, establish military base", 24 October 2013.

# BIBLIOGRAPHY

*Al-Sharq al-Awsat*, "Former Libyan defence minister says 'army must be under civilian authority'", 7 October 2015, BBC Monitoring.

*Al-Shorfa*, "Qatari government workers and military personnel receive salary increases", 15 September 2011, http://al-shorfa.com/en_GB/articles/meii/features/main/2011/09/15/feature-02, last accessed 21 July 2016.

*Al-Wasat*, "Yemeni military official allegedly starts establishment of new army", 21 May 2015, BBC Monitoring.

Amnesty International, "Lebanon: Security forces using excessive force against protestors must be held to account", 29 August 2015, https://www.amnesty.org/en/latest/news/2015/08/lebanon-security-forces-using-excessive-force-against-protestors-must-be-held-to-account/, last accessed 21 July 2016.

Amnesty International, "The Battle for Libya: Killings, Disappearances and Torture", London 2011, http://www.amnesty.org/en/library/info/MDE19/025/2011/en, last accessed 21 July 2016.

Arab Center for Research and Policy Studies, "The Arab Opinion Index 2011", http://english.dohainstitute.org/release/5083cf8e-38f8-4e4a-8bc5-fc91660608b0, last accessed 21 July 2016.

Arab Contractors, "President Sisi Inaugurated Marshal Hussein Tantawi Mosque in the Fifth Settlement", 9 March 2015, http://www.arabcont.com/English/News/Release-2015-971%20.aspx, last accessed 21 July 2016.

*The Arabist*, "Sisi's speech to the army, and Morsi", 15 July 2013, http://arabist.net/blog/2013/7/15/sisis-speech-to-the-army-and-morsi, last accessed 21 July 2016.

*Arab News*, "Conscription call by grand mufti finds strong support from intellectuals", 17 April 2015, http://www.arabnews.com/featured/news/733766, last accessed 21 July 2016.

————, "Lebanese Army seals Parliament after Syria-linked demonstrations", 22 June 2013, http://www.arabnews.com/news/455765, last accessed 21 July 2016.

*Arabian Business*, "Saudi rules out imminent military conscription", 14 August 2014, http://www.arabianbusiness.com/saudi-rules-out-imminent-military-conscription-561278.html#.Vzs0G0akxJg, last accessed 21 July 2016.

————, "UAE monthly household income revealed", 3 February 2009, http://www.arabianbusiness.com/uae-monthly-household-income-revealed-80418.html, last accessed 21 July 2016.

*ArabianBusiness.com*, "Saudi Arabia to raise wages for most military", 31 August 2010, http://www.arabianbusiness.com/saudi-arabia-raise-wages-for-most-military-345848.html, last accessed 21 July 2016.

*Asharq Al-Awsat*, "Hadi, Salih and the Huthis Share Army Capabilities", 20 March 2015, BBC Monitoring.

————, "Yemeni army leaders to reform military after takeover of Aden from pro-Huthis", 4 August 2015, BBC Monitoring.

*Associated Press*, "Mauritania army stages coup; junta takes charge", 6 August 2008, http://web.archive.org/web/20080812110822/http://ap.google.com/article/ALeqM5hmqqO8XJixmimcunkNvDYctnppTgD92CQJ180, last accessed 21 July 2016.

*The Australian*, "Gaddafi's Libyan Army collapsing, say defectors", 5 June 2011, http://www.theaustralian.com.au/news/world/gaddafis-libyan-army-collapsing-say-defectors/story-e6frg6so-1226069500257, last accessed 21 July 2016.

Azar, Fabiola and Etienne Mullet, "Muslims and Christians in Lebanon: Common Views on Political Issues", *Journal of Peace Research*, Vol. 39, No. 6, 2002.

Baaklini, Abdo I., "Civilian Control of the Military in Lebanon: A Legislative Perspective", in Claude Welch (ed.), *Civilian Control of the Military: Theory and Cases from Developing Countries* (Albany, NY: State University of New York Press, 1976).

*Babnet Tunisie*, "Tunisie: L'association d'anciens militaires dénonce l'exploitation médiatique de la souffrance des familles des victimes du terrorisme", 7 June 2013, http://www.babnet.net/cadredetail-66419.asp, last accessed 21 July 2016.

Bache, William, "Transferring American Military Values to Iraq", *Middle East Review of International Affairs*, Vol. 11, No. 3, 2007.

Barak, Oren, "Commemorating Malikiyya: Political Myth, Multiethnic Identity and the Making of the Lebanese Army", *History and Memory*, Vol. 13, No. 1, 2001.

————, "Towards a Representative Military? The Transformation of the Lebanese Officer Corps", *Middle East Journal*, Vol. 60, No. 1, 2006.

————, *The Lebanese Army: a National Institution in a Divided Society* (Albany, NY: SUNY Press, 2009).

Bartov, Omer, *Hitler's Army: Soldiers, Nazis and War in the Third Reich* (New York: Oxford University Press, 1991).

Batatu, Hanna, "Some Observations on the Social Roots of Syria's Ruling, Military Group and the Causes for its Dominance", *Middle East Journal*, Vol. 35, No. 3, 1981.

BBC Monitoring, "Saudi mufti urges compulsory military service of youths—pan-Arab daily report", Al-Quds al-Arabi, 11 April 2015.

————, "Saudi paper highlights benefits of military conscription, urges state to recruit", 11 February 2016, Al-Watan.

————, "Syria's Al-Asad salutes army for 'heroism, sacrifice', says confident of victory", 1 August 2013.

————, "Syrian leader gives speech on war, terrorism, role of West and media—full text", 27 July 2015.

———, "Syrian military, security forces to cast their votes 'for the first time'", 28 March 2016, Syrian State TV.

———, "Syrian President condemns West, vows to survive protests", 11 January 2012.

———, "We will engage in dialogue—Syria's al-Asad", 6 January 2013.

*BBC News*, "Bloodless coup in Libya", 1 September 1969, http://news.bbc.co.uk/onthisday/hi/dates/stories/september/1/newsid_3911000/3911587.stm, last accessed 21 July 2016.

———, "Egypt: Army warns it will not allow 'dark tunnel'", 8 December 2012, http://www.bbc.com/news/world-middle-east-20651896, last accessed 21 July 2016.

———, "Profile: Khamis Ghaddafi", 4 September 2011, http://www.bbc.co.uk/news/world-africa-14723041, last accessed 21 July 2016.

———, "Top Yemeni general, Ali Mohsen, backs opposition", 21 March 2011, http://www.bbc.com/news/world-middle-east-12804552, last accessed 21 July 2016.

Be'eri, Eliezer, "The Waning of the Military Coup in Arab Politics", *Middle Eastern Studies*, Vol. 18, No. 1, Jan. 1982.

———, *Army Officers in Arab Politics and Society* (New York: Praeger, 1970).

Beattie, Kirk J., "Egypt: Thirty-Five Years of Praetorian Politics", in Constantine Danopoulos (ed.), *Military Disengagement from Politics* (London: Routledge, 1988).

Beinin, Joel, *Workers and Peasants in the Modern Middle East* (New York: Cambridge University Press, 2001).

Belkin, Aaron and Evan Schofer, "Toward a Structural Understanding of Coup Risk", *Journal of Conflict Resolution*, Vol. 47, No. 5, Oct. 2003.

Ben-Dor, Gabriel, "Civilianization of Military Regimes in the Arab World", *Armed Forces and Society*, Vol. 1, No. 3, 1975.

Bin Muhammad, Ghazi, *The Tribes of Jordan at the at the Beginning of the Twenty-first Century* (Amman: Rutab, 1999).

Bligh, Alexander, "The Jordanian Army: Between Domestic and External Challenges", in Barry Rubin and Thomas A. Keaney (eds), *Armed Forces in the Middle East: politics and strategy* (Portland, OR: Frank Cass, 2002).

Bou Nassif, Hicham, "'Second-Class': The Grievances of Sunni Officers in the Syrian Armed Forces", *Journal of Strategic Studies*, Vol. 38, No. 5, 2015.

———, "Wedded to Mubarak: The Second Careers and Financial Rewards of Egypt's Military Elite, 1981–2011", *Middle East Journal*, Vol. 67, No. 4, 2013.

Bou-Nacklie, N. E., "*Les troupes spéciales*: religious and ethnic recruitment, 1916–1946", *International Journal for Middle East Studies*, Vol. 25, No. 4, 1993.

Bove, Vincenzo and Jennifer Brauner, "The Demand for Military Expenditure in Authoritarian Regimes", Birkbeck Working Papers in Economics and Finance, No. 1106, Oct. 2011.

Bove, Vincenzo and Roberto Nisticò, "Coups d'état and Defence Spending: a Counterfactual Analysis", Centre for Studies in Economics and Finance, Department of Economics, University of Naples, July 2014, http://www.csef.it/WP/wp366.pdf, last accessed 21 July 2016.

Boyne, Sean, "Lebanon rebuilds its army", *Jane's Intelligence Review*, Vol. 7, No. 3, 1995.

Bröckling, Ulrich and Michael Sikora (eds), *Armeen und ihre Deserteure. Vernachlässigte Kapitel einer Militärgeschichte der Neuzeit* (Göttingen: Vandenhoeck and Ruprecht, 1998).

Brooks, Risa A., "Abandoned at the Palace: Why the Tunisian Military Defected from the Ben Ali Regime in January 2011", *Journal of Strategic Studies*, Vol. 36, No. 2, 2013.

———, "An Autocracy at War: Explaining Egypt's Military Effectiveness, 1967 and 1973", *Security Studies*, Vol. 15, No. 3, 2006.

———, *Political–Military Relations and the Stability of Arab Regimes*, Adelphi Paper 324 (Oxford: International Institute for Strategic Studies, 1998).

———, *Shaping Strategy: the civil–military politics of strategic assessment* (Princeton: Princeton University Press, 2008).

*Business Insider*, "11 photos showing King Abdullah II of Jordan being a total badass", 5 February 2015, http://uk.businessinsider.com/king-abduallh-of-jordan-is-a-total-badass-2015-2?r=USandIR=T, last accessed 21 July 2016.

*Channel 1 TV*, "Egyptian defence minister says army is united", 24 July 2013, BBC Monitoring.

*Christian Science Monitor*, "Nasser purges air force", 27 June 1969.

Civil–Military Fusion Centre, "The Libyan rebels: evolution of a fighting force", July 2011.

*CNN*, "Shadowy Iraq office accused of sectarian agenda", 1 May 2007, http://edition.cnn.com/2007/WORLD/meast/05/01/iraq.office/, last accessed 21 July 2016.

Collier, Paul, *Wars, Guns and Votes: Democracy in Dangerous Places* (New York: HarperCollins, 2009).

Collier, Paul and Anke Hoeffler, "Military Spending and the Risks of Coups d'Etat", Centre for the Study of African Economies, Department of Economics, Oxford University, Oct. 2007, http://users.ox.ac.uk/~econpco/research/pdfs/MilitarySpendingandRisksCoups.pdf, last accessed 21 July 2016.

———, "On economic causes of civil war", *Oxford Economic Papers*, Vol. 50, No. 4, 1998.

Cook, Steven A., *Ruling but not Governing: The Military and Political Development in Egypt, Algeria and Turkey* (Baltimore, MD: Johns Hopkins University Press, 2007).

———, *The Struggle for Egypt: From Nasser to Tahrir Square* (Oxford: Oxford University Press, 2012).

Cooley, John, *Libyan Sandstorm: The Complete Account of Qaddafi's Revolution* (New York: Holt, Rinehart and Winston, 1982).

Cooper, Mark N., "The Demilitarisation of the Egyptian Cabinet", *International Journal of Middle East Studies*, Vol. 14, No. 2, 1982.

Cordesman, Anthony, "Inexcusable Failure: Progress in Training the Iraqi Army and Security Forces as of Mid-July 2004", Center for Strategic and International Studies, 20 July 2004.

———, "The US Transition in Iraq: Iraqi Forces and US Military Aid", Center for Strategic and International Studies, 21 October 2010.

Cronin, Stephanie, "Tribes, Coups and Princes: Building a Modern Army in Saudi Arabia", *Middle Eastern Studies*, Vol. 49, No. 1, 2013.

*Daily Beast*, "Egyptians: Stop Calling Our Revolution a Coup", 7 October 2013, http://www.thedailybeast.com/articles/2013/07/10/egyptians-stop-calling-our-revolution-a-coup.html, last accessed 21 July 2016.

*Daily News Egypt*, "Al-Sisi inaugurates housing, infrastructure projects across Egypt", 6 February 2016, http://www.dailynewsegypt.com/2016/02/06/al-sisi-inaugurates-housing-infrastructure-projects-across-egypt/, last accessed 21 July 2016.

———, "Al-Sisi urges Egyptians to cycle", 13 June 2014, http://www.dailynewsegypt.com/2014/06/13/al-sisi-urges-egyptians-cycle/, last accessed 21 July 2016.

———, "Cabinet ministers must start work at 7am: Mehleb", 17 June 2014, http://www.dailynewsegypt.com/2014/06/17/cabinet-ministers-must-start-work-7am-mehleb/, last accessed 21 July 2016.

———, "Name change angers activists", 10 November 2012, http://www.dailynewsegypt.com/2012/11/10/name-change-angers-activists/, last accessed 21 July 2016.

*Daily Star*, "Assad: Syrian army fatigued but will prevail", 27 July 2015.

*Daily Star Lebanon*, "Army scores highest on Lebanese trust index poll", 14 August 2014, http://www.dailystar.com.lb/News/Lebanon-News/2014/Aug-14/267244-army-scores-highest-on-lebanese-trust-index-poll.ashx#ixzz3Hdq5AyVl, last accessed 21 July 2016.

———, "Lebanese break through army cordon with roses", 5 March 2005, http://www.dailystar.com.lb/News/Lebanon-News/2005/Mar-01/4994-lebanese-break-through-army-cordon-with-roses.ashx#axzz3HdBPJGlB, last accessed 21 July 2016.

*Daily Telegraph*, "Battle to retake Basra was 'Complete Disaster'", 20 April 2008, http://www.telegraph.co.uk/news/worldnews/1896183/Battle-to-retake-Basra-was-complete-disaster.html, last accessed 21 July 2016.

# BIBLIOGRAPHY

Dann, Uriel, *Iraq under Qassem: A Political History, 1958–1963* (New York: Praeger, 1969).

————, *King Hussein and the Challenge of Arab Radicalism, Jordan 1955–1967* (Oxford: Oxford University Press, 1989).

*Defense Industry Daily*, "All Over Again: Egypt Looks Beyond the USA for New Arms", 7 April 2016, http://www.defenseindustrydaily.com/all-over-again-egypt-looks-beyond-the-usa-for-new-arms-019091/ last accessed 21 July 2016.

*Defense News*, "Egypt Military Winds Down Sinai Campaign Against IS", 23 September 2015, http://www.defensenews.com/story/defense/international/mideast-africa/2015/09/23/egypt-military-winds-sinai-campaign/72689540/, last accessed 21 July 2016.

————, "Egypt, France to Sign Arms Deal Mid-April", 6 April 2016, http://www.defensenews.com/story/defense/policy-budget/industry/2016/04/06/egypt-france-fighter-jet-frigate-satellite/82695674/, last accessed 21 July 2016.

Department of Defense, "Measuring Stability and Security in Iraq", Report to Congress In accordance with the Department of Defense Supplemental Act 2008 Section 9204, Public Law 110–252, (Washington, DC, Dec. 2009).

*Direct Info*, "Tunisie—ANC: Les militaires victimes de l'affaire de Barraket Essahel réhabilités par la loi", 13 June 2014, http://directinfo.webmanagercenter.com/2014/06/13/tunisie-anc-les-militaires-victimes-de-laffaire-de-barraket-essahel-rehabilites-par-la-loi/, last accessed 21 July 2016.

————, "Tunisie: Accorder ou non le droit de voter et de se porter candidats aux militaires", 4 November 2015, http://directinfo.webmanagercenter.com/2015/11/04/tunisie-accorder-le-droit-de-vote-aux-militaires-et-aux-securitaires-implique-loctroi-du-droit-de-se-porter-candidat/, last accessed 21 July 2016.

Dodge, Toby, *Iraq: From War to Authoritarianism* (London: International Institute for Strategic Studies/Routledge, 2012).

Droz-Vincent, Philippe, "From Political to Economic Actors: The Changing Role of Middle Eastern Armies", in Oliver Schlumberger (ed.), *Debating Arab Authoritarianism: Dynamics and Durability in Nondemocratic Regimes* (Stanford, CA: Stanford University Press, 2007).

————, "Le militaire et le politique en Egypte", *Monde arabe, Maghreb Machrek*, No. 165, July/Sept. 1999.

Drysdale, Alasdair, "Ethnicity in the Syrian Officer Corps: A Conceptualisation", *Civilisations*, Vol. 29, Nos. 3/4, 1979.

*Echourouk El Youmi*, "Algerian former counterterrorism chief charged with breaching military rules", 1 October 2015, BBC Monitoring.

*Economist, The*, "Cracks in the army: Defections from Bashar Assad's armed forces are growing", 29 October 2011.

*Egypt Independent*, "Army will control 60% of Egypt's national entity for tele-communications", 11 May 2015, http://www.egyptindependent.com/news/newspaper-army-will-control-60-egypt-s-national-entity-telecommunications, last accessed 21 July 2016.

Ehud Ya'ari, "Sadat's Pyramid of Power", *Jerusalem Quarterly*, No. 14, Winter 1980.

Eisenstadt, Michael, "Like a Phoenix from the Ashes? The Future of Iraqi Military Power", Policy Papers, No. 36 (Washington, DC: Washington Institute for Near East Policy, 1993) http://www.washingtoninstitute.org/uploads/Documents/pubs/PP_36_FutureofIraqiMilitaryPower.pdf, last accessed 21 July 2016.

El Kurd, Dana, "The Jordanian Military: A Key Regional Ally", *Parameters*, Vol. 44, No. 3, 2014.

Elaph, "Syrian dissident urges army to overthrow al-Asad", 5 September 2013, BBC Monitoring.

El-Edroos, Syed Ali, *The Hashemite Arab Army 1908–1979* (Amman: The Publishing Committee, 1980).

*El-Khabar*, "…changes in the army will be met with resistance, attempts to oppose…", 14 October 2015, BBC Monitoring.

———, "Algerian opposition not convinced of army neutrality regarding elections", 18 February 2014, BBC Monitoring.

———, "Algerian opposition parties form alliance, urge army to be neutral", 18 April 2013, BBC Monitoring.

El-Khazen, Farid, *The Breakdown of the State in Lebanon, 1967–1976* (London: I. B. Tauris, 2000).

Engel, Andrew, "Libya's Divided Security Establishment: Who Commands?", *War on the Rocks*, 20 February 2014, http://warontherocks.com/2014/02/libyas-divided-security-establishment-who-commands/, last accessed 21 July 2016.

Enloe, Cynthia, *Ethnic Soldiers* (Athens: University of Georgia Press, 1980).

*Eshourouk El Youmi*, "Algerian president dismisses senior officers in military expenditure control", 21 September 2014, BBC Monitoring.

Fahmy, Khaled, *All the Pasha's Men: Mehmed Ali, his army and the making of modern Egypt* (Cairo: American University in Cairo Press, 2003).

Farcau, Bruce W., *The Coup: Tactics in the Seizure of Power* (London: Praeger, 1994).

Fattah, Khaled, "A political history of civil–military relations in Yemen", *Alternative Politics*, Special Issue 1, November 2010.

Fattah, Khaled, "Ensuring the Success of Yemen's Military Reforms", Carnegie Europe, 13 December 2012, http://carnegieeurope.eu/publications/?fa=50349, last accessed 21 July 2016.

Fearon, James D. and David Laitin, "Ethnicity, Insurgency, and Civil War", *American Political Science Review*, Vol. 97, No. 1, 2003.

————, "The Civil–Military Problematique: Huntington, Janowitz, and the Question of Civilian Control", *Armed Forces and Society*, Vol. 23, No. 2, 1996.

————, *Armed Servants: Agency, Oversight and Civil–Military Relations* (Cambridge, MA: Harvard University Press, 2003).

Federal Research Division of the Library of Congress, Country Studies Series, "Jordan Personnel: Composition, Recruitment, and Training", 1989.

Feith, Douglas, *War and Decision* (New York: Harper, 2008).

*Financial Times*, "Egyptians become victims of soaring crime rate", 1 May 2013, http://www.ft.com/intl/cms/s/0/7ffac226-adab-11e2-a2c7–0014 4feabdc0.html#axzz2xWywGjZl, last accessed 21 July 2016.

Finer, Samuel E., *The Man on Horseback: The role of the military in politics* (Boulder, CO: Westview, 1988).

*Foreign Policy*, "How Maliki Ruined Iraq", 19 June 2014, http://foreignpolicy. com/2014/06/19/how-maliki-ruined-iraq/?wp_login_redirect=0, last accessed 21 July 2016.

————, "How to get Egypt's Generals Back on Our Side", 5 January 2015, http://foreignpolicy.com/2015/01/05/how-to-get-egypts-generals-back-on-our-side-sisi-military-us-foreign-policy/, last accessed 21 July 2016.

————, "The Egyptian Republic of Retired Generals", 8 May 2012, http:// mideastafrica.foreignpolicy.com/posts/2012/05/08/the_egyptian_ republic_of_retired_generals, last accessed 21 July 2016.

————, "The Wikipedia war over Egypt's 'Coup'", 7 July 2013, http://blog. foreignpolicy.com/posts/2013/07/07/the_wikipedia_war_over_egypts_ coup, last accessed 21 July 2016.

Frisch, Hillel, *The Palestinian Military: Between Militias and Armies* (New York: Routledge, 2008).

Furr, Ann and Muwafaq Al-Serhan, "Tribal Customary Law in Jordan", *South Carolina Journal of International Law and Business*, Vol. 4, No. 2, Spring 2008.

Galetovic, Alexander and Ricardo Sanhueza, "Citizens, Autocrats, and Plotters: A Model and New Evidence on Coups d'État", *Economics and Politics*, Vol. 12, No. 2, 2000.

Gallup, "Egypt from Tahrir to Transition", April 2011, http://www.gallup. com/poll/157046/egypt-tahrir-transition.aspx, last accessed 21 July 2016.

Garçon, José and Pierre Affuzi, "L'armée algérienne: le pouvoir de l'ombre", *Pouvoirs*, No. 86, 1998.

Gaub, Florence, "Multi-ethnic Armies in the Aftermath of Civil War: Lessons Learned from Lebanon", *Defence Studies*, Vol. 7, No. 1, 2007.

————, "Libya in Limbo: How to Fill the Security Vacuum", NATO Defense College Research Report, 31 August 2011.

————, "Syria's Military: Last Man Standing?", Carnegie Europe, 29 July 2014, http://carnegieeurope.eu/strategiceurope/?fa=56274, last accessed 21 July 2016.

————, "The Libyan Armed Forces between Coup-Proofing and Repression", *Journal of Strategic Studies*, Vol. 36, No. 2, 2013.

————, "Whatever happened to Yemen's army?", EUISS brief 9, 2015, http://www.iss.europa.eu/uploads/media/Brief_9_Yemen.pdf.

————, *Military Integration after Civil Wars: Multiethnic Armies, Identity and Post-Conflict Reconstruction* (London: Routledge, 2010).

Gawrych, George W., "The Egyptian High Command in the 1973 War", *Armed Forces and Society*, Vol. 13, No. 4, 1987.

Geddes, Barbara, "How Autocrats Defend Themselves Against Armed Rivals", SSRN eLibrary, 2009.

Gerges, Fawaz A., "Egypt and the 1948 War: internal conflict and regional ambition", in Eugene L. Rogan and Avi Shlaim (eds), *The War for Palestine: Rewriting the History of 1948*, Cambridge Middle East Studies 15, 2nd edn (Cambridge: Cambridge University Press, 2007).

Gèze, François, "Armée et nation en Algérie: l'irrémédiable divorce?", *Hérodote*, No. 1 2005.

Glassmyer, Katherine and Nicholas Sambanis, "Rebel–Military Integration and Civil War Termination", *Journal of Peace Research*, Vol. 45, No. 3, 2008.

Gordon, Joel, *Nasser's Blessed Movement: Egypt's Free Officers and the July Revolution* (Oxford: Oxford University Press, 1992).

Gotowicki, Stephen H., "The Role of the Egyptian Military in Domestic Society", US Army, Foreign Military Studies Office, 1997, http://fmso.leavenworth.army.mil/documents/egypt/egypt.htm, last accessed 21 July 2016.

Grewal, Sharan, "A quiet revolution: The Tunisian Military after Ben Ali", Carnegie Middle East Center, 24 February 2016.

*Guardian*, "Egypt imposes anti-terror law that punishes 'false' reporting of attacks", 17 August 2015, http://www.theguardian.com/world/2015/aug/17/egyptian-president-ratifies-law-to-punish-false-reporting-of-terror-attacks, last accessed 21 July 2016.

————, "Egypt 'suffering worst economic crisis since 1930s'", 16 May 2013, http://www.theguardian.com/world/2013/may/16/egypt-worst-economic-crisis-1930s, last accessed 21 July 2016.

————, "Egyptian police go on strike", 10 March 2013, http://www.theguardian.com/world/2013/mar/10/egypt-police-strike, last accessed 21 July 2016.

————, "Iraqi army not ready to take over until 2020, says country's top general", 12 August 2010, http://www.theguardian.com/world/2010/aug/12/iraqi-army-not-ready-general, last accessed 21 July 2016.

————, "Saudi pilots receive online death threats after air strikes on Isis", 24 September 2014, http://www.theguardian.com/world/2014/sep/24/saudi-pilots-online-death-threats-twitter-air-strikes-isis, last accessed 21 July 2016.

*Gulf News*, "Ex-military raises profile in new Egypt parliament", 6 December 2015, http://gulfnews.com/news/mena/egypt/ex-military-raises-profile-in-new-egypt-parliament-1.1632584, last accessed 21 July 2016.

Gutteridge, William, *Military Institutions and Power in the New States* (London: Pall Mall Press, 1964).

*Haaretz*, "ISIS Top Brass Is Iraqi Army's Former Best and Brightest", 8 August 2015, http://www.haaretz.com/israel-news/1.670177, last accessed 21 July 2016.

————, "The root of Egypt's coup: Morsi giving free hand to Sinai Islamists", 18 July 2013, http://www.haaretz.com/news/middle-east/1.536623, last accessed 21 July 2016.

Halpern, Manfred, "Egypt and the New Middle Class: Reaffirmations and New Explorations", *Comparative Studies in Society and History*, Vol. 11, No. 1, 1969.

————, *The Politics of Social Change in the Middle East and North Africa* (Santa Monica: RAND, 1963).

Harkabi, Yehoshofat, "Basic Factors in the Arab Collapse during the Six-Day War", *Orbis*, Vol. 11, No. 3, 1967.

Haykel, Bernard, Thomas Hegghammer and Stéphane Lacroix (eds), *Saudi Arabia in Transition: Insights on Social, Political, Economic and Religious Change* (New York: Cambridge University Press, 2015).

Henderson, Darryl, *Cohesion: The Human Element in Combat* (Washington, DC: National Defense University Press, 1985).

Hill, The, "US to help Iraq security for another 10 years, says general", 17 January 2008, http://thehill.com/homenews/administration/4510-us-to-help-iraq-security-for-another-10-years-says-general, last accessed 21 July 2016.

Hirst, David, "The Terror from Tikrit", *Guardian*, 26 November 1971.

Horowitz, Donald, *Ethnic Groups in Conflict* (Los Angeles: University of California Press, 1985).

Hosmer, Stephen, *Why the Iraqi Resistance to the Coalition Invasion was so Weak* (Santa Monica: RAND, 2007).

Hoyt, Timothy D., "Social Structure, Ethnicity, and Military Effectiveness: Iraq, 1980–2004", in Risa A. Brooks and Elizabeth A. Stanley (eds), *Creating Military Power: the sources of military effectiveness* (Stanford, CA: Stanford University Press, 2007).

Huntington, Samuel P., "Civilian Control of the Military: A Theoretical Statement", in Heinz Elau et al. (eds), *Political Behavior: A Reader in Theory and Research* (Glencoe, IL: Free Press, 1956).

————, *Political Order in Changing Societies* (New Haven: Yale University Press, 1968).

————, *The Soldier and the State: The Theory and Politics of Civil–military Relations* (Cambridge, MA: Belknap Press of Harvard University Press, 1957).

Hurewitz, J. C., *Middle East Politics: The Military Dimension* (Boulder, CO: Westview Press 1969).

*Hürriyet Daily News*, "Egypt promotes junior corps impatient over military failure", 15 August 2012, http://www.hurriyetdailynews.com/egypt-promotes-junior-corps-impatient-over-military-failure.aspx?pageID=238andnID=27820andNewsCatID=352, last accessed 21 July 2016.

*Independent*, "Iraqi officers pay dear for West's coup fiasco", 17 February 1998, http://www.independent.co.uk/news/iraqi-officers-pay-dear-for-wests-coup-fiasco-1145298.html, last accessed 21 July 2016.

————, "Libyan commander 'attempted a coup'", 24 October 1993, http://www.independent.co.uk/news/world/libyan-commander-attempted-a-coup-1512701.html, last accessed 21 July 2016.

Institute for the Study of War, "The Regime's Military Capabilities: Part 1", 26 May 2015, http://iswresearch.blogspot.fr/2015/05/the-regime-military-capabilities-part-1.html, last accessed 21 July 2016.

International Crisis Group, "Holding Libya Together", Middle East/North Africa Report No. 115, 14 December 2011, http://www.crisisgroup.org/~/media/Files/Middle%20East%20North%20Africa/North%20Africa/115%20Holding%20Libya%20Together%20-%20Security%20Challenges%20after%20Qadhafi.pdf, last accessed 21 July 2016.

————, "Loose Ends: Iraq's Security Forces between US Drawdown and Withdrawal", Middle East Report No. 99, 26 October 2010, http://www.crisisgroup.org/~/media/Files/Middle%20East%20North%20Africa/Iraq%20Syria%20Lebanon/Iraq/99%20Loose%20Ends%20-%20Iraqs%20Security%20Forces%20between%20US%20Drawdown%20and%20Withdrawal.pdf, last accessed 21 July 2016.

————, "Lost in Transition: The World According to Egypt's SCAF", Middle East/North Africa Report No. 121, 24 April 2012, http://www.crisisgroup.org/~/media/files/middle%20east%20north%20africa/north%20africa/egypt/121-lost-in-transition-the-world-according-to-egypts-scaf.pdf, last accessed 21 July 2016.

————, "Yemen's Military–Security Reform: Seeds of a New Conflict?", Middle East Report No. 139, 4 April 2013, http://www.crisisgroup.org/en/regions/middle-east-north-africa/iraq-iran-gulf/yemen/139-yemens-military-security-reform-seeds-of-new-conflict.aspx, last accessed 21 July 2016.

International Institute for Strategic Studies, *The Military Balance 2008* (London: Routledge, 2008).

————, *The Military Balance 2010* (London: Routledge, 2010).

————, *The Military Balance 2011* (London: Routledge, 2011).

————, *The Military Balance 2014* (London: Routledge, 2014).

Israel Program for Scientific Translations, *Middle East Record Volume 2, 1961* (Tel Aviv: Tel Aviv University, 1962).

Jackman, Robert W., "Politicians in Uniform: Military Governments and Social Change in the Third World", *American Political Science Review*, Vol. 70, No. 4, 1976.

Jahr, Christoph, "'Der Krieg zwingt die Justiz, ihr Innerstes zu revidieren': Desertion und Militärgerichtsbarkeit im Ersten Weltkrieg", in Ulrich Bröckling, Ulrich and Michael Sikora (eds), *Armeen und ihre Deserteure. Vernachlässigte Kapitel einer Militärgeschichte der Neuzeit* (Göttingen: Vandenhoeck and Ruprecht, 1998).

Janowitz, Morris, *Military Institutions and Coercion in the Developing Nations* (Chicago: University of Chicago Press, 1977).

————, *Sociology and the Military Establishment* (Beverly Hills: Sage Publications, 1974).

————, *The Professional Soldier: A Social and Political Portrait* (New York: Collier Macmillan, 1960).

Jeune Afrique, "Le général Ammar, l'homme qui a dit non", 7 February 2011, http://www.jeuneafrique.com/192799/politique/le-g-n-ral-ammar-l-homme-qui-a-dit-non/, last accessed 21 July 2016.

————, "Tunisie: la torture de l'ère Ben Ali en procès", 2 December 2011, http://www.jeuneafrique.com/189037/societe/tunisie-la-torture-de-l-re-ben-ali-en-proc-s/ last accessed 21 July 2016.

*Jordan Times*, "Jordan marks Arabisation of army today", 29 February 2016, http://www.jordantimes.com/news/local/jordan-marks-arabisation-army-today, last accessed 21 July 2016.

————, "Jordan military committed to defending all Arab causes–King", 2 November 2014, http://www.jordantimes.com/news/local/jordan-military-committed-defending-all-arab-causes-%E2%80%94-king#sthash.RczSoPVg.dpuf, last accessed 21 July 2016.

————, "Overwhelming majority trusts army, security agencies", 30 September 2014, http://jordantimes.com/overwhelming-majority-trusts-army-security-agencies, last accessed 21 July 2016.

Kamrava, Mehran, "Military professionalization and civil–military relations in the Middle East", *Political Science Quarterly*, Vol. 115, No. 1, 2000.

*Kapitalis*, "Tunisie. Les putschistes de 1962 sont-ils des 'martyrs'?", 8 September 2012, http://www.kapitalis.com/politique/11650-tunisie-les-putschistes-de-1962-sont-ils-des-lmartyrsr.html, last accessed 21 July 2016.

Kechichian, Joseph A., *Succession in Saudi Arabia* (New York: Palgrave, 2001).

Ketchley, Neil, "The army and the people are one hand!" Fraternisation and the 25th January Egyptian Revolution", *Comparative Studies in Society and History*, Vol. 56, No. 1, 2014.

Khaddour, Kheder, "Assad's Officer Ghetto: Why the Syrian Army Remains Loyal", Carnegie Middle East Center, 4 November 2015.

————, "Strength in Weakness: The Syrian Army's Accidental Resilience", Carnegie Middle East Center, 14 March 2016.

Khadduri, Majid, "The Role of the Military in Iraqi Society", in Nettleton Fisher (ed.), *The Military in the Middle East* (Columbus: Ohio State University Press, 1963).

Khorma, Tamer, "The Myth of the Jordanian Monarchy's Resilience to the Arab Spring", Comments 33, Stiftung Wissenschaft und Politik, July 2014.

Khuri, Fuad I. and Gerald Obermeyer, "The Social Bases for Military Intervention in the Middle East", in Catherine McArdle Kelleher (ed.), *Political Military Systems: Comparative Perspectives* (London: Sage Publications, 1974).

King, Anthony, "The Word of Command: Communication and Cohesion in the Military", *Armed Forces and Society*, Vol. 32, No. 4, July 2006.

Knight, Malcolm, Norman Loayza and Delano Villanueva, "The Peace Dividend: Military Spending Cuts and Economic Growth", Policy Research Working Paper 1577 (Washington, DC: World Bank and International Monetary Fund, 1996).

Knights, Michael, "The Military Role in Yemen's Protests: Civil–Military Relations in the Tribal Republic", *Journal of Strategic Studies*, Vol. 36, No. 2, 2013.

Koonings, Kees and Dirk Kruijt, *Political Armies* (London: Zed Books, 2002).

Kratochwil, Friedrich V., *Rules, Norms and Decisions: On the conditions of practical and legal reasoning in international relations and domestic affairs* (Cambridge: Cambridge University Press, 1990).

*L'Expression*, "Algeria's chief of staff reiterates army's refusal to engage in politics", 25 June 2014, BBC Monitoring.

*L'Orient–Le Jour*, "Chamel Roukoz, l'homme qui commande les commandos", 7 September 2015, http://www.lorientlejour.com/article/942891/chamel-roukoz-lhomme-qui-commande-les-commandos.html, last accessed 21 July 2016.

*La Croix*, "Émile Lahoud: Un Marin en Eaux Troubles", 1 December 1989.

*LA Times*, "Coup attempt, military purge reported in Iraq: as many as 200 executed after move against President Hussein in January, dissidents assert", 8 February 1989, http://articles.latimes.com/1989–02–08/news/mn-2132_1_coup-attempt, last accessed 21 July 2016.

*LA Times*, "Weapons imports to Syria surged sevenfold in 10 years, report says", 20 March 2012, http://latimesblogs.latimes.com/world_now/

2012/03/syria-weapons-increase-imports-russia.html, last accessed 21 July 2016.

Landis, Joshua, "Syria and the Palestine War: fighting King Abdullah's 'Greater Syria Plan'", in Eugene L. Rogan and Avi Shlaim (eds), *The War for Palestine: Rewriting the History of 1948*, Cambridge Middle East Studies 15, 2nd edn (Cambridge: Cambridge University Press, 2007).

*Le Matin Algérie*, "Saïd Bouteflika est un 'malade mental', affirme le général à la retraite Benhadid", 23 September 2015.

*Leaders*, "Pourquoi les agents des Corps Armés ne doivent pas bénéficier du droitdevote",17April2014,http://www.leaders.com.tn/article/13849-pourquoi-les-agents-des-corps-armes-ne-doivent-pas-beneficier-du-droit-de-vote, last accessed 21 July 2016.

Lebanese Army Operate, https://www.youtube.com/watch?v=4OGUg72r E5Y, last accessed 21 July 2016.

Leon, Gabriel, "Loyalty for Sale? Military Spending and Coups d'Etat", *Public Choice*, Vol. 159, Nos. 3–4, 2014.

Lewin, Leif, *Self-Interest and Public Interest in Western Politics* (Oxford: Oxford University Press, 1991).

*Libya al-Ahrar TV*, "Libyan army commands reject House of Representatives' decisions", 24 August 2014, BBC Monitoring.

———, "Libyan officers at Mu'aytiqah airbase oppose appointment of new chief of staff", 29 August 2014, BBC Monitoring.

*Libya Herald*, "Haftar appointed army commander, promoted Colonel-General—Libyan official", 5 February 2015, BBC Monitoring.

———, "Libya army chief says removed senior official due to incompetence, betrayal", 25 June 2015, BBC Monitoring.

———, "Libyan Air Force commander sacked for publicly supporting Maj-Gen Haftar", 21 March 2014, BBC Monitoring.

———, "Libyan HoR creates position of army commander-in-chief—paper", 19 February 2015, BBC Monitoring.

———, "Security is under control—Interior Minister Sheikh", 26 July 2013.

Lieutenant Colonel Carl D. Grunow, US Army, "Advising Iraqis: Building the Iraqi Army", *Military Review*, July–Aug. 2006.

Linz, Juan J., "The Perils of Presidentialism", *Journal of Democracy*, Vol. 1, No. 1, 1990.

Londregan, John B. and Keith T. Poole, "Poverty, the Coup Trap, and the Seizure of Executive Power", *World Politics*, Vol. 42, No. 2, 1990.

Luckham, A. R., "A Comparative Typology of Civil–Military Relations", *Government and Opposition*, Vol. 6, No. 1, 1971.

Luttwak, Edward, *Coup d'État: A Practical Handbook* (Harmondsworth: Penguin Books, 1968).

MacCoun, Robert, "What is Known about Unit Cohesion and Military Performance", in Bernard D. Rostker et al. (eds), *Sexual Orientation and US Military Personnel Policy: Options and Assessment* (Santa Monica: RAND, 1993).

————, Elizabeth Kier and Aaron Belkin, "Does Social Cohesion Determine Motivation in Combat? An Old Question with an Old Answer", *Armed Forces and Society*, Vol. 32, No. 4, 2006.

*Mada Masr*, "Calls for Sisi's nomination a public sentiment, says military spokesperson", 22 September 2013, http://www.madamasr.com/news/calls-sisi%E2%80%99s-nomination-public-sentiment-says-military-spokesperson, last accessed 21 July 2016.

————, "Companies clash with military over ad rights", 19 October 2015, http://www.madamasr.com/sections/politics/companies-clash-military-over-ad-rights, last accessed 21 July 2016.

————, "Polls show high approval ratings for Sisi after first 100 days in office", 22 September 2014, http://www.madamasr.com/news/polls-show-high-approval-ratings-sisi-after-first-100-days-office, last accessed 21 July 2016.

————, "The Armed Forces and Egypt's Land", 27 April 2016, http://www.madamasr.com/sections/economy/armed-forces-and-egypts-land, last accessed 21 July 2016.

*Magharebia*, "Les Tunisiens manifestent leur soutien à l'armée", 2 August 2013, http://magharebia.com/fr/articles/awi/features/2013/08/02/feature-01, last accessed 21 July 2016.

Malsagne, Stéphane, "L'armée libanaise dans la guerre de Palestine (1948–1949): vers un renouveau historiographique", *Confluences Méditerranée*, No. 65, Spring 2008.

————, *Fouad Chéhab, 1902–1973: Une figure oubliée de l'histoire libanaise* (Paris: Editions Karthala, 2011).

Manning, Frederick, "Morale, unit cohesion, and esprit de corps", in Reuven Gal and D. Mangelsdorff (eds), *Handbook of Military Psychology* (Chichester: John Wiley, 1991).

Margold, Stella, "Agrarian Land Reform in Egypt", *American Journal of Economics and Sociology*, Vol. 17, No. 1, 1957.

Marlowe, David, "Cohesion, Anticipated Breakdown, and Endurance in Battle: Considerations for Severe and High Intensity Combat", unpublished draft (Washington, DC: Walter Reed Army Institute of Research, 1979).

Marr, Phebe, *The Modern History of Iraq* (Boulder, CO: Westview Press, 2012).

Marshall, Shana, "The Egyptian Armed Forces and the remaking of an economic empire", 15 April 2015, Carnegie Middle East Center, http://carnegie-mec.org/2015/04/15/egyptian-armed-forces-and-remaking-of-economic-empire, last accessed 21 July 2016.

Martinez, Luis, *The Algerian Civil War, 1990–1998* (London: Hurst & Co., 2000).

————, *The Libyan Paradox* (New York: Columbia University Press, 2007).

McLaurin, R. D., "From professional to political: the redecline of the Lebanese Army", *Armed Forces and Society*, Vol. 17, No. 4, 1991.

Meddeb, Hamza, "Conscription Reform Will Shape Tunisia's Future Civil–Military Relations", 21 October 2015, Carnegie Endowment for International Peace, http://carnegieendowment.org/syriaincrisis/?fa=61704, last accessed 21 July 2016.

*MENA News Agency*, "Army combats monopoly in Egyptian markets", 29 August 2014, BBC Monitoring.

————, "Army commanders approve Egyptians' will to name Al-Sisi for president", 11 January 2014, BBC Monitoring.

————, "Egypt Armed Forces warns against publishing 'memoirs' of ex-military officials", 28 September 2013, BBC Monitoring.

————, "Egypt's Cairo governor names schools after army, police 'martyrs'", 19 January 2014, BBC Monitoring.

————, "Egypt's news agency lists national projects implemented by army", 10 June 2015, BBC Monitoring.

————, "Egypt's police pursue Brotherhood member for creating anti-army Facebook page", 5 February 2015, BBC Monitoring.

————, "Egypt's Sisi assigns army with evacuating lands of new capital", 19 March 2015, BBC Monitoring.

————, "Egypt's Sisi decides that army help police in protecting facilities", 27 October 2014, BBC Monitoring.

————, "Egypt's Sisi orders army to end road construction by 6 Aug", 7 June 2015, BBC Monitoring.

————, "Egypt's Sisi orders army to revamp Heart Institute in month", 7 June 2015, BBC Monitoring.

————, "Egypt's Sisi says Armed Forces projects provide job opportunities for civilians", 4 December 2014, BBC Monitoring.

————, "Egypt's Sisi supports print book named 'Best soldiers on earth'", 10 February 2014, BBC Monitoring.

————, "Egyptian Armed Forces open centre for monitoring media coverage of referendum", 14 January 2014, BBC Monitoring.

————, "Egyptian army operates buses to cope with uncontrolled rise in transport fare", 7 July 2014, BBC Monitoring.

————, "Egyptian army takes part in reducing food prices", 6 December 2015, BBC Monitoring.

————, "Egyptian court refuses to force Sisi to run for president", 29 December 2013, BBC Monitoring.

————, "Egyptian leader issues decree to give exceptional pension to former soldiers", 16 October 2014, BBC Monitoring.

————, "Egyptian police arrest Facebook admin for instigating against army", 7 April 2014, BBC Monitoring.

BIBLIOGRAPHY

————, "Egyptian President opens upgraded Armed Forces factories", 14 May 2015, BBC Monitoring.

————, "Egyptian university to 'sack' students over 'insulting' army ", 27 October 2014, BBC Monitoring.

*Middle East Eye*, "Egypt hunts former army officer over assassination of prosecutor general", 3 July 2015, http://www.middleeasteye.net/news/egypt-hunts-former-army-officer-over-assassination-prosecutor-general-513 631553, last accessed 21 July 2016.

————, "Egypt to dismiss preachers who criticise army or police during Eid sermons", 16 July 2015, http://www.middleeasteye.net/news/egypt-dismiss-preachers-who-criticise-police-or-army-during-eid-sermons-21761084, last accessed 21 July 2016.

————, "Head of Libya's army: 'no control' over government-funded rebels", 11 August 2014, http://www.middleeasteye.net/news/head-libyas-army-no-control-over-government-funded-rebels-221789896, last accessed 21 July 2016.

————, "Libya army command 'loyal' to constitutional legitimacy", 20 May 2014, http://www.middleeasteye.net/news/libya-army-command-loyal-constitutional-legitimacy-230572364, last accessed 21 July 2016.

————, "Observers point toward discord in Sisi's visit to Sinai barracks", 8 July 2015, http://www.middleeasteye.net/news/observers-point-toward-disaccord-sisis-visit-sinais-military-barracks-1464347557, last accessed 21 July 2016.

*Middle East Eye*, "Sami Anan: Former chief of staff with ambition to replace Egypt's Sisi", 1 December 2015, http://www.middleeasteye.net/news/profile-egypts-former-army-chief-staff-sami-anan-publishing-tbc-431751869, last accessed 21 July 2016.

*Middle East Eye*, "Syria to raise army salaries to fight 'economic migration'", 7 October 2015, http://www.middleeasteye.net/news/syria-raise-army-salaries-fight-economic-migration-65331448, last accessed 21 July 2016.

*Middle East Monitor*, "Egyptian military expands control over economy", 26 January 2015, https://www.middleeastmonitor.com/20150126-egyptian-military-expands-control-over-economy/, last accessed 21 July 2016.

Middle Eastern Values Study, "The Birthplace of the Arab Spring: Values and Perceptions of Tunisians and a Comparative Assessment of Egyptian, Iraqi, Lebanese, Pakistani, Saudi, Tunisian, and Turkish Publics", 2014, http://mevs.org/files/tmp/Tunisia_FinalReport.pdf, last accessed 21 July 2016.

Miewald, Robert D., "Weberian Bureaucracy and the Military Model", *Public Administration Review*, Vol. 30, No. 2, 1970.

Ministry of National Defence, Tunisia, *The Tunisian Armed Forces* (Tunis: Alif, Les Editions de la Méditerranée, 1996).

*Mosaique FM*, "Chawki Gaddes: Les agents de sécurité et les militaires ont le droit de voter", 22 April 2014, http://archivev2.mosaiquefm.net/fr/index/a/ActuDetail/Element/36209, last accessed 21 July 2016.

Moskos, Charles C., "From Institution to Occupation: Trends in Military Organisation", *Armed Forces and Society*, Vol. 4, No. 1, 1977.

———, "The All-Volunteer Military: Calling, Profession, or Occupation?", *Parameters*, Vol. 7, No. 1, 1977.

Mosse, George L., *Fallen Soldiers: Reshaping the Memory of the World Wars* (Oxford: Oxford University Press, 1990).

Moussa, Nayla, "Loyalties and Group Formation in the Lebanese Officer Corps", Carnegie Middle East Center, 3 February 2016, http://carnegie-mec.org/2016/02/03/loyalties-and-group-formation-in-lebanese-officer-corps/itga, last accessed 21 July 2016.

Nasser, Gamal Abdel, *Egypt's Liberation: The Philosophy of the Revolution* (Washington, DC: Public Affairs Press, 1955).

*National, The*, "Army and police officers' Dh100,000 pension gap", http://www.thenational.ae/news/uae-news/army-and-police-officers-dh100–000-pension-gap last accessed 21 July 2016.

———, "Libya to spend billions on defence", 24 March 2013, http://www.thenational.ae/business/industry-insights/aviation/libya-to-spend-billions-on-defence, last accessed 21 July 2016.

———, "Libya Army Officers want Chief dismissed", 24 April 2013, http://www.thenational.ae/news/world/africa/libya-army-officers-want-chief-dismissed, last accessed 21 July 2016.

National News Agency of the Lebanese Republic, "Jumblatt: History shall do Sleiman justice", 5 May 2014, http://www.nna-leb.gov.lb/en/show-news/26254/Jumblatt-History-shall-do-Sleiman-justice, last accessed 21 July 2016.

*National Libyan TV*, "Libyan General Chief of Staff Office urges forces to obey ousted chief", 24 August 2014, BBC Monitoring.

Nerguizian, Aram, "Between Sectarianism and Military Development: The Paradox of the Lebanese Armed Forces", in Bassel F. Salloukh et al. (eds), *The Politics of Sectarianism in Postwar Lebanon* (London: Pluto Press, 2015).

New Arab, "Syria Army conscription and poor conditions stir anger", 11 November 2015, https://www.alaraby.co.uk/english/news/2015/11/13/syria-army-conscription-and-poor-conditions-stir-anger, last accessed 21 July 2016.

*New York Times*, "Army Ousts Egypt's President; Morsi is Taken into Military Custody", 3 July 2013, http://www.nytimes.com/2013/07/04/world/middleeast/egypt.html?pagewanted=alland_r=0, last accessed 21 July 2016.

———, "Chief of Tunisian Army Pledges his Support for 'the Revolution'", 24 January 2011, http://www.nytimes.com/2011/01/25/world/africa/25tunis.html?_r=0, last accessed 21 July 2016.

————, "Egypt Launches Airstrike in Libya Against ISIS Branch", 26 February 2015, http://www.nytimes.com/2015/02/17/world/middleeast/isis-egypt-libya-airstrikes.html?_r=0, last accessed 21 July 2016.

————, "Egypt Lifts a Junior Corps Impatient Over Military Failure", 13 August 2012, http://www.nytimes.com/2012/08/14/world/middleeast/purge-by-morsi-shows-impatience-within-egypts-military.html?pagewanted=all, last accessed 21 July 2016.

————, "Egypt Stability Hinges on a Divided Military", 5 February 2011, http://www.nytimes.com/2011/02/06/world/middleeast/06military.html?_r=0, last accessed 21 July 2016.

————, "Egypt's New Leader Spells Out Terms for US–Arab Ties", 22 September 2012, http://www.nytimes.com/2012/09/23/world/middleeast/egyptian-leader-mohamed-morsi-spells-out-terms-for-us-arab-ties.html?pagewanted=alland_r=0, last accessed 21 July 2016.

————, "Facing Militants With Supplies Dwindling, Iraqi Soldiers Took to Phones", 26 September, 2014, http://www.nytimes.com/2014/09/27/world/middleeast/facing-isis-with-few-supplies-iraqi-soldiers-took-to-phones.html, last accessed 21 July 2016.

————, "Fateful Choice on Iraq Army Bypassed Debate", 17 March 2008, http://www.nytimes.com/2008/03/17/world/middleeast/17bremer.html?pagewanted=alland_r=0, last accessed 21 July 2016.

————, "Iraq Army Woos Deserters Back to War on ISIS", 28 September 2014, http://www.nytimes.com/2014/09/29/world/middleeast/iraq-army-woos-deserters-back-to-war-on-isis.html?_r=0, last accessed 21 July 2016.

————, "Libya: Minister of Defence to be Dismissed", 27 June 2013, http://www.nytimes.com/2013/06/28/world/africa/libya-minister-of-defense-to-be-dismissed.html?_r=0, last accessed 21 July 2016.

————, "Minister Sees Need for US help in Iraq until 2018", 15 January 2008, http://www.nytimes.com/2008/01/15/world/middleeast/15military.html?_r=0, last accessed 21 July 2016.

————, "More Than 1,000 in Iraq's Forces Quit Basra Fight", 4 April 2008, http://www.nytimes.com/2008/04/04/world/middleeast/04iraq.html, last accessed 21 July 2016.

————, "Ready or Not, Iraq's Military Prepares to Stand on its Own", 28 June 2009, http://www.nytimes.com/2009/06/28/weekinreview/28nordland.html, last accessed 21 July 2016.

————, "Rebels in Libya Gain Power and Defectors", 27 February 2011, http://www.nytimes.com/2011/02/28/world/africa/28unrest.html?pagewanted=all, last accessed 21 July 2016.

————, "Recordings Suggest Emirates and Egyptian Military Pushed Ousting of Morsi", 1 March 2015, http://www.nytimes.com/2015/03/

02/world/middleeast/recordings-suggest-emirates-and-egyptian-military-pushed-ousting-of-morsi.html?_r=0, last accessed 21 July 2016.

———, "Succession Gives Army a Stiff Test in Egypt", 11 September 2010, http://www.nytimes.com/2010/09/12/world/middleeast/12egypt.html?_r=0, last accessed 21 July 2016.

———, "Text of Colonel Reese's Memo", 30 July 2009, http://www.nytimes.com/2009/07/31/world/middleeast/31advtext.html?pagewanted=all and _r=0, last accessed 21 July 2016.

———, "Their Jobs in Jeopardy, Iraqi Troops Demand Pay", 25 May 2003, http://www.nytimes.com/2003/05/25/international/worldspecial/25IRAQ.html, last accessed 21 July 2016.

———, "US and Iraqis tell of a coup attempt against Baghdad", 3 July 1992, http://www.nytimes.com/1992/07/03/world/us-and-iraqis-tell-of-a-coup-attempt-against-baghdad.html, last accessed 21 July 2016.

*Nile News TV*, "Egyptian Armed Force will not be part of political scene, ruling", 1 July 2013, BBC Monitoring.

Nordlinger, Eric A., "Soldiers in Mufti: The Impact of Military Rule upon Economic and Social Change in the Non-Western States", *American Political Science Review*, Vol. 64, No. 4, December 1970.

———, *Soldiers in Politics: Military Coups and Governments* (Upper Saddleback River, NJ: Prentice Hall, 1977).

Northcote Parkinson, Cyril, "Parkinson's Law: The Pursuit of Progress", *The Economist*, 19 November 1955.

*NOW Lebanon*, "A State of Minds: Lebanon in Numbers—Views on President Suleiman's term", 22 July 2014, https://now.mmedia.me/lb/en/a-state-of-minds/556942-views-on-president-suleimans-term last accessed, 21 July 2016.

———, "Nine Unforgettable Years: A Tribute to President Emile Lahoud", 25 November 2007, https://now.mmedia.me/lb/en/archive/Nine-Unforgettable-Years-A-Tribute-to-President-Emile-Lahoud21320, last accessed 21 July 2016.

Ohl, Dorothy et al., "For Money or Liberty? The political economy of military desertion and rebel recruitment in the Syrian civil war", Carnegie Middle East Center, 24 November 2015.

O'Kane, Rosemary, "Coups d'Etat in Africa: A Political Economy Approach", *Journal of Peace Research*, Vol. 30, No. 3, 1993.

Osman, Tarek, *Egypt on the Brink: From the Rise of Nasser to Mubarak* (New Haven: Yale University Press: 2010).

Pargeter, Alison, *Libya: The Rise and Fall of Qaddafi* (New Haven: Yale University Press, 2012).

Parker, Richard B., *The Politics of Miscalculation in the Middle East* (Bloomington: Indiana University Press, 1993).

Pelletiere, Stephen C. and Douglas V. Johnson, *Lessons learned: The Iraq–Iran War*, Vol. I (Carlisle Barracks, PA: Strategic Studies Institute, US Army War College, 1991).

Perlmutter, Amos, "Egypt and the Myth of the New Middle Class: A Comparative Analysis", *Comparative Studies in Society and History*, Vol. 10, No. 1, October 1967.

———, "From Obscurity to Rule: The Syrian Army and the Ba'th Party", *Western Political Quarterly*, Vol. 22, 1969.

———, "The Praetorian State and the Praetorian Army: Toward a Taxonomy of Civil–Military Relations in Developing Polities", *Comparative Politics*, Vol. 1, No. 3, 1969.

Pew Research Center, "Egyptians embrace revolt leaders, religious parties and military, as well", 25 April 25 2011, http://www.pewglobal.org/2011/04/25/egyptians-embrace-revolt-leaders-religious-parties-and-military-as-well/, last accessed 21 July 2016.

———, "One year after Morsi's ouster, divides persist on El-Sisi, Muslim Brotherhood", 22 May 2014, http://www.pewglobal.org/2014/05/22/one-year-after-morsis-ouster-divides-persist-on-el-sisi-muslim-brother-hood/, last accessed 21 July 2016.

———, "Egyptian military gets higher ratings than most political parties", 1 July 2013, http://www.pewresearch.org/fact-tank/2013/07/01/egyptian-military-gets-higher-ratings-than-most-political-parties/ last accessed, 21 July 2016.

Pfiffner, James P., "US Blunders in Iraq: De-Baathification and Disbanding the Army", *Intelligence and National Security*, Vol. 25, No. 1, 2010.

Picard, Elizabeth, "Arab Military in Politics: from Revolutionary Plot to Authoritarian Regime", in Giacomo Luciani (ed.), *The Arab State* (London: Routledge, 1990).

———, "The Demobilization of the Lebanese Militias", Centre for Lebanese Studies, 1999.

Pilster, Ulrich and Tobias Boehmelt, "Coup-Proofing and Military Effectiveness in Interstate Wars, 1967–1999", *Conflict Management and Peace Science*, Vol. 28, No. 4, 2011.

Pollack, Kenneth M., *Arabs at War: Military Effectiveness, 1948–1991* (Lincoln: University of Nebraska Press, 2002).

Powell, Jonathan, "Coups and Conflict: The Paradox of Coup-Proofing", dissertation, University of Kentucky, 2012.

Powell, Jonathan and Clayton L. Thyne, "Global instances of coups from 1950 to 2010: A new dataset", *Journal of Peace Research*, Vol. 48, No. 2, 2011.

Pritchett, Lant and Frauke de Weijer, "Fragile States: Stuck in a Capability Trap?", World Development Report 2011, Background Paper, October 2010.

# BIBLIOGRAPHY

Pye, Lucian, "Armies in the Process of Political Modernization", in John J. Johnson (ed.), *The Role of the Military in Underdeveloped Countries* (Princeton: Princeton University Press, 1962).

Quandt, William B., "Algerian Military Development: The Professionalization of a Guerrilla Army", March 1972, RAND Corporation, http://www.rand.org/pubs/papers/P4792.html, last accessed 21 July 2016.

Quinlivan, James T., "Coup-Proofing: Its Practice and Consequences in the Middle East", *International Security*, Vol. 24, No. 2, 1999.

Rabinovich, Itamar and Haim Shaked, *Middle East Contemporary Survey, 1984–1985* (Boulder, CO: Westview Press, 1987).

Report of the Independent Commission on the Security Forces of Iraq, 6 September 2007, http://media.csis.org/isf.pdf, last accessed 21 July 2016.

*Reuters*, "Egypt army: will not use violence against citizens", 31 January 2011, http://www.reuters.com/article/2011/01/31/egypt-army-idAFLDE70U2JC20110131, last accessed 21 July 2016.

———, "How Mosul fell: An Iraqi general disputes Baghdad's story", 14 October 2014, http://uk.reuters.com/article/2014/10/14/uk-mideast-crisis-gharawi-special-report-idUKKCN0I30ZA20141014, last accessed 21 July 2016.

———, "Saudi king orders one-month salary bonus for security personnel", 29 April 2015, http://www.reuters.com/article/saudi-military-bonuses-idUSL5N0XQ1S020150429, last accessed 21 July 2016.

———, "Some 5.000 militia men join new Libyan army", 15 February 2012, http://www.reuters.com/article/2012/02/15/us-libya-militias-idUSTRE81E23H20120215, last accessed 21 July 2016.

———, "Son's unit may be one of Gaddafi's last lines of defense", 25 February 2011, http://www.reuters.com/article/2011/02/25/us-libya-commandos-idUSTRE71N8GT20110225, last accessed 21 July 2016.

———, "UPDATE 1-Egypt army: will not use violence against citizens", 31 January 2011, http://www.reuters.com/article/2011/01/31/egypt-army-idAFLDE70U2JC20110131, last accessed 21 July 2016.

Roll, Stephan, "The Military and the Muslim Brotherhood: Will a Power-sharing Agreement be Reached in Egypt?" SWP Comments, February 2012, http://www.swp-berlin.org/en/publications/swp-comments-en/swp-aktuelle-details/article/egypt_military_and_muslim_brotherhood.html, last accessed 21 July 2016.

Romero, Juan, *The Iraqi Revolution of 1958: A Revolutionary Quest for Unity and Security* (New York: University Press of America, 2011).

Rondé, André, "L'Armée libanaise et la restauration de l'Etat de droit", *Revue Droit et Défense*, No. 2, 1998.

Rose, Arnold M., "The social psychology of desertion from combat", *American Sociological Review*, Vol. 16, No. 5, 1951.

# BIBLIOGRAPHY

Safran, Nadav, *Saudi Arabia: The Ceaseless Quest for Security* (Cambridge, MA: Belknap Press, 1985).

Salibi, Kamal, *The Modern History of Jordan* (London: I. B. Tauris, 1993).

*Sarasota Herald Tribune*, "Egyptian Army Officers said arrested in Purge", 16 January 1954.

Sassoon, Joseph, *Saddam Hussein's Ba'th Party: Inside an Authoritarian Regime* (New York: Cambridge University Press, 2012).

Schiff, Rebecca L., *The Military and Domestic Politics: A concordance theory of civil–military relations* (New York: Routledge, 2009).

Seale, Patrick, *Asad of Syria: The Struggle for the Middle East* (Los Angeles: University of California Press, 1988).

Shils, Edward, "The Military in the Political Development of the New States", in John J. Johnson (ed.), *The Role of the Military in Underdeveloped Countries* (Princeton: Princeton University Press, 1967).

Shils, Edward A. and Morris Janowitz, "Cohesion and Disintegration in the Wehrmacht in World War II", *Public Opinion Quarterly*, Vol. 2, Summer 1948.

Siebold, Guy, "Military Group Cohesion", in Thomas W. Britt, Amy B. Adler, Carl Andrew Castro (eds), *Military Life: The Psychology of Serving in Peace and Combat*, Vol. 1 (Westport: Praeger Security International, 2006).

Singh, Naunihal, *Seizing Power: The Strategic Logic of Military Coups* (Baltimore, MD: Johns Hopkins University Press, 2014).

Snow, Peter, *Hussein: A Biography* (London: Barrie and Jenkins, 1972).

Souaidia, Habib, *La Sale Guerre: Le témoignage d'un ancien officier des forces spéciales de l'armée algérienne, 1992–2000* (Paris: La Découverte, 2001).

Special Inspector General for Iraq Reconstruction, Quarterly Report to the United States Congress, 30 April 2008.

———, Quarterly Report to the United States Congress, 30 July 2010.

Springborg, Robert, "The President and the Field Marshal: Civil–Military Relations in Egypt Today", *Middle East Report*, July–Aug. 1987.

St John, Ronald Bruce, *Historical Dictionary of Libya* (Lanham, MD: Scarecrow Press, 1998).

Stanton, Neville, Christopher Baber and Don Harris, *Modelling Command and Control: Event Analysis of Systemic Teamwork* (Aldershot: Ashgate, 2008).

*Stars and Stripes*, "Iraqi army remains on defensive as extent of June debacle becomes clearer", 14 July 2014, http://www.stripes.com/news/middle-east/iraqi-army-remains-on-defensive-as-extent-of-june-debacle-becomes-clearer-1.293417, last accessed 21 July 2016.

Tal, Lawrence, *Politics, the Military and National Security in Jordan, 1955–1967* (Basingstoke: Palgrave, 2002).

Taylor, William C., *Military Responses to the Arab Uprisings and the Future of Civil–Military Relations in the Middle East* (New York: Palgrave Macmillan, 2014).

# BIBLIOGRAPHY

Telhami, Shibley, "2012: Public Opinion Survey", Anwar Sadat Chair for Peace and Development, University of Maryland, http://www.brookings.edu/~/media/research/files/reports/2012/5/21%20egyptian%20elections%20poll%20telhami/egypt_poll_results, last accessed 21 July 2016.

Tell, Tariq, "Early Spring in Jordan: The Revolt of the Military Veterans", Carnegie Middle East Center, 4 November 2015.

Thompson, William R., "Toward Explaining Arab Military Coups", *Journal of Political and Military Sociology*, Vol. 2, No. 2, 1974.

Thyne, Clayton L. and Jonathan Powell, "Coup d'état or Coup d'Autocracy? How Coups Impact Democratisation, 1950–2008", *Foreign Policy Analysis*, 2014.

*Time*, "How Disbanding the Iraqi Army Fueled ISIS", 28 May 2015, http://time.com/3900753/isis-iraq-syria-army-united-states-military/, last accessed 21 July 2016.

Torrey, Gordon H., *Syrian Politics and the Military, 1945–1958* (Columbus: Ohio State University Press, 1964).

*Tripoli Post*, "Nations' Feedback on Libyan Uprising", 23 February 2011, http://tripolipost.com/articledetail.asp?c=1andi=5463, last accessed 21 July 2016.

*Tunisie Numerique*, "Tunisie—Le centre Carter pour le droit au vote des militaires et agents de l'ordre", 22 April 2014, http://www.tunisienumerique.com/tunisie-le-centre-carter-pour-le-droit-au-vote-des-militaires-et-agents-de-lordre/219304, last accessed 21 July 2016.

————, "Tunisie: Identification des corps de 5 personnes ayant pris part au putsch de décembre 1962", 5 September 2012, http://www.tunisienumerique.com/tunisie-identification-des-corps-de-5-personnes-ayant-pris-part-au-putsch-de-decembre-1962/142217, last accessed 21 July 2016.

Ucko, David H., "Militias, tribes and insurgents: The challenge of political integration in Iraq", in Mats Berdal and David H. Ucko (eds), *Reintegrating Armed Groups after Conflict: Politics, Violence and Transition* (New York: Routledge, 2009).

United Nations Human Rights Council, "Report of the International Commission of Inquiry on Libya", New York, 2 March 2012, www.ohchr.org%2FDocuments%2FHRBodies%2FHRCouncil%2FRegularSession%2FSession19%2FA_HRC_19_68_en.docandei=6VxrT_3RFMXOsgaU2pGtAgandusg=AFQjCNFQAOsidSQiRewVmC5_8gxQtSOGdA, last accessed 21 July 2016.

US Congress, House, Armed Services Committee, Subcommittee on Oversight and Investigations Hearing, Development of Operational Capability of the Iraqi Security Forces (110th Congress, 1st sess., 12 June 2007), Lieutenant General Martin F. Dempsey, former Commanding General, Multi-National Security Transition Command–Iraq, the coalition command responsible for recruiting, training, and equipping the Iraqi Security Forces.

————, Hearing on Iraqi Security Forces, Non-Government Perspectives (110th Congress, 1st sess., 28 March 2007) Dr Anthony Cordesman testimony.

US Department of Defence, "2011 Demographics: Profile of the Military Community", November 2010, http://www.militaryonesource.mil/12038/MOS/Reports/2011_Demographics_Report.pdf, last accessed 21 July 2016.

————, *Dictionary of Military Terms and Acronyms* (Seattle: Praetorian Press, 2011).

van Dam, Nikolaos, "Middle Eastern Political Clichés: 'Tikriti' and 'Sunni Rule' in Iraq; 'Alawi Rule' in Syria: A Critical Appraisal", *Orient*, Vol. 21, No. 1, 1980.

Vandergriff, Donald E., "Officer Manning: Armies of the past", www.johns-militaryhistory.com%2FVandergriff_Officers_Briefing.pptandei=9vK_U9DZE-2W0QWY04HABQandusg=AFQjCNE2Jfp2k4dyKeaYbojHKld NmvGo0Qandsig2=sI3pRt8vl5q11jybm2lYJQ, last accessed 21 July 2016.

Vandewalle, Dirk, *A History of Modern Libya* (New York: Cambridge University Press, 2012).

————, *Libya Since Independence: Oil and State-Building* (Ithaca, NY: Cornell University Press, 1998).

Vatikiotis, P. J., *Politics and the Military in Jordan: a study of the Arab Legion 1921–1957* (London: Frank Cass, 1967).

WAL, "Libyan officers, soldiers in Al-Jufrah express support for combating 'terrorism'", 21 May 2014, BBC Monitoring.

Wall Street Journal, "Iraqis Face Uncertain Future as US Ends Combat Mission", 27 August 2010, http://www.wsj.com/articles/SB100014240 52748704913704575453303215595156, last accessed 21 July 2016.

————, "Yemen Leader Moves to Unify Fractured Fighting Force", 29 July 2015, http://www.wsj.com/articles/yemen-leader-moves-to-unify-frac-tured-fighting-force-1438225287, last accessed 21 July 2016.

Ware, L. B., "The Role of the Tunisian Military in the Post-Bourguiba Era", *Middle East Journal*, Vol. 39, No. 1, 1985.

*Washington Post*, "The US military is back training troops in Iraq, but it's a little different this time", 8 January 2015, http://www.washingtonpost.com/world/the-us-military-is-back-training-troops-in-iraq-but-its-a-little-dif-ferent-this-time/2015/01/08/11b9aa58–95f2–11e4–8385–8662933 22c2f_story.html, last accessed 21 July 2016.

Watson, Bruce Allen, *When Soldiers Quit: Studies in Military Disintegration* (London: Praeger, 1997).

Weber, Max, *On Charisma and Institution Building* (Chicago: University of Chicago Press, 1968).

# BIBLIOGRAPHY

Weiler, Robert S., "Eliminating Success During Eclipse II: An Examination of the Decision to Disband the Iraqi Military", United States Marine Corps, Command and Staff College, March 2009, http://www.dtic.mil/dtic/tr/fulltext/u2/a511061.pdf, last accessed 21 July 2016.

Welch, Claude, "Civilian Control of the Military: Myth and Reality", in Claude Welch (ed.), *Civilian Control of the Military: Theory and Cases from Developing Countries* (Albany, NY: State University of New York Press, 1976).

Welch, Claude E. and Arthur K. Smith, *Military Role and Rule: Perspectives on Civil–Military Relations* (Belmont: Duxbury Press, 1974).

Whitman, Elizabeth, "The Awakening of the Syrian Army: General Husni al-Za'im's Coup and Reign, 1949", senior thesis, Columbia University, April 2011.

Whynes, David, *The Economics of Third World Military Expenditure* (London: Macmillan Press, 1979).

Wiking, Staffan, *Military Coups in Sub-Saharan Africa: How to justify illegal assumptions of power* (Uppsala: Scandinavian Institute of African Studies, 1983), http://www.diva-portal.org/smash/get/diva2:278002/FULL-TEXT01.pdf, last accessed 21 July 2016.

Witty, David M., "A Regular Army in Counterinsurgency Operations: Egypt in North Yemen, 1962–1967", *Journal of Military History*, Vol. 65, No. 2, April 2001.

Wolpin, Miles D., "The military as a conservative socio-political force: Marxian and non-Marxian Perspectives" in Miles D. Wolpin (ed.), *Militarism and Social Revolution in the Third World* (Allanheld, Osmun, 1981).

Wong, Leonard et al., "Why They Fight: Combat Motivation in the Iraq War", Strategic Studies Institute, July 2003, http://www.strategicstudiesinstitute.army.mil/pdffiles/PUB179.pdf, last accessed 21 July 2016.

Woods, Kevin M., Williamson Murray, Elizabeth A. Nathan, Laila Sabara and Ana M. Venegas, *Saddam's Generals: Perspectives of the Iran–Iraq War* (Alexandria, VA: Institute for Defense Analyses, 2011).

*Yemen Fox*, "Mutiny inside Yemen's special forces", 22 November 2014, BBC Monitoring.

———, "President urges Partnership with Huthi Group", 18 November 2014, BBC Monitoring.

*Yemen Observer*, "Marib Tribal Men Demand Recruiting 85 Thousand People", 27 November 2014, BBC Monitoring.

*Yemen Post*, "Al-Subaihi slams army chiefs, Huthi militias", 28 November 2014, BBC Monitoring.

———, "Hadi Reinstates, Promotes 8009 Officers, Soldiers from South", 24 November 2014, BBC Monitoring.

———, "Yemen officially including Huthi militants within forces", 23 November 2014, BBC Monitoring.

# BIBLIOGRAPHY

*Yemen Times*, "Rebels in Disguise", 16 October 2014, BBC Monitoring.

Zisser, Eyal, "The Syrian Army: Between the Domestic and the External Fronts", *Middle East Review of International Affairs Journal*, Vol. 5, No. 1, 2001.

Zogby Research Services, "Egyptian Attitudes in the post-Tamarrud, post-Morsi Era", July 2013, http://b.3cdn.net/aai/6eaeff56ba538229a3_gom6bhktx.pdf, last accessed 21 July 2016.

————, "Egyptian Attitudes: September 2013", http://static.squarespace.com/static/52750dd3e4b08c252c723404/t/5294bf5de4b013dda087d0e5/1385480029191/Egypt%20October%202013%20FINAL.pdf%20%20t, last accessed 21 July 2016.

————, "Tunisia: Divided and Dissatisfied with Ennahda", 2013, http://b.3cdn.net/aai/b8cc8e61b78158d847_8pm6b1oog.pdf, last accessed 21 July 2016.

Zuk, Gary and William R. Thompson, "The Post-Coup Military Spending Question: A Pooled Cross-Sectional Time Series Analysis", *American Political Science Review*, Vol. 76, No. 1, 1982.

# INDEX

# INDEX

# INDEX

# INDEX

INDEX

# INDEX